ATM Switching Systems

For a complete listing of the *Artech House Telecommunications* Library,
turn to the back of this book.

ATM Switching Systems

Thomas M. Chen
Stephen S. Liu

Artech House
Boston • London

Library of Congress Cataloging-in-Publication Data
Chen, Thomas M.
ATM switching systems / Thomas M. Chen, Stephen S. Liu
Includes bibliographical references and index.
ISBN 0-89006-682-5 (acid-free paper)
1. Asynchronous transfer mode.   I. Liu, Stephen S.   II. Title
TK5105.35.C47 1995   94-44500
621.382—dc20   CIP

A catalogue record for this book is available from the British Library

Chen, Thomas M.
ATM Switching Systems
I. Title   II. Liu, Stephen S.
621.382

ISBN 0-89006-682-5

© 1995 ARTECH HOUSE, INC.
685 Canton Street
Norwood, MA 02062

International Standard Book Number: 0-89006-682-5
Library of Congress Catalog Card Number: 94-44500

10 9 8 7 6 5 4 3 2

For my parents Janet and Houpen, my sister Judy, and Robin
(T.C.)

For Lily, Joshua, and Joseph
(S.L.)

Contents

Preface

We are living in interesting times. The entire landscape of telecommunications—services, technologies, regulations, and competition—is fluid and changing daily. For about a century, the Bell system in the U.S. had experienced steady but unspectacular growth. New technologies such as digital switching and fiber optics were incorporated to modernize the network, but Ma Bell remained essentially a telephone system with "plain old telephone service." The picture changed dramatically in 1984 when the Bell system was fragmented into several smaller but more independent and competitive companies. The shock waves from the massive reorganization are still shaking out the telecommunications and related industries today.

In this milieu, asynchronous transfer mode (ATM) made a splash in 1988 and has rolled like a tsunami. For telephone companies eager to expand beyond plain old telephone service, ATM points a way towards new services and business opportunities. But as promising as ATM is, it has yet to deliver on a large scale outside of research labs and field trials. Although the future of ATM appears increasingly secure, large-scale deployment is fraught with a degree of risk and uncertainty.

The reason for this uncertainty is not because ATM is a mystical new technology (despite some of the hype). As we will see, ATM is a new name for a specific implementation of fast packet switching and asynchronous time-division concepts that have been widely researched for many years. As a concept, ATM is well-understood as a streamlined switching and multiplexing method capable of transporting all types of information with high throughput and low delays. A tremendous amount of research has demonstrated the feasibility of ATM switching, and commercial ATM switches of all sorts and sizes are now being deployed.

It has become clear that the uncertainties are related to implementation—namely, economics and operations. ATM networks, like any type of network, involve more than simply transferring information between users. Behind the services seen by users are (typically complex and labor-intensive) monitoring and control systems for operating and managing the network. Network control and management (for example, traffic control) are especially complicated in ATM because of its statistical, cell-based nature.

Thus, ATM switches are much more than a switching fabric that transfers cells from its inputs to its outputs. This book examines ATM switches as a *system* (in which the fabric is one component) containing control and management functions. Surprisingly, the relationship between ATM switching and network control has not been examined previously in depth, and we believe this has limited the understanding in both areas. The objective of this monograph is to relate the two areas in a common theoretical framework by developing a general ATM switching system model. The switch model is *functional* and not specific to any implementation. It is intended to facilitate the study of the impact of signaling, operations and maintenance, network management, and traffic control on the switching system design and performance.

This book is intended to be self-contained for readers with different backgrounds in communications networks. It is organized into two parts. The first part, consisting of Chapters 1 through 4, provides the relevant technical background information on ATM. These chapters lay the necessary foundation for the construction of the switch model in the second part. Readers already familiar with ATM can proceed directly to the second part, which consists of Chapters 5 through 10. These chapters develop a top-down view of the functional blocks of the ATM switch model. The relationship among all chapters is shown in the diagram.

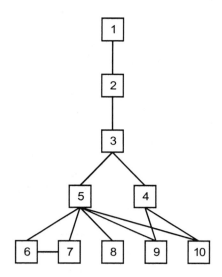

Chapter 1 is optional and intended for those readers who are interested in an overview of the "big picture." The chapter begins with a brief history of the public telephone network and packet-switched data networks. The idea of a single digital network offering integrated services is presented. ATM is introduced as one element of the envisioned future broadband network; other elements include the emerging technologies of SONET/SDH, metropolitan area networks, and the intelligent network.

Chapter 2 is an introduction to the ATM concept in detail. The status of ITU-T (formerly known as CCITT) standards and ATM industry agreements are summarized. The chapter covers the basic functions of the ATM layer. ATM switching systems are viewed as network elements that route, buffer, and process the information flows in the ATM layer. These information flows are described in the next chapter.

Chapter 3 covers the layered structure of the B-ISDN protocol reference model. Its representation of the user, control, and management planes implies three different types of information flows in ATM networks: user data (transparent to the network), signaling information for call/connection control, and management information for the efficient operation of the network. Each type of information flow is described in detail. This chapter is supplemented by more background material in Chapter 4, but readers who wish to could proceed to Chapter 5.

Chapter 4 is an overview of traffic control and resource management which, in addition to the OAM and network management functions described in Chapter 3, are necessary for the efficient operation of ATM networks. The early part of the chapter discusses the objectives and general principles, and the latter part covers the basic mechanisms of resource management, connection admission control, usage/network parameter control, and congestion control. The material will be useful for Chapter 9 and parts of Chapters 6 and 10.

Beginning the second part of the book, Chapter 5 applies the background information from the previous chapters towards the development of a functional switch model. This chapter outlines five major functional blocks in the model: input modules, output modules, cell switch fabric, connection admission control, and system management. It provides a high-level guide to the remaining chapters, which are devoted to the details in each functional block.

The input module is the subject of Chapter 6. The basic function of the input module is extraction of ATM cells from the physical layer signal, which is presumed to be SONET, and processing of the cells in preparation for routing through the fabric. Most of the chapter consists of a comprehensive review of SONET. The remainder of the chapter describes the necessary cell processing. It is noted that the input module may contain some functions distributed from the connection admission control and system-management functional blocks; this point is followed up later in Chapters 9 and 10.

Closely tied with Chapter 6, Chapter 7 investigates the output module, which is a counterpart of the input module in that it handles the egress of traffic rather than ingress. The output module performs many of the reverse functions of the input module. Like the input module, the output module may contain some distributed connection admission control and system-management functions. It is simpler than the input module, however, because the ATM-layer processing in the input module is more complicated.

Chapter 8 is devoted to the cell switch fabric, which performs the essential buffering and routing functions in the switch. General design principles are illustrated through four prototypical approaches. Other functions of the cell switch fabric are concentration, expansion, copying, and multicasting. In addition, the cell switch fabric needs buffer management, which consists of space/time priorities to allow sensitivity to traffic with different cell delay and cell loss requirements.

Chapter 9 examines the functional block for connection admission control. This handles the exchange and processing of signaling messages with users and other switches following high-layer signaling protocols. In response to new connection requests, connection admission control has the responsibility of making decisions about call acceptance and the required amount of resources. Because of the intensive processing involved, it is observed that the functions may be partially distributed to the input modules and output modules to improve performance.

The functional block for system management is the subject of the Chapter 10. It is generally responsible for managing the internal operation of the switching system and supporting the network-wide management activities. It handles the OAM and network management functions described in Chapter 3 and traffic management (excluding connection admission control) in Chapter 4. It is observed that some management functions may be desired within the input modules and output modules in order to improve performance by alleviating the processing burden on the centralized system management block. It is an interesting problem for future study.

Acknowledgments

This book is the result of research work initiated by Phil Matthews and Demos Kostas at GTE Telephone Operations. We are grateful for the exchange of ideas and discussions with our colleagues at GTE Laboratories. In particular, we wish to thank Dr. Dean Casey for his support and Dr. Vijay Samalam for reviewing an earlier draft. Finally, we are grateful to the editorial staff at Artech House, who provided encouragement and kept us on track.

Introduction

1

1.1 ORGANIZATION OF THE BOOK

For interested readers, this chapter describes the "big picture" context for the *asynchronous transfer mode* (ATM) concept. It begins by tracing highlights from the past century of progress in the public telephone network and packet-switched data networks. The latter part of the chapter introduces the notion of an integrated services digital network and presents a vision of the future public switched network. Many in the telecommunications industry anticipate that the future public switched network will be based on ATM and other technologies mentioned in this chapter.

Readers interested specifically in ATM may wish to proceed to the introduction to the ATM concept in Chapter 2. Chapter 2 summarizes the functions of the ATM layer specified in international standards and industry agreements. Chapter 3 covers the B-ISDN protocol reference model as a representation of the different types of information flows in ATM networks. Chapter 4 is an overview of traffic control principles and functions. Chapters 2 through 4 together provide the technical background information on ATM needed for the architecture study in the later chapters.

Beginning the second part of the book, Chapter 5 applies the information from the previous chapters towards the construction of a general ATM switch model. It outlines five major functional blocks in the switch model, which are treated in more detail in the remaining chapters. Chapters 6 through 10 cover the functions of the input module, output module, cell switch fabric, connection admission control, and system management, respectively.

1.2 HISTORICAL BACKGROUND

In the past, separate telecommunications networks have been specially designed for different services. For instance, the public switched telephone network has been developed for conversational speech; data networks for computer communications; and broadcast networks for television. While these networks are very capable of supporting their intended services, they are generally not well suited for other services that are inherently different in such network requirements as bandwidth, holding times, end-to-end delays, and error rates.

The idea of a single ubiquitous network providing all services in an integrated manner has existed for some time. In a sense, this notion was suggested by AT&T's first president, Theodore Vail, in his vision of "one policy, one system, universal service" [1], and it has been recently restated [2]. Implementation has been hindered by the lack of the necessary technology and public demand for integrated services. In recent years, however, there has been increasing demand from multimedia applications, which involve the processing and exchange of information in the various media of text, audio, and images. In addition, research in high-speed switching, fiber optics, and new protocols have demonstrated the technical feasibility of integrated services networks.

Research in the past few years has led to the concept of ATM as a possible means to realize an integrated services network. It will become evident in this chapter that ATM represents a dramatic change in the evolution of the public switched telephone network. It combines characteristics of both conventional packet switching and circuit switching. Not only does ATM imply a major change in the network facilities, but for the first time, the network will be designed to provide much more than plain old telephone service.

1.2.1 The Early Telephone Network

In 1820, Hans Christian Oersted discovered that connecting and disconnecting a battery at one end of a wire caused a compass needle to flip at the other end (by changing the electromagnetic field). Thus it became possible to telegraph a message encoded as a series of electromagnetic changes along a wire. Essentially telegraphy was the first means of transmitting text in digital form, and it is ironic that the telephone network is returning to its roots, in a sense, by changing into a digital network.

Alexander Graham Bell was searching for a method for a "harmonic telegraph," an instrument to send multiple tones simultaneously over a single wire, when he invented the telephone in 1876 [1]. At the transmitting telephone, the speaker's voice would cause a stretched membrane to vibrate. The membrane would vibrate an attached magnetized reed and generate an electrical current. At the receiving telephone, the reverse operation would take place to regenerate the voice sounds. Bell had demonstrated point-to-point analog transmission of speech.

After the Bell Telephone Company was established in 1877, it soon became necessary to develop a switching network to efficiently interconnect the multiplying number of telephone subscribers. Initially, call connections were established and managed by human operators at manual switchboards. Over the years, switchboards were replaced by automatic electromechanical switches and then modern electronic switching systems with stored program control [3,4]. For more than a century, the Bell telephone system (and now its divested Bell operating companies) has been continually improving the network facilities, but the basic principles of *circuit switching* have remained intrinsic to the telephone network [5]. In circuit switching, a connection with fixed bandwidth is reserved for a call for its entire duration. An advantage is that an established call is unaffected by other calls. A disadvantage is that any unused bandwidth will be wasted. While these traits are appropriate for speech, they are not ideal for data.

1.2.2 Data Networks

As computers became more commonplace, the telephone network began to be used for the transmission of digital information between machines (typically between a computer and a remote terminal). Although the telephone network was designed for analog speech, it was also attractive for machine-to-machine communications because of its ubiquity and convenience. Digital information required the use of modems (modulators/demodulators), which converted the digital signals into analog signals before transmission and back into digital after transmission. In the 1940s, experimental modems built at the Air Force Cambridge Research Laboratory were able to demonstrate a transmission rate of 1,300 bits per second (bps) over unconditioned analog telephone lines [6]. The rates of modems have since been improved to beyond 14.4 thousand bits per second (Kbps), but the rate is fundamentally limited by the nominal 4-kHz voiceband channel.

The escalating needs of the data-processing community at some point exceeded the limited capabilities of modems. Furthermore, circuit switching was clearly inefficient for the exchange of intermittent short bursts of data. A different type of network using *packet switching* was developed in the 1960s for exchanging messages between computers [7]. Packet switching is analogous to the store-and-forward method of mail delivery in the postal system. Source information is segmented, and each segment is encapsulated with a header to form a packet, similar to putting a letter into an envelope. The packet header contains information used for routing, error control, and flow control. At each switch, incoming packets are buffered, their headers are processed, and the packets are transmitted to the appropriate next switch.

Packet switching was originally conceived by Paul Baran of the Rand Corporation in 1964 as a distributed switching system for survivable military communications [8]. In 1966, Donald Davies at the National Physical Laboratory in the U.K. independently devised a message switching network. In 1967,

Lawrence Roberts and others at the Advanced Research Projects Agency (ARPA) began their pioneering work on the ARPANET to link together time-shared research computers in a nationwide network [6]. Operational since 1969, ARPANET has demonstrated a phenomenal rate of expansion (now a part of the worldwide Internet), stimulated the development of numerous other packet-switched networks worldwide, and germinated new applications such as the popular electronic-mail service.

These packet-switched networks typically leased 56-Kbps transmission links from the telephone network. In order to ensure reliable and correct packet delivery, conventional packet switching protocols are quite complicated with extensive error control and flow control functions [9]. Consequently, packet switches are processing-intensive and typically limited to throughputs of thousands of packets per second with packet delays on the order of 50–100 ms [10].

1.2.3 Packet-Switched Speech

Some experiments in packet-switched speech were undertaken in the 1970s, for example in the ARPANET [11,12]. Because speech is sensitive to end-to-end delay whereas nonreal-time data is sensitive to errors, it was widely taken for granted that circuit switching was most appropriate for speech while packet switching was most suitable for data [13]. However, there are a number of compelling reasons to consider packet switching for speech. First, speech is bursty in the sense that it consists of talkspurts separated by silence intervals [14]. If packets are generated only during talkspurts, statistical multiplexing by packet switching can reduce bandwidth usage by approximately 50%–60% depending on the method of speech activity detection [12]. Second, packet switching allows the use of layered (or embedded) speech coding, which separates speech information into packets of different priorities [11,14]. The least important speech information (within the lowest priority packets) is lost first during network congestion, resulting in a graceful degradation in speech quality. Finally, packet switching can transport speech and data in a common manner using the same transmission and switching facilities.

In the packet speech experiments, a number of significant problems were encountered [12]. The main problem was that the conventional data protocols involved extensive error-control and flow-control procedures, and consequently they were processing-intensive. Packet switches had limited throughputs and lengthy packet delays. For speech, the protocols could be much simpler. While error control and flow control are needed for reliable delivery of data packets, speech is much more tolerant of errors and loss of information [14]. A second problem was significant end-to-end delays consisting of: packetization delay in filling packets (typically 1,000–2,000 bits) with encoded speech information; random queueing delays at each switch; packet processing delays at each switch; and a buffering delay at the receiver to compensate for the variability of queueing delays. A third problem was the recovery of lost or late speech information [11]. Finally, it was found that flow-control strategies for data were not appropriate for speech [14].

Overall it was learned that although packet switching was feasible for speech in principle, major modifications in the existing protocols and packet switches would be necessary in order to achieve an acceptable quality of voice service. These experiences would contribute later to the development of the ATM concept.

1.3 EVOLUTION TO INTEGRATED SERVICES

In the previous section, we saw the development of the analog circuit-switched telephone network and digital packet-switched data networks. The success of data networks demonstrated several things: the capabilities of digital technology, the feasibility of packet switching, and the significance of data traffic. In addition, experiments in packet speech showed the feasibility of packet-switching delay-sensitive information.

These developments are influencing the evolution of the public switched telephone network today. Digital technology is increasing the performance and capabilities of the network. Considerable progress has been made in the conversion of all switching and transmission facilities from analog to digital. The *integrated digital network* (IDN) refers to the "integration" of digital switching and digital transmission to realize synergistic benefits in cost and performance.

The digital infrastructure will bring the notion of a single network providing all services closer to reality. The IDN will facilitate the addition of data services and packet switching, and it will evolve into a single digital network providing a wide variety of voice and data services. The *integrated services digital network* (ISDN) refers to the "integration" of different services through a common user-network interface.

1.3.1 Integrated Digital Network

Digital transmission became feasible in the late 1950s as solid-state electronics became increasingly economical and reliable. Digital transmission has many advantages over analog transmission—it is less sensitive to noise, easier to regenerate, easier to incorporate signaling, easier to multiplex, and simpler to monitor performance [3]. Furthermore, speech information in digital form can be computer processed and stored within the network. Digital signal processing of speech has become very economical and robust [11].

Digital transmission has been deployed extensively into the network [3]. The T1-carrier, a 1.544-Mbps digital transmission line carrying 24 time-division multiplexed (TDM) voice channels of 64 Kbps each, was introduced in 1962 for interoffice transmission. There now exists a digital hierarchy consisting of T1,

T1C, T2, T3, and upwards, which define groups of 1.544-Mbps bitstreams that are time-division multiplexed together.

Telephone switches in the U.S. were analog until the 1976 introduction of the first digital switch, AT&T's No. 4 ESS (electronic switching system). When analog switching is used with analog transmission, signals are frequency-division multiplexed (FDM) onto interoffice trunks. At the tandem switch, incoming FDM signals are demultiplexed and demodulated by channel banks, routed through a space-division switch, and then multiplexed and modulated again. This process is costly and accumulates noise through a series of switches. When digital transmission is used with analog switching, there is an additional cost of analog/digital conversions.

The No. 4ESS allowed the direct connection between the switch and digital transmission lines eliminating the need for costly analog/digital conversions. In addition, there is a synergy in the combination of digital switching and digital transmission. When switching and transmission are both digital, the multiplexer/demultiplexer channel banks are not necessary because incoming TDM signals need not be demultiplexed before the digital switch. Time-division multiplexing and time-division switching operations turn out to be very similar, and hence individual signals can be time-division switched without first demultiplexing them [15,16]. Thus, digital transmission combined with digital switching eliminates a great deal of equipment and improves performance compared with the equivalent analog equipment [17].

The IDN "integrates" digital switching and digital transmission to realize benefits in cost and performance. The public switched telephone network is well in progress toward the IDN, especially in interoffice facilities. In the near future, virtually all transmission and switching in the network will be digital.

1.3.2   Integrated Services Digital Network

The IDN will evolve towards the ISDN to maximize use of the digital infrastructure to include data services in addition to voice services [18]. The ISDN concept originated in 1971 but international standards for ISDN were adopted much later by the *International Telecommunication Union-Telecommunication Standardization Sector* (ITU-T, known as CCITT until March 1993) in the 1984 and 1988 I-Series Recommendations [16,19–21].

The ISDN concept is characterized by:

- End-to-end digital connectivity;
- A wide range of services, including voice and nonvoice services;
- A limited set of standard user-network interfaces.

The IDN will be enhanced with data-handling capabilities by means of a packet-switching subnetwork that will be functionally separate from the circuit-switched network. More capabilities will be added to the IDN until it eventually offers a wide range of digital voice and nonvoice services such as data, facsimile, teletext, videotex, and teleconferencing. The objective of ISDN is to *integrate* user access to these services through a common set of interfaces.

Interfaces will be based on these ISDN channels:

- 64-Kbps B channel for user information;
- 16- or 64-Kbps D channel for user information and signaling;
- 384-Kbps H0 channel;
- 1.536-Mbps H11 channel;
- 1.920-Mbps H12 channel.

The 64-Kbps basic rate was derived from the simple encoding scheme consisting of sampling 4 kHz voice signals at 8,000 samples per second, with 8 bits per sample.

A crucial component of ISDN is the standardized user-network interface [22]. Conceptually, the interface provides user access to a *digital pipe*, which can be filled by any mix of traffic up to the capacity of the pipe [18]. Within the network, the different types of traffic are separated and handled by appropriate service-specific subnetworks as shown in Figure 1.1. The current ISDN standards specify two types of user interfaces: a 144-Kbps *basic* rate access and a 1.536-Mbps *primary* rate access. The basic rate interface consists of 2 B channels and a 16-Kbps D channel (often referred to as "2B+D"). The primary rate interface consists of 23 B channels and a 64-Kbps D channel (often called "23B+D").

The current state of progress towards ISDN is summarized in [23]. Generally the deployment of ISDN has been slower than expected for a number of reasons: slow completion of standards, limited availability of services to the public, lack of interoperability between different manufacturers' switches, in-

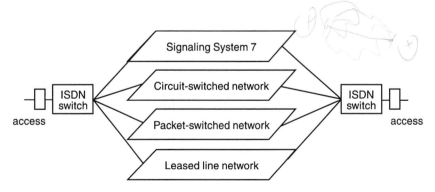

Figure 1.1 Integrated user access to service-specific subnetworks in ISDN.

sufficient end-user applications to justify modification of existing facilities, and confusion between vendors and potential users [10]. Furthermore, there is an inherent inflexibility in the ISDN user interfaces. Rates lower than 64 Kbps must be adapted up to that rate either by being stuffed with extraneous bits or by being combined with other lower rates to make up 64 Kbps. Similarly, rates between basic access and primary access must be adapted up to the primary access rate either by being stuffed with bits or by being combined with other rates to make up a primary access rate.

1.3.3 Signaling System Number 7

A major component of ISDN is a general-purpose common channel signaling system called *signaling system number 7* (SS7) described in the ITU-T 1984 Red Books and 1988 Blue Books [16,24,25]. Compared to in-band signaling, common channel signaling has several advantages, including faster call set-up and more flexibility to meet future functional needs. *CCITT number 6* and AT&T's *common channel interoffice signaling* were common channel signaling systems developed in the 1970s for international and national network signaling, respectively. Both have become outdated and have been succeeded by SS7, which is used for the network signaling between ISDN switches.

In SS7, signaling messages are exchanged through an overlaid packet-switching network independent from the ISDN transport network for user information. The signaling network consists of signaling points interconnected by signaling links. A signaling point is any node in the signaling network capable of generating, terminating, or relaying SS7 control messages. Signaling points may be service switching points (SSP), service control points (SCP), or signaling transfer points (STP). SSPs are switching systems with stored program control that interface with the SS7 network. SCPs are centralized, fault-tolerant, transaction-processing databases containing call-handling information that is accessed when additional function processing is required for the service requested by the customer. STPs are high-capacity, reliable packet switches for routing SS7 control messages. Figure 1.2 shows an example of SCPs and SSPs interconnected by STPs and signaling links.

The deployment of SS7 is currently very active as part of the transition to ISDN and the intelligent network (discussed in Section 1.4.4). To date, more than a thousand switches in the U.S. have been modified for SSP functions. Over a hundred STPs have been installed. Several dozen SCPs are in service handling millions of calls daily [26].

1.4 BROADBAND ISDN

While ISDN is being implemented, it has already been overtaken by the rapid progress in lightwave technology, which makes possible the enticing prospect

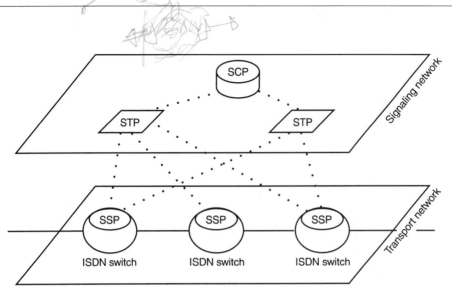

Figure 1.2 Signaling system number 7.

of offering broadband services to business and residential users. Fiber optics is theoretically capable of transmission rates up to 10^{15} bps over one kilometer with extremely low error rates [2]. Hence there is potentially abundant transmission capacity for voice, data, and video services including distributive entertainment video, video telephony, and videoconferencing [27].

Since 1985, the ITU-T Study Group 13 (formerly CCITT Study Group XVIII) has focused its attention on the introduction of broadband services at rates of 150 Mbps and higher into ISDN to create broadband ISDN (B-ISDN). The prefix is included to distinguish it from ISDN, which is now referred to as narrowband ISDN. B-ISDN is envisioned to be a highly flexible network with integrated transport supporting broadband services as well as narrowband services.

1.4.1 Synchronous Optical Network/Synchronous Digital Hierarchy

An important part of B-ISDN is the specification of the *synchronous optical network* (SONET) standard for the physical layer in the U.S. [28,29]. The original SONET proposal was submitted by Bell Communications Research (Bellcore) to the T1X1 Subcommittee in 1985 to allow optical midspan meets between different manufacturers' equipment. With worldwide participation among manufacturers, network providers, and researchers, an initial standards specification was drafted by the T1X1 Subcommittee in 1988 [30,31] and a (mostly) compatible version was adopted by the ITU-T in 1988 under the name of *synchronous digital hierarchy* (SDH) [32–34].

SONET is a modular family of rates and formats for interfaces used in optical networks. The standard defines:

- A synchronous frame structure for a basic signal at rate 51.84 Mbps (155.52 Mbps in SDH);
- A byte-interleaved scheme to create a family of rates and formats consisting of integer multiples of the basic signal;
- Layered overhead and embedded data communication channels for operations and maintenance;
- A procedure for automatic protection switching.

SONET/SDH has gained widespread support because it provides compatibility between equipment from different manufacturers, simple multiplexing and demultiplexing, direct access to lower speed tributaries without the need to first demultiplex the entire high-speed signal, abundant set of operations and maintenance capabilities, and easy extension to future higher bit rates.

The discussion of the SONET standard will be deferred to Chapter 6, where it is covered in much more detail.

1.4.2 Asynchronous Transfer Mode

It would have been natural to extend the circuit-switched ISDN by defining new higher rates, and for a time it was assumed that multi-rate circuit switching referred to as *synchronous transfer mode* (STM) would become the basis for B-ISDN. However, there were some critics of ISDN who believed that the rigid channel structures of STM could not provide the required flexibility for future services, nor was it efficient for variable bit-rate information [35–38]. Furthermore, it was observed that overlaid circuit switching and packet switching facilities, as in ISDN, would not yield the economies possible (in principle) from truly integrated transport. Hence there were arguments for a single service-independent transport technique, and the pivotal question became which switching technique could provide the required flexibility and efficiency [39].

As mentioned earlier, experiments in packet-switched speech had demonstrated the feasibility of the idea but encountered a number of implementation issues, such as complicated protocols and slow packet switches. However, the conceptual advantages of packet switching remained attractive. In the early 1980s, the experiences contributed to an experimental version of packet switching modified with the objectives of very high throughput, fast packet processing, and minimal queueing delays [40–42]. The modified version, called *fast packet switching*, is based on these ideas:

- Modern digital transmission is high-speed and very reliable; therefore, the role of the subnetwork can be simplified by removing error-control and flow-control functions from lower protocol layers to be performed on an end-to-end basis as needed by a particular service.

- The technique should be connection-oriented in order to simplify packet processing.
- The simplified protocols can be processed faster in hardware to increase the packet switch throughput and reduce packet delays.

At the same time, experiments were conducted with the same concept under the name of asynchronous time-division (ATD) switching [43–45].

In 1988, the ITU-T standardized a form of the fast packet and ATD switching concepts under the new name of *asynchronous transfer mode* (ATM) to distinguish it from conventional packet switching, and the organization designated ATM as the target switching and multiplexing approach for B-ISDN [46]. In ATM, information is transported by means of streams of short fixed-length packets called cells, which are asynchronous time-division multiplexed. It is expected to be capable of effectively emulating any service and thus provide high-throughput, low-delay, service-independent transport for all types of traffic. In contrast to the overlaid networks in Figure 1.1, Figure 1.3 illustrates an ATM subnetwork for B-ISDN with an SS7 signaling network. The SS7 network will likely continue to be used for network signaling for some time. It is shown in dashed lines because ATM switches are as capable of carrying signaling messages as STPs, and hence the STPs will eventually become redundant. In the long term, the ATM subnetwork may replace the STPs to carry network signaling information as well as user data.

The advantages of ATM are believed to be:

- Flexibility to support existing services and unforeseen future services;
- Dynamic bandwidth allocation;
- Integrated transport of all information types;
- Efficient utilization of network resources by statistical sharing.

Whether all of these anticipated benefits can be realized as the ATM concept moves to practical implementation is an important question [47].

The disadvantages are that cells may suffer variable delays through the network or may be lost. The network must ensure the quality of service, in terms of cell delays and cell loss rate, required by the users. In addition, considerable processing is involved in converting user information into and from the ATM cell format, and in carrying cells at high rates through each switch.

The discussion of the ATM concept will be continued in Chapter 2.

1.4.3 Metropolitan Area Networks

It is worthwhile to mention metropolitan area networks (MANs) because they are a technology related to ATM and will likely have an important role in the

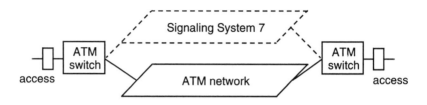

Figure 1.3   B-ISDN with ATM subnetwork and SS7 signaling network.

evolution towards B-ISDN. Local area networks (LANs) have been typically 10-Mbps Ethernets and 4-Mbps token rings, but LAN technology is migrating towards higher speeds exemplified by 100-Mbps *fiber distributed data interface* (FDDI) [48]. A MAN is essentially a very large LAN with access protocols that are less sensitive to network size, designed for more users, and nominally optimized to an area 50 km in diameter. Like a LAN, MANs are based on multiple access of a shared medium. Unlike LANs, MANs may support digital voice services, which have a large influence on the design of the MAN [49]. Another difference is that MANs are considered to be part of the public switched network.

MANs have been the subject of study in the IEEE 802.6 Working Group of IEEE Project 802. In 1990, *distributed queue dual bus* (DQDB) was adopted for the IEEE 802.6 MAN standard [50], based on the original *queued packet and synchronous exchange* (QPSX) proposal by Telecom Australia. DQDB is a physical dual ring that functions as dual unidirectional buses. Each station has two-port interfaces to both buses which operate in opposite directions. The dual buses allow a unique distributed queueing mechanism for scheduling transmissions on each bus that is equivalent in operation to a single queue. When a station wants to transmit (downstream) on bus A, for example, it makes a reservation request (upstream) on bus B. The upstream stations will monitor the request and allow an empty slot to pass downstream on bus A to be seized by the requesting station. Each station maintains up/down counters to keep track of its position in the distributed queue so that it seizes the appropriate empty slots for transmission. By this distributed queue mechanism, the utilization can reach nearly 100%.

MANs are expected to be important to introduce broadband data services and ease the introduction of B-ISDN, and therefore the MAN and ATM standards have been intentionally aligned [51]. The cell formats are the same in length, with minor differences in the header formats. A public wide-area connectionless data service based on the DQDB protocol, called *switched multimegabit data services* (SMDS), is currently being offered by most service providers. Direct ATM access through MANs is also being considered.

1.4.4 Intelligent Network

Although not related specifically to B-ISDN, the *intelligent network* (IN) concept is an important part of the envisioned future public network with far-reaching implications and goals. Modern switching systems, beginning with the 1ESS in 1965, have stored program control. When service changes must be made or new services are introduced, it is a painstaking process to make changes in the complex proprietary software of each switch, and there is a possibility that services may exhibit different behaviors in different switching systems [26].

In development since the mid-1980s, the basic idea underlying the IN is the separation of the service logic from the network transport facilities, with a vendor-independent interface between them. The service logic would reside in centralized databases (the SCPs mentioned earlier) and accessed through the signaling network, namely SS7. This separation would allow service changes to be implemented centrally, quickly, uniformly, and independently of proprietary switching systems.

The first phase of the IN, designated as intelligent network 1 or IN/1 by Bellcore, consists of switching systems, SCPs, SS7 for accessing the SCPs, and operations systems (OS) for network management and maintenance. Bellcore developed a plan to expand the IN/1 architecture, called IN/2, and a modest near-term subset of IN/2, designated as IN/1+. These plans were abandoned when Bellcore convened the Multi-Vendor Interactions (MVI) Forum in 1989 between Bellcore, the regional Bell operating companies, and vendors. The MVI Forum has produced a plan called the *advanced intelligent network* (AIN).

IN has also been the subject of study of ITU-T Study Group 11 in collaboration with Study Group 13. The initial set of technical recommendations referred to as IN Capability Set 1 (CS1) was completed in December 1991 with the objective of deployment in 1993 [52]. The ITU-T is currently working on follow-on plans called CS2.

Since IN is not directly relevant to the remainder of this book, readers interested in more details are referred to [26,53–56].

References

[1]   Boettinger, H., *The Telephone Book,* New York: Stearn Publishers Ltd., 1983.
[2]   Mayo, J., "The Evolution Toward Universal Information Services," *Telephony,* Vol. 208, March 4, 1985, pp. 40–50.
[3]   Bellamy, J., *Digital Telephony,* New York: John Wiley & Sons, 1982.
[4]   Rey, R., ed., *Engineering and Operations in the Bell System,* 2nd ed., Murray Hill, NJ: AT&T Bell Laboratories, 1983.
[5]   Joel, A., Jr., "Circuit-Switching Fundamentals," in *Fundamentals of Digital Switching* (J. McDonald, ed.), New York: Plenum Press, 1983.

[6]   Green, P., Jr., "Computer Communications: Milestones and Prophecies," *IEEE Communications Magazine,* Vol. 22, May 1984, pp. 49–63.

[7]   Heggestad, H., "An Overview of Packet-Switching Communications," *IEEE Communications Magazine,* Vol. 22, April 1984, pp. 24–31.

[8]   Roberts, L., "The Evolution of Packet Switching," *Proc. of the IEEE,* Vol. 66, Nov. 1978, pp. 1,307–1,313.

[9]   Tanenbaum, A., *Computer Networks,* 2nd ed., Englewood Cliffs, NJ: Prentice-Hall, 1989.

[10] Kleinrock, L., "ISDN—The Path to Broadband Networks," *Proc. of the IEEE,* Vol. 79, Feb. 1991, pp. 112–117.

[11] Gold, B., "Digital Speech Networks," *Proc. of the IEEE,* Vol. 65, Dec. 1977, pp. 1,636–1,658.

[12] Weinstein, C., and J. Forgie, "Experience with Speech Communications in Packet Networks," *IEEE J. on Selected Areas in Communications,* Vol. SAC-1, Dec. 1983, pp. 963–980.

13]   Ross, M., "Circuit versus Packet Switching," *Fundamentals of Digital Switching* (J. McDonald, ed.), New York: Plenum Press, 1983.

[14] Bially, T., et al., "Voice Communication in Integrated Digital Voice and Data Networks," *IEEE Trans. on Communications,* Vol. COM-28, Sept. 1980, pp. 1,478–1,489.

[15] Stallings, W., *Data and Computer Communications,* New York: Macmillan, 1985.

[16] Stallings, W., *ISDN and Broadband ISDN,* 2nd ed., New York: Macmillan, 1992.

[17] McDonald, J., "Digital Networks," in *Fundamentals of Digital Switching* (J. McDonald, ed.), New York: Plenum Press, 1983.

[18] Dorros, I., "ISDN," *IEEE Communications Magazine,* Vol. 19, March 1981, pp. 16–19.

[19] Decina, M., and E. Scace, "CCITT Recommendations on the ISDN: A Review," *IEEE J. on Selected Areas in Communications,* Vol. SAC-4, May 1986, pp. 320–325.

[20] Habara, K., "ISDN: A Look at the Future Through the Past," *IEEE Communications Magazine,* Vol. 26, Nov. 1988, pp. 25–32.

[21] Kano, S., et al., "ISDN Standardization," *Proc. of the IEEE,* Vol. 79, Feb. 1991, pp. 118–123.

[22] Gifford, W., "ISDN User-Network Interfaces," *IEEE J. on Selected Areas in Communications,* Vol. SAC-4, May 1986, pp. 343–348.

[23] Wu, W., and A. Livne, "ISDN: A Snapshot," *Proc. of the IEEE,* Vol. 79, Feb. 1991, pp. 103–111.

[24] Jabbari, B., "Common Channel Signaling System Number 7 for ISDN and Intelligent Networks," *Proc. of the IEEE,* Vol. 79, Feb. 1991, pp. 155–169.

[25] Modarressi, A., and R. Skoog, "An Overview of Signaling System No. 7," *Proc. of the IEEE,* Vol. 80, April 1992, pp. 590–606.

[26] Robrock II, R., "The Intelligent Network—Changing the Face of Telecommunications," *Proc. of the IEEE,* Vol. 79, Jan. 1991, pp. 7–20.

[27] Spears, M., "Broadband ISDN Switching Capabilities from a Services Perspective," *IEEE J. on Selected Areas in Communications,* Vol. SAC-5, Oct. 1987, pp. 1,222–1,230.

[28] Ballart, R., and Y-C. Ching, "SONET: Now It's the Standard Optical Network," *IEEE Communications Magazine,* Vol. 27, March 1989, pp. 8–15.

[29] Boehm, R., "Progress in Standardization of SONET," *IEEE LCS Magazine,* Vol. 1, May 1990, pp. 8–16.

[30] ANSI, *American National Standard for Telecommunications—Digital Hierarchy Optical Rates and Formats Specifications,* T1.105–1988, 1988.

[31] ANSI, *American National Standard for Telecommunications—Digital Hierarchy Optical Interface Specifications, Single Mode,* T1.106–1988, 1988.

[32] ITU-T Rec. G.707, *Synchronous Digital Hierarchy Bit Rates,* Melbourne, Nov. 14–25, 1988.

[33] ITU-T Rec. G.708, *Network Node Interface for the Synchronous Digital Hierarchy,* Melbourne, Nov. 14–25, 1988.

[34] ITU-T Rec. G.709, *Synchronous Multiplexing Structure,* Melbourne, Nov. 14–25, 1988.

[35] DePrycker, M., "Evolution from ISDN to BISDN: A Logical Step Towards ATM," *Computer Communications,* Vol. 12, June 1989, pp. 141–146.

[36] Minzer, S., "Toward an International Broadband ISDN Standard," *Telecommunications*, Vol. 21, Oct. 1987, pp. 94–112.

[37] Turner, J., "Design of an Integrated Services Packet Network," *IEEE J. on Selected Areas in Communications*, Vol. SAC-4, Nov. 1986, pp. 1,373–1,380.

[38] Turner, J., "New Directions in Communications (or Which Way to the Information Age?)," *IEEE Communications Magazine*, Vol. 24, Oct. 1986, pp. 8–15.

39] Chen, T., and D. Messerschmitt, "Integrated Voice/Data Switching," *IEEE Communications Magazine*, Vol. 26, June 1988, pp. 16–26.

[40] Kirton, P., et al., "Fast Packet Switching for Integrated Network Evolution," *1987 Int. Switching Symp.*, Phoenix, March 15–20, 1987, pp. B6.2.1–7.

[41] Luderer, G., et al., "Wideband Packet Switching Technology for Switching Systems," *1987 Int. Switching Symp.*, Phoenix, March 15–20, 1987, pp. B6.1.1–7.

[42] Turner, J., and L. Wyatt, "A Packet Network Architecture for Integrated Services," *GLOBE-COM'83*, San Diego, Nov. 28–Dec. 1, 1983, pp. 2.1.1–6.

[43] Dieudonne, M., and M. Quinquis, "Switching Techniques for Asynchronous Time Division Multiplexing (or Fast Packet Switching)," *1987 Int. Switching Symp.*, Phoenix, March 15–20, 1987, pp. B5.1.1–6.

[44] Gonet, P., et al., "Asynchronous Time-Division Switching: The Way to Flexible Broadband Communication Networks," *1986 Int. Zurich Seminar on Digital Communications*, March 9–11, 1986, pp. 141–148.

[45] Plehiers, P., et al., "Evolution towards a Belgian Broadband Experiment," *1987 Int. Switching Symp.*, Phoenix, March 15–20, 1987, pp. B5.3.1–8.

[46] ITU-T Rec. I.121, *Broadband Aspects of ISDN*, Melbourne, Nov. 14–25, 1988.

[47] Aaron, M., and M. Decina, "Asynchronous Transfer Mode or Synchronous Transfer Mode or Both?" *IEEE Communications Magazine*, Vol. 29, Jan. 1991, pp. 10–13.

[48] Chlamtac, I., and W. Franta, "Rationale, Directions, and Issues Surrounding High-Speed Networks," *Proc. of the IEEE*, Vol. 78, Jan. 1990, pp. 94–120.

[49] Mollenauer, J., "Standards for Metropolitan Area Networks," *IEEE Communications Magazine*, Vol. 26, April 1988, pp. 15–19.

[50] IEEE Standard 802.6, *Distributed Queue Dual Bus (DQDB) Subnetwork of a Metropolitan Area Network*, Dec. 1990.

[51] Byrne, W., et al., "Evolution of Metropolitan Area Networks to Broadband ISDN," *IEEE Communications Magazine*, Vol. 29, Jan. 1991, pp. 69–82.

[52] Duran, J., and J. Visser, "International Standards for Intelligent Networks," *IEEE Communications Magazine*, Vol. 30, Feb. 1992, pp. 34–42.

[53] Bellcore, *Advanced Intelligent Network Release 1 Proposal*, special report SR-NPL-001509, issue 1, Nov. 1989.

[54] Bellcore, *Advanced Intelligent Network Release 1 Baseline Architecture*, special report SR-NPL-001555, issue 1, March 1990.

[55] Bellcore, *Advanced Intelligent Network Release 1 Network and Operations Plan*, special report SR-NPL-001623, issue 1, June 1990.

[56] Berman, R., and J. Brewster, "Perspectives on the AIN Architecture," *IEEE Communications Magazine*, Vol. 30, Feb. 1992, pp. 27–32.

Asynchronous Transfer Mode 2

2.1 INTRODUCTION

Chapter 1 presented a broad picture of the circuit-switched telephone network and packet-switched data networks. It traced the course of evolution of the public telephone network towards the IDN, ISDN, and broadband ISDN. This chapter begins the introduction to asynchronous transfer mode (ATM) which will continue through Chapters 3 and 4. The material is based largely on documents from the ITU-T (formerly CCITT) [1–11], ATM Forum [12], and Bellcore [13–17]. For interested readers, many tutorials on ATM can be readily found, for example [18–34]. Section 2.2 relates the position of ATM within the B-ISDN protocol reference model. For the purpose of discussion, a distinction is made between the ATM concept and its implementation in the standards. The principles of the ATM concept are reviewed in Section 2.3, followed by an overview of ATM standards in Section 2.4. The remainder of this chapter introduces several topics in ATM networking that will be covered in detail in later chapters.

The previous chapter mentioned the notion of "integration" in the context of the IDN and ISDN. Integration in the network can be realized at different, and increasingly difficult, levels: traffic integration in physical transmission, service integration in user access, and traffic integration in switching. The IDN, ISDN, and broadband ISDN are examples of networks with different levels of integration. Conceptually, ATM is a method capable of achieving integration at all of these levels in B-ISDN.

Integration at the level of physical transmission can be realized simply by means of multiplexing. For decades, traffic in the public switched telephone network have shared high-speed interoffice trunks by frequency- or time-division multiplexing. In the IDN, traffic will be time-division multiplexed to share digital transmission facilities.

ISDN is an example of service integration at the level of user access. It will support circuit-switched B channels and packet-switched D channels accessed through a common set of standardized user-network interfaces. Although the

17

services are provided by functionally separate subnetworks, users are presented with the perception of a single network.

If broadband services are initially introduced into ISDN as another overlay subnetwork, it will become inefficient to administer and maintain a number of separate service-specific subnetworks and their operations support systems. It will also be costly to add or change subnetworks as services need to be introduced or changed. In principle, it would be much more efficient (and therefore economical) to operate and maintain a single service-independent subnetwork capable of supporting a wide range of services. Changes in the mix of services would not necessarily require a change in the subnetwork. This principle of traffic integration at the switching level underlies the envisioned B-ISDN concept, and ATM is the switching method chosen for the service-independent subnetwork.

2.2 BROADBAND ISDN

As described in ITU-T standards, broadband ISDN is a network architecture evolving from ISDN based on extensions of ISDN principles [1]. It provides a range of narrowband and broadband voice, data, video, and multimedia services. Services may be distributive or interactive, constant bit-rate (CBR) or variable bit-rate (VBR), and connection-oriented or connectionless. In support of these services, the network provides virtual connections that may be point-to-point or multipoint, symmetric or asymmetric, unidirectional or bidirectional, and switched or (semi) permanent [2,3]. A B-ISDN call may consist of a number of virtual connections that can be negotiated, established, modified, and terminated separately or together.

A fundamental part of the B-ISDN specification is the protocol reference model shown in Figure 2.1 [4]. The B-ISDN protocol reference model consists of three parts:

- User plane for the transfer of user information;
- Control plane for connection control functions;
- Management plane for network supervision functions.

This chapter discusses only the user plane as it embodies the concept of integration at the levels of transmission, user access, and switching. The protocol reference model and its planes are the topic of Chapter 3.

The user plane represents the protocols for carrying information between users through the network. Like the widely known open systems interconnection (OSI) reference model, the user plane has a hierarchical layered structure. Instead of the seven layers of the OSI model, the user plane consists of these four layers:

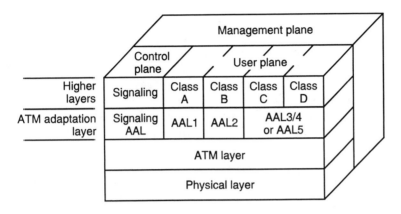

Figure 2.1 B-ISDN protocol reference model.

- Higher layers;
- ATM adaptation layer;
- ATM layer;
- Physical layer.

(The correspondence between these layers and the seven OSI layers is under study.) Each layer uses the services of the lower layers and in turn provides services to the layer above it. The layered structure allows independence in the design and implementation of each layer; for example, ATM may be used on different physical media, such as optical fiber or twisted pair copper.

User services are supported at the highest layer of the user plane. For didactic purposes, four classes of services have been identified by the ITU-T [6]. Class A refers to connection-oriented constant bit-rate services, such as circuit emulation or CBR speech. Classes B to D are variable bit-rate services. Class B service is connection-oriented with a timing relation required between source and destination, e.g., VBR video. Class C service is connection-oriented without a timing relation requirement—typically connection-oriented data such as X.25 and signaling. Class D refers to connectionless services; for example, connectionless data from local area networks (LANs) and metropolitan area networks (MANs).

The *ATM adaptation layer* (AAL) supports all classes of services above the service-independent ATM layer [6,7,13]. AAL functions are service-specific and were originally designated as types 1 to 4 corresponding to service classes A to D. However, AAL3 and AAL4 have been merged into a single AAL3/4, and a new AAL5 has been adopted as a simpler version of AAL3/4 for VBR data services. For reference, AAL1, AAL3/4, and AAL5 are described in Appendixes A through C (note AAL2 has not been defined in the standards yet).

The AAL consists of two sublayers: the *convergence sublayer* (CS) and the *segmentation and reassembly* (SAR) sublayer. The CS is a service-dependent interface specification that can include multiplexing, error control, cell-loss detection, and timing recovery. The SAR sublayer divides the variable-length information from the CS into ATM cells for the ATM layer and reconstructs ATM cells into the original CS data units. Specific functions of the different AALs are delineated in the appendixes. In all cases, AAL functions are performed only at the edges of the network, and AAL information is carried within the ATM cell (information field) transparently by the ATM layer.

ATM was briefly introduced in Section 1.4.2. The ATM layer accepts data units from the AAL ready for cell encapsulation (generation and concatenation of the header) and delivers information to the AAL after cell decapsulation (extraction and processing of the header). The primary function of the ATM layer is sequential end-to-end transfer of ATM cells according to the ATM protocol information contained in their cell headers. The layer is service-independent in that the cell information fields are carried transparently and could contain any type of user data or network information. Further details of the ATM layer are postponed until the next section.

Below the ATM layer, the physical layer is responsible for the transmission of ATM cells as bitstreams across a physical medium. This layer is divided into a *physical medium* (PM) sublayer and *transmission convergence* (TC) sublayer. The PM sublayer provides transmission of a bitstream with associated timing information and line coding depending on the particular physical medium. The TC sublayer consists of transmission functions independent of the physical medium, including:

- Transmission frame generation and recovery;
- Frame adaptation (mapping cells into and from the frame payload);
- Cell delineation (identification and recovery of cell boundaries);
- Cell header error-check processing and generation;
- Cell rate decoupling (inserting and extracting empty cells).

The functions of the physical layer based on SONET are discussed in Chapter 6.

The implication of the hierarchical structure of the user plane in the B-ISDN protocol reference model is illustrated in Figure 2.2. Conceptually different services are supported above the service-independent ATM subnetwork through the AAL, which converts between the user application-specific information and ATM cells. Thus, services can be added or changed in the higher layers without necessitating changes in the functions of the underlying ATM subnetwork. Clearly this is an important advantage when the future mix of services is dynamic and difficult to predict. This motivation for ATM may be summarized as *flexibility to add and change services*. Additionally, a single subnetwork offers *simpler operations and administration* compared to multiple subnetworks.

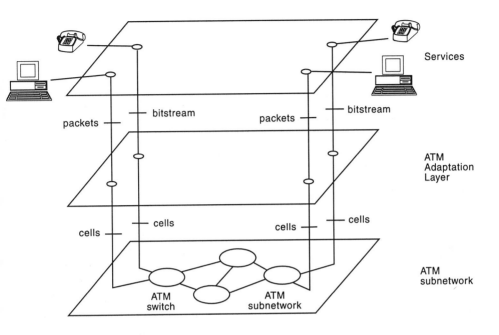

Figure 2.2 Conceptual view of different services supported above a service-independent ATM subnetwork.

2.3 ATM CONCEPT

In ATM, *asynchronous* does not refer to physical transmission, which will in fact be synchronous in B-ISDN (e.g., SONET/SDH). Asynchronous refers to the manner in which bandwidth is allocated among connections and users. Bandwidth is divided into time slots of fixed length. These time slots are allocated for user information as needed and therefore do not have predetermined temporal positions (within a periodic frame, for example). Instead of identification of the connection by temporal position, time slots are identified with explicit prefix labels. *Transfer mode* is a term intended to signify that it is a multiplexing and switching technique.

The ATM concept is defined by a number of principles:

- All information is carried in the form of fixed-length data units called cells, which consist of a header and an information field (sometimes called payload).
- ATM is connection-oriented, and cells in the same virtual connection maintain their sequential order.

- Traffic sources may generate cells as needed—i.e., without predetermined temporal positions—and therefore cells have explicit labels (a field in the header) for connection identification.
- The main function of the cell header is identification of cells belonging to the same virtual connection.
- The identifier labels have only local significance (they are not explicit addresses) and are translated at each switch.
- The information field is carried transparently; for instance, no error control is performed on the information field.
- Cell streams are asynchronous time-division multiplexed.

It can be seen that ATM specifies the method of information exchange across the *user-network interface* (UNI) as well as the mode of multiplexing and switching within the network. Furthermore, ATM is a technique for integrating all traffic at the levels of transmission, user access, and switching.

For the UNI, the main advantage of ATM is that it allows dynamic bandwidth allocation; that is, bandwidth is given to traffic sources as needed (at the granularity of cells). In comparison, bandwidth allocation by the *synchronous transfer mode* (STM) technique, where periodic time slots are reserved for connections, would limit the interface to a rigid set of fixed rates. ATM permits variable bit-rate interfaces without precluding constant bit-rate interfaces. This motivation for ATM may be described as *flexibility in user access.*

As a multiplexing technique, ATM is potentially capable of more efficient utilization of transmission facilities compared to synchronous TDM. In synchronous TDM, a periodic frame consisting of short time slots (usually byte-size) is defined on a transmission link, and connections sharing the link are reserved fixed time slot positions in each frame. It is apparent that bandwidth will be wasted if the traffic is bursty and contains idle periods. This inefficiency can be prevented in asynchronous TDM where time slots are allotted to connections as needed. However, a prefix label is needed for each time slot to identify the connection. As a consequence, the time slots are larger than bytes so that the labels consume a smaller fraction of the total bandwidth. Also, processing is required for each time slot, and buffering is required to resolve contention. ATM is an example of this labeled asynchronous TDM technique in that identifier labels in the cell header have only local, and not end-to-end, significance. As a multiplexing technique, ATM is motivated by the *potential for efficient utilization.*

As a switching technique compared to STM (or multirate circuit switching), the main advantage of ATM is that it *avoids the necessity of peak rate allocation* as in STM. Another difference is that ATM involves network processing of cells, whereas STM carries traffic transparently through the network. This is a disadvantage in terms of processing burden but allows greater network control over routing, error control, flow control, copying, and priorities. Considering priorities, for example, each cell can be assigned delay and loss priorities. By means of priorities, the network can exercise control over the preferential treatment of one traffic class relative to another class at the levels of virtual connections or individual cells. Thus, as a switching technique, ATM may be motivated by the capability for *granular and flexible control of network traffic*.

There are basically two undesirable consequences of the asynchronous nature of ATM. Since network resources are not reserved, congestion is possible when an excessive amount of traffic contends for limited buffer resources, making it necessary to lose cells. Another consequence is variable cell delays through the network caused mainly by random queueing delays at each switch and multiplexer. Hence the concept of *quality of service* (QOS), in terms of cell delays and cell loss rate, is fundamental to discussions of ATM [8]. It is intended that B-ISDN will provide multiple QOS classes of virtual connections to support a range of traffic types with different QOS requirements. Support of multiple traffic classes and protection of their QOS, while simultaneously maximizing statistical sharing and utilization of network resources, is the most difficult challenge in the implementation of ATM.

2.4 ATM STANDARDS

It is worthwhile to distinguish between the ATM concept and its realization in standards. ATM standards attempt to specify an implementation of ATM that ensures conformance and interoperability among all organizations. The ATM standards are the result of cooperation among telecommunications organizations around the world and between different standards bodies, including CCITT Study Group XVIII on B-ISDN, IEEE 802.6 Working Group on MANs, Study Group XI on signaling, and Study Groups XV and XVII on video coding.

The Telecommunication Standardization Sector (ITU-T, known as the CCITT until March 1993) of the *International Telecommunication Union* (ITU), and in particular ITU-T Study Group 13 (formerly, CCITT Study Group XVIII), has been responsible for B-ISDN since 1985. The first milestone was the 1988 Recommendation I.121, which established ATM as the target transfer mode for B-ISDN and provided a guideline for subsequent ATM standards. It signified a drastic change in the direction of the public network evolution, contrary to the initial assumption that STM would be adopted in the natural migration from narrowband ISDN. Indeed, debates about the relative merits of ATM and STM have continued despite the broad acceptance of ATM as the long-term goal [35].

Since 1988, the usual approval procedures have been accelerated in recognition of commercial driving factors. This has allowed standards recommendations to be approved within a four-year study period instead of only at the end. The objective was a sufficient set of specifications for deployment of basic ATM services in the 1993–1995 timeframe. Major 1990–1992 recommendations are listed in Table 2.1. The general areas of deliberation have been the ATM technique, AAL, services, network aspects, interfaces, and operations and maintenance (OAM). New recommendations are expected to include resolution of control issues such as signaling, resource management, OAM, and network performance [19].

Table 2.1
Major 1990–1992 ITU-T Recommendations

I.121	Broadband aspects of ISDN
I.150	B-ISDN ATM functional characteristics
I.211	B-ISDN service aspects
I.311	B-ISDN general network aspects
I.321	B-ISDN protocol reference model and its applications
I.327	B-ISDN functional architecture
I.361	B-ISDN ATM-layer specification
I.362	B-ISDN ATM adaptation layer functional description
I.363	B-ISDN ATM adaptation layer specification
I.371	Traffic control and congestion control in B-ISDN
I.413	B-ISDN user-network interface
I.432	B-ISDN user-network interface physical-layer specification
I.610	B-ISDN operation and maintenance principles and functions

In the U.S., B-ISDN is the subject of the T1S1 Technical Subcommittee of the *American National Standards Institute* (ANSI). The European counterpart is the NA5 Committee of the *European Telecommunications Standards Institute* (ETSI). In addition, the ATM Forum is an international consortium of service providers, users, and equipment vendors dedicated to promoting interoperability among equipment from different vendors and timely deployment of ATM services. The ATM Forum is not chartered to set standards, but many of its members also participate in official standards organizations. Begun in 1991 with only six members, membership has exceeded 500 by May 1994. In 1993, the ATM Forum completed specifications on the UNI [12]. Currently work is progressing in several Forum working groups on services, signaling, interfaces, traffic control, network management, testing, and internetworking.

The single most important ATM standard concerns the definition of the cell header [5]. The standardized ATM cell format for the UNI and *network node interface* (NNI) is shown in Figure 2.3. It is a 53-byte cell format consisting of a 5-byte header and 48-byte information field. The cell length is a compromise between a proposal developed by ANSI for a 5-byte header and 64-byte information field and another proposal put forth by ETSI for a 4-byte header and 32-byte information field [32]. A major consideration was the packetization delay for voice. A shorter cell involves less delay to fill a cell with encoded speech information. On the other hand, a longer cell may be advantageous because more time is available to process each cell header, capacity utilization may be improved, and less cost is incurred in segmentation and reassembly and other AAL functions.

The accepted cell-header format reflects in large part the T1S1 proposal. At the UNI, the fields are:

- Generic flow control (GFC);
- Virtual path identifier (VPI);
- Virtual channel identifier (VCI);
- Payload type (PT);
- Cell loss priority (CLP);
- Header error control (HEC).

The GFC field is not present at the NNI; instead, the four bits are included in the VPI field. The ETSI proposal also contained fields for VPI/VCI, payload type, and HEC, but no fields for priorities or GFC.

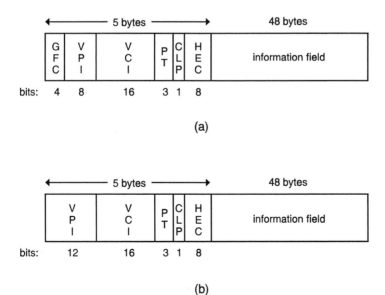

Figure 2.3 ATM cell format at (a) UNI and (b) NNI.

ANSI proposed the GFC field to provide a mechanism for the flow control of multiple user terminals connected to a shared access link. The intention was to allow user interface configurations similar to those used in LANs and MANs, which is clearly more of a consideration for data traffic. The precise use of the GFC field has not been determined in standards yet. Initially, the GFC field will be set to all zeros and have no effect on the flow rates of B-ISDN terminals [12]. It is overwritten by ATM switches and not transported through the network.

The VPI and VCI fields constitute a label to identify the virtual connection at the virtual path (VP) and virtual channel (VC) levels, respectively. These VPI/VCI values have only local significance and are translated at each ATM switch. VPs and VCs are explained in more detail in Section 2.5.2. At the UNI, 24 bits are available for the VPI/VCI. The number of VPI/VCI bits in use is determined between the user and network at the time of service subscription (but the specific VPI/VCI values are assigned per connection); the other bits are set to zero. Certain codes for the VPI/VCI fields are reserved for special uses; these are listed in Tables 2.2 and 2.3.

Table 2.2
Pre-assigned Cell Header Values at UNI

Use	GFC	VPI	VCI	PT	CLP
Unassigned cell	AAAA	00000000	00000000 00000000	XXX	0
Metasignaling*	AAAA	YYYYYYYY	00000000 00000001	0A0	C
General broad-cast signaling*	AAAA	YYYYYYYY	00000000 00000010	0AA	C
Point-to-point signaling*	AAAA	YYYYYYYY	00000000 00000101	0AA	C
Segment OAM F4 flow cell	AAAA	AAAAAAAA	00000000 00000011	0A0	A
End-to-end OAM F4 flow cell	AAAA	AAAAAAAA	00000000 00000100	0A0	A
Segment OAM F5 flow cell[†]	AAAA	AAAAAAAA	AAAAAAAA AAAAAAAA	100	A
End-to-end OAM F5 flow cell[†]	AAAA	AAAAAAAA	AAAAAAAA AAAAAAAA	101	A
Resource man-agement cell[†]	AAAA	AAAAAAAA	AAAAAAAA AAAAAAAA	110	A

Use	GFC	VPI	VCI	PT	CLP
ILMI cell[‡]	AAAA	00000000	00000000 00010000	AAA	0
SMDS[§]	AAAA	00000000	00000000 00001111	0A0	A
Idle cell[‖]	0000	00000000	00000000 00000000	000	1
Physical-layer OAM cell[#]	0000	00000000	00000000 00000000	100	1
Reserved for use by physical layer	PPPP	00000000	00000000 00000000	PPP	1

Key:
A = Available for use by appropriate ATM-layer function.
X = "Don't care."
C = Source will set CLP = 0 but may be changed by network.
P = Available for use by physical layer.

Notes:
* These VCI field values are reserved for user signaling. When VPI field YYYYYYYY = 0, these VCI values are reserved for user-to-local-exchange signaling. When VPI field YYYYYYYY is not 0, these VCI values are reserved for user signaling to other signaling entities (e.g., other users).
† Any VCI value except 0.
‡ Interim local management interface (ILMI) cell is defined by ATM Forum. Sender will set CLP = 0. Receiver will process ILMI cells with CLP = 1 as ILMI cells and as any other CLP = 1 cells.
§ Proposed default value for switched multimegabit data service (SMDS).
‖ Used by cell-based physical layer for cell delineation and cell-rate decoupling. Idle cells are not passed to ATM layer.
Used by cell-based physical layer for F1-F3 OAM flows.

Table 2.3
Pre-assigned Cell Header Values at NNI

Use	VPI	VCI	PT	CLP
Unassigned cell	000000000000	00000000 00000000	XXX	0
Point-to-point signaling	AAAAAAAAAAAA	00000000 00000101	0AA	C
Segment OAM F4 flow cell	AAAAAAAAAAAA	00000000 00000011	0A0	A

Table 2.3 (continued)

Use	VPI	VCI	PT	CLP
End-to-end OAM F4 flow cell	AAAAAAAAAAAA	00000000 00000100	0A0	A
Segment OAM F5 flow cell*	AAAAAAAAAAAA	AAAAAAAA AAAAAAAA	100	A
End-to-end OAM F5 flow cell*	AAAAAAAAAAAA	AAAAAAAA AAAAAAAA	101	A
Resource management cell*	AAAAAAAAAAAA	AAAAAAAA AAAAAAAA	110	A
Idle cell†	000000000000	00000000 00000000	000	1
Physical-layer OAM cell‡	000000000000	00000000 00000000	100	1
Reserved for use by physical layer	000000000000	00000000 00000000	PPP	1

Key:
A = Available for use by appropriate ATM-layer function.
X = "Don't care."
C = Source will set CLP = 0 but may be changed by network.
P = Available for use by physical layer.

Notes:
* Any VCI value except 0.
† Used by cell-based physical layer for cell delineation and cell rate decoupling. Idle cells are not passed to ATM layer.
‡ Used by cell-based physical layer for F1-F3 OAM flows.

The main purpose of the PT field is to distinguish between cells containing user data and network information. Codes for the PT field are listed in Table 2.4. For user-data cells, the field can be used by the network to indicate that congestion has been detected. The field also allows the ATM layer users (e.g., AAL) to specify two types of user cells; this distinction is carried transparently by the ATM layer. For network information cells, the payload contains information for network supervision functions depending on the particular type of cell. Examples of network information cells (such as OAM cells) can be found in Chapter 3.

Table 2.4
PT Field Codes

PT code	Meaning
000	User data cell, congestion not experienced, AAI = 0*
001	User data cell, congestion not experienced, AAI = 1*
010	User data cell, congestion experienced, AAI = 0*
011	User data cell, congestion experienced, AAI = 1*
100	Segment OAM F5 flow cell
101	End-to-end OAM F5 flow cell
110	Resource-management cell
111	Reserved for future functions

* ATM-user-to-ATM-user indication (AAI) is used only by ATM layer users (e.g., AAL) to distinguish two types of cells; this distinction is transparent to ATM layer.

The CLP bit allows a two-level loss priority (CLP = 0 for high, CLP = 1 for low) to be specified explicitly for individual cells. Low loss priority cells should be discarded before cells of high loss priority if congestion occurs and necessitates a loss of cells. A certain minimum capacity should be guaranteed for high loss priority cells. Cell loss priority is expected to be useful primarily for VBR video or voice to distinguish between crucial (e.g., frame synchronization) and less important information. The CLP bit may also be set by the network under appropriate conditions, referred to as cell tagging (explained in Chapter 4).

No header field is defined for explicit service (or delay) priorities, but service priorities may be associated implicitly with a VP or VC (within the VPI/VCI translation tables at each ATM switch, for instance). The service priority remains constant and the same for all cells of a particular VP or VC. In contrast, notice that cell loss priority may be indicated explicitly for each cell.

The HEC field uses a cyclic redundancy check for error protection of the cell header (the information field is not protected against errors in the ATM layer). It provides single bit-error correction and multiple bit-error detection; for details about the HEC procedure, refer to Chapter 6. Cells with detected but uncorrected header errors are discarded. Header error control is actually considered part of the physical layer because the HEC field is also used for cell delineation (as explained in Chapter 6).

The ATM technique applies to the exchange of information across the UNI and NNI reference points as described in [9,10,17]. The access rate of the UNI is 155.52 Mbps (symmetric in both directions) or 622.08 Mbps (symmetric or 155.52 Mbps in the other direction). In the 155.52 Mbps access, the bit rate available for cell transport is 149.76 Mbps. The actual rate of exchange of cells across the UNI is negotiated between user and network during a connection establishment procedure (see Section 2.5.3). The remainder of the transmission capacity is filled by idle (unassigned) cells. The capacity for cell transport in the 622.08-Mbps access is under study. The transmission rates of the NNI are also 155.52 Mbps and 622.08 Mbps.

The physical layer of the UNI may be cell-based (unframed or sometimes called *pure ATM*) or SONET/SDH-based (framed) [10]. The NNI will be SONET/SDH-based. The cell-based interface is defined as a continuous stream of cells without an external frame structure. Overhead cells are inserted among user data cells for performance monitoring and OAM functions. Synchronization is performed cell by cell, and cell delineation uses the HEC field (refer to Chapter 6). As long as the HEC calculation does not indicate an error, cell alignment is assumed to be properly maintained. A string of detected errors would indicate a loss of cell alignment and cause the initiation of a hunting procedure to recover alignment.

In the 155.52-Mbps SONET-based interface, the cell streams are mapped into the payload of SONET STS-3c frames (or STM-1 frames in the case of SDH). This frame is 125 microseconds consisting of 9 rows of 270 bytes each. The first 9 columns of bytes are transport overhead and another column contains path overhead, which leaves 260 columns of payload capacity for the transport of cells. More details are covered in Chapter 6.

2.5 ATM NETWORKING

An ATM network may be considered a collection of ATM network elements (switches, crossconnects, multiplexers, concentrators) interconnected by transmission facilities which together provide the information transport functions of the ATM layer and physical layer. In addition, the ATM network supports the relevant call control and network management functions. This section overviews the general network aspects in the areas of:

- Cell transport;
- Virtual path and virtual channel connections;
- Connection admission control;
- Traffic control;
- ATM-layer management.

2.5.1 ATM-Layer Cell Transport

The primary responsibility of an ATM network is the cell transport functions of the ATM layer. The ATM layer receives 48-byte data units from the AAL or ATM-layer management. These are encapsulated with header information into cells. The ATM layer provides end-to-end sequential connection-oriented transport of the cells according to the protocol information in their headers. The transport of user cells with an agreed quality of service (QOS) and throughput is often called the ATM bearer service. The handling of cells containing network information depends on the particular cell type and its function (see Chapter 3).

The transport of cells in the ATM layer involves:

- Cell encapsulation and decapsulation;
- Insertion and extraction of idle (unassigned) cells;
- Cell header processing (including VPI/VCI translation);
- Cell forwarding (routing and buffering);
- Multiplexing and concentration;
- Cell copying;
- Generic flow control at the UNI.

These functions will be discussed in more detail throughout the remainder of the book.

2.5.2 Virtual Paths and Virtual Channels

As the VPI and VCI labels in the cell headers indicate, cell transport in ATM networks is connection-oriented at the levels of VPs and VCs, as shown in Figure 2.4. A virtual channel is a generic term for a unidirectional communication capability for ATM cell transport, or essentially a virtual circuit. A VC is identified by the combined VPI/VCI label. A VC link is said to exist between two consecutive points where the VCI value is translated. A VC connection (VCC) is a concatenation of consecutive VC links with endpoints and connecting points. A continuous portion of a VCC is called a VC segment. A VCC has attributes that are negotiated between the user and network at the time of VCC establishment, such as QOS and throughput. Their attributes remain constant during the connection unless they are renegotiated. Cells within a VC maintain their sequential order.

VCC endpoints and connecting points may be a VC switch or VC crossconnect. Cells are routed according to their VCI labels. A VC switch has call-processing capabilities, whereas a VC crossconnect is controlled by network management. A VCC endpoint is also where the cell information field is exchanged between the ATM layer and its user (e.g., AAL or ATM-layer manage-

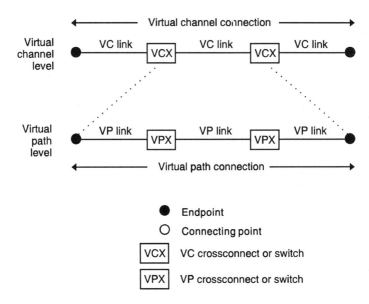

Figure 2.4 ATM-layer connections at VC and VP levels.

ment). VCCs may be switched or (semi) permanent. Switched VCCs are established through signaling, while (semi) permanent VCCs are established through network management. Initially, VCCs are expected to be (semi) permanent, with switched VCCs to be implemented later as signaling standards are further developed.

A collection of VCs traversing the same route may be switched and managed more easily as a group, which is referred to as a virtual path. A VP is identified by the VPI label. A VP link exists between two consecutive points where the VPI value is translated. A VP connection (VPC) is a concatenation of consecutive VP links. A continuous portion of a VPC is called a VP segment. Like a VCC, a VPC has attributes such as QOS and throughput. The QOS, however, is constrained to meet the most demanding QOS of VCs within the VPC. Cells within a VP maintain their sequential order.

VPC endpoints and connecting points may be a VP switch or VP crossconnect. Cells are routed according to their VPI labels. Like VCCs, VPCs may be (semi) permanent under control of network management or switched by means of signaling. VPCs are expected to be (semi) permanent initially, with switched VPCs to possibly appear in the future.

2.5.3 Connection Admission Control

As mentioned, cell transport in ATM networks is connection-oriented at the levels of VPs and VCs. Semipermenant VPCs/VCCs are controlled by network management; switched VPCs/VCCs are negotiated, established, modified, and terminated by means of signaling. Specific connection control functions in ATM networks include:

- Exchanging and processing signaling information;
- Connection admission or rejection;
- Resource allocation and routing determination;
- VPI/VCI assignment and removal.

During *connection admission control* (CAC), the user specifies the source traffic characteristics and QOS requirements. The network determines whether it can provide a VCC or VPC of an appropriate QOS class and throughput. If the traffic contract is agreed between the user and network, the network proceeds to allocate the necessary resources (such as setting up the appropriate VPI/VCI translation entries at each switch). The network also establishes the set of traffic parameters to be measured and enforced for the connection, which is referred to as input policing or *usage parameter control* (UPC).

Connection admission and rejection is the primary means for controlling traffic flows in ATM. Unlike conventional packet switching, there is no protocol mechanism in ATM for link-level flow control. It is widely believed that conventional link-level flow control using feedback is not feasible at the high speeds of ATM networks, nor is it appropriate for real-time traffic. However, this might change for *best effort* types of services being studied in the ATM Forum and elsewhere.

CAC and signaling procedures are described in detail in Chapters 3 and 9.

2.5.4 Traffic Control

After a connection is established, the network is responsible for maintaining the agreed QOS and the user is responsible for conformance to the negotiated traffic contract [8]. However, congestion may still occur due to statistical multiplexing. In order to protect the QOS from all connections, the network will rely on several mechanisms to control the flows of traffic. The primary means of control is CAC at the VPC/VCC level. Examples of traffic control functions at the cell level have been identified as:

- Usage parameter control (monitoring and enforcing the input traffic rate);
- Explicit forward congestion notification (using the PT field);
- Selective cell discarding (according to the CLP bit);
- Implicit service priorities.

Traffic control is the subject of Chapter 4.

2.5.5 ATM-Layer Management

While traffic control is concerned with traffic flows causing problems of congestion, the service provider must ensure the proper and efficient operation of the network facilities. ATM-layer management concerns the general functions of monitoring the network behavior and status, detection and analysis of troubles, and system protection and repair. A major part of ATM-layer management is operations and maintenance (OAM) [11]. Current OAM standards cover fault management and performance management. Further details of ATM-layer management and OAM are discussed in Chapter 3.

2.6 ATM SWITCHING

In general ATM switching systems are network elements that support the cell transport, connection control, and management functions of ATM networks as delineated in Section 2.5. While standards specify the ATM-layer and physical-layer functions of ATM networks, they do not specify their implementation at the switch level. The standards deliberately allow the switch architecture to be designed by the network provider or equipment vendors.

In fact, many different switch architecture designs are possible, and no single design appears to be universally superior. However, a generic architectural model of an ATM switching system can be inferred from the required network functions. This architecture model is the main objective of Chapters 5 through 10. The objective is a model that will be useful for advancing studies of ATM performance and implementation; it is not our intention to recommend any particular design implementation.

In Chapter 3, it will be seen that the B-ISDN protocol reference model implies three types of information flows in ATM networks related to user data, connection control, and network management. To handle these information flows, ATM switching systems will contain functional blocks responsible for cell transport, connection control, and system management. Various traffic control functions, as discussed in Chapter 4, will also be embedded within the switch architecture components. Based on these functional requirements, a generic switch architecture model is developed in Chapter 5. Its individual components are examined in detail in Chapters 6 through 10.

2.7 CONCLUSIONS

The ATM concept is a promising switching and multiplexing approach that has the potential to integrate different types of traffic—voice, data, and video—at the switching level. A wide range of services can be supported above a single

ATM subnetwork through different ATM adaptation layers. An ATM network offers these advantages:

- Flexibility to add and change services without changing the underlying subnetwork;
- Simpler operations and administration than multiple subnetworks;
- Dynamic bandwidth allocation;
- Potential for efficient utilization;
- No necessity for peak-rate allocation;
- Potential for granular and flexible control of network traffic.

On the other hand, the asynchronous nature of ATM can result in cell loss and variable cell delays in the network. QOS, in terms of cell loss rate and cell delays, is fundamental to discussions of ATM. Support of multiple traffic classes with different QOS requirements, while maximizing statistical sharing and utilization of network resources, is a difficult challenge in the implementation of ATM.

An implementation of ATM is specified in international standards and industry agreements. The ATM cell format consists of a 5-byte header and 48-byte information field. The main purpose of the cell header is identification of the virtual path and virtual channel. Other header fields allow identification of the payload type, forward-congestion indication, cell loss priority, and header error control.

An ATM network carries out the information transport functions of the ATM layer and physical layer. Although cell transport is its main responsibility, the network also has important functions related to CAC, traffic control, and network management. ATM switching systems are network elements that support these functions. While standards specify the network functions, they do not specify their implementation at the switch level.

The introduction to ATM will continue through Chapters 3 and 4. From this background information, a functional switch architecture model is developed in Chapter 5. Its individual components are examined in detail in the remaining chapters.

References

[1] ITU-T Rec. I.121, *Broadband Aspects of ISDN*, Melbourne, Nov. 14–25, 1988.
[2] ITU-T Rec. I.150, *B-ISDN Asynchronous Transfer Mode Functional Characteristics*, Helsinki, March 1–12, 1993.
[3] ITU-T Rec. I.311, *B-ISDN General Network Aspects*, Helsinki, March 1–12, 1993.
[4] ITU-T Rec. I.321, *B-ISDN Protocol Reference Model and Its Application*, Geneva, April 5, 1991.
[5] ITU-T Rec. I.361, *B-ISDN ATM-Layer Specification*, Helsinki, March 1–12, 1993.

[6]   ITU-T Rec. I.362, *B-ISDN ATM Adaptation Layer (AAL) Functional Description*, Helsinki, March 1–12, 1993.

[7]   ITU-T Rec. I.363, *B-ISDN ATM Adaptation Layer (AAL) Specification*, Helsinki, March 1–12, 1993.

[8]   ITU-T Rec. I.371, Traffic Control and Congestion Control in B-ISDN, Helsinki, March 1–12, 1993.

[9]   ITU-T Rec. I.413, *B-ISDN User-Network Interface*, Helsinki, March 1–12, 1993.

[10] ITU-T Rec. I.432, *B-ISDN User-Network Interface—Physical-Layer Specification*, Helsinki, March 1–12, 1993.

[11] ITU-T Rec. I.610, *B-ISDN Operation and Maintenance Principles and Functions*, Helsinki, March 1–12, 1993.

[12] ATM Forum, *ATM User-Network Interface Specification Version 3.0*, Sept. 10, 1993.

[13] Bellcore, *Asynchronous Transfer Mode (ATM) and ATM Adaptation Layer (AAL) Protocols Generic Requirements*, TA-NWT-001113, Issue 2, July 1993.

[14] Bellcore, *Generic Requirements for Exchange SVC Cell Relay Service*, TA-NWT-001501, Issue 1, Dec. 1993.

[15] Bellcore, *Generic Requirements for Exchange PVC Cell Relay Service*, TA-TSV-001408, Issue 1, Aug. 1993.

[16] Bellcore, *Broadband ISDN Switching System Generic Requirements*, TA-NWT-001110, Issue 2, Aug. 1993.

[17] Bellcore, *Broadband ISDN User to Network Interface and Network Node Interface Physical-Layer Generic Criteria*, TA-NWT-001112, Issue 1, Aug. 1992.

[18] Byrne, W., et al., "Broadband ISDN Technology and Architecture," *IEEE Network*, Vol. 27, Jan. 1989, pp. 23–28.

[19] Day, A., "International Standardization of B-ISDN," *IEEE LTS*, Vol. 2, Aug. 1991, pp. 13–20.

[20] Delisle, D. and L. Pelamourgues, "B-ISDN and How It Works," *IEEE Spectrum*, Vol. 28, Aug. 1991, pp. 39–42.

[21] DePrycker, M., "Evolution from ISDN to BISDN: A Logical Step Towards ATM," *Computer Communications,* Vol. 12, June 1989, pp. 141–146.

[22] DePrycker, M., *Asynchronous Transfer Mode: Solution for Broadband ISDN*, New York: Ellis Horwood, 1991.

[23] Dupraz, J. and M. DePrycker, "Principles and Benefits of the Asynchronous Transfer Mode," *Electrical Communications*, Vol. 64, 1990, pp. 116–123.

[24] Frantzen, V., and R. Handel, "A Solid Foundation for Broadband ISDN," *Telcom Report International*, Vol. 14, 1991, pp. 24–27.

[25] Frantzen, V., and R. Handel, "Networking Aspects of Broadband ISDN," *Telcom Report International*, Vol. 14, 1991, pp. 28–31.

[26] Gechter, J., and P. O'Reilly, "Conceptual Issues for ATM," *IEEE Network*, Vol. 3, Jan. 1989, pp. 14–16.

[27] Hac, A. and H. Mutlu, "Synchronous Optical Network and Broadband ISDN Protocols," *Computer*, Nov. 1989, pp. 26–34.

[28] Handel, R., "Evolution of ISDN Towards Broadband ISDN," *IEEE Network*, Vol. 3, Jan. 1989, pp. 7–13.

[29] Lane, J., "ATM Knits Voice, Data on Any Net," *IEEE Spectrum*, vol. 31, Feb. 1994, pp. 42–45.

[30] Le Boudec, J.-Y., "The Asynchronous Transfer Mode: A Tutorial," *Computer Networks and ISDN Systems*, Vol. 24, 1992, pp. 279–309.

[31] McQuillan, J., "Cell Relay Switching," *Data Communications*, Sept. 1991, pp. 58–69.

[32] Minzer, S., "Broadband ISDN and Asynchronous Transfer Mode (ATM)," *IEEE Communications Magazine*, Vol. 27, Sept. 1989, pp. 17–57.

[33] Rider, M., "Protocols for ATM Access Networks," *IEEE Network*, Vol. 3, Jan. 1989, pp. 17–22.

[34] Sykas, E., et al., "Overview of ATM Networks: Functions and Procedures," *Computer Communications*, Vol. 14, Dec. 1991, pp. 615–626.

[35] Aaron, M., and M. Decina, "Asynchronous Transfer Mode or Synchronous Transfer Mode or Both?" *IEEE Communications Magazine,* Vol. 29, Jan. 1991, pp. 10–13.

Information Flows in ATM 3

3.1 INTRODUCTION

The previous chapter introduced the ATM concept and presented its basic principles. The implementation of ATM in industry standards was reviewed. The chapter provided a general description of ATM networks and introduced some topics that will be revisited in more detail in the next few chapters. ATM switching systems can be viewed as network elements that relay, store, generate, and process all types of information flowing in the network. These flows are handled in different ways and imply different functions within ATM switches. Therefore, an understanding of information flows is essential to a study of ATM switching systems. This chapter focuses on the various types of information flows in ATM networks, as they are represented by the B-ISDN protocol reference model. The three planes of the protocol reference model—user plane, control plane, and management plane—are covered in Sections 3.2 to 3.4, respectively.

The B-ISDN protocol reference model is shown in Figure 3.1. It may be recalled from Section 2.2 that the protocol reference model consists of three parts [1]:

- User plane for the transfer of user application information;
- Control plane for call and connection-control functions;
- Management plane for network-supervision functions.

Specific types of information flows are associated with each plane, in particular:

- User data (transparent to the ATM network);
- Signaling information related to calls and connections;
- Management information concerning network status and performance.

This chapter examines in detail the different types of ATM cells related to these information flows: user data cells, signaling cells, *operations and maintenance* (OAM) cells, and *interim local management interface* (ILMI) cells.

After this chapter, the introduction to ATM will be concluded with Chapter 4 on traffic control and resource management. The background information in Chapters 1 through 4 will be applied to the development of a general functional ATM switch model in Chapter 5.

3.2 USER PLANE

The user plane was discussed in Section 2.2; it is recapped briefly here. The hierarchical structure of the user plane consists of the physical layer, the ATM layer, the ATM adaptation layer, and higher layers. The physical layer provides point-to-point transmission of ATM cells as bitstreams across a physical medium (e.g., optical fiber). The ATM layer relies on the services of the physical layer to provide end-to-end sequential transport of user data cells according to the ATM protocol information in their cell headers. The AAL supports different user applications above the ATM layer by converting between the application-specific data and the ATM cell format.

The physical and ATM layers are subdivided into the levels shown in Figure 3.2, which will be important for the discussion of the management plane. The physical layer is subdivided into three levels: transmission path, digital section, and regenerator section [2]. A transmission path is defined between points where the ATM layer accesses the physical layer. The endpoints of a transmission path perform cell delineation, cell header error control, and assembly/disassembly of the payload of the transmission system. A digital section extends between network elements that assemble and disassemble continuous bitstreams. A regenerator section is a portion of a digital section be-

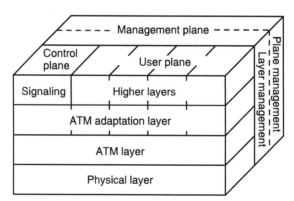

Figure 3.1 B-ISDN protocol reference model.

tween two points of signal regeneration. In the SONET-based physical layer, the transmission path, digital section, and regenerator section levels correspond to the defined SONET path, line, and section levels (see Chapter 6).

The ATM layer is subdivided into the virtual path and virtual channel levels as described in Section 2.5.2. The main purpose of the ATM cell header is identification of the virtual path and virtual channel connection. By means of the VPI/VCI fields, user data cells are associated with VP and VC connections that have negotiated attributes of QOS and throughput. VPC/VCC connecting points may be ATM switches or crossconnects that perform the ATM-layer cell transport functions overviewed in Section 2.5.1. Other fields in the ATM cell header shown in Figure 2.3 allow for identification of the payload type, forward congestion indication, cell loss priority, and header error control.

It is important to note that the information fields of user data cells are carried transparently by the network. User data is converted into the cell payload through various service-specific AALs, as described in Section 2.2 and Appendixes A through C. In contrast to user data cells, other types of cells may contain payloads that must be processed by ATM switches.

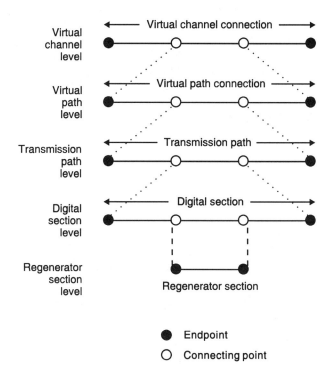

Figure 3.2 Levels of the physical and ATM layers.

3.3 CONTROL PLANE

The control plane in Figure 3.1 represents call and connection-control functions related to the establishment, supervision, and release of switched VPCs/VCCs. Switched VPCs/VCCs are controlled by means of signaling whereas (semi) permanent VPCs/VCCs are under the control of network management. Signaling is currently a subject of active study within standards organizations because call control will be more complicated in B-ISDN than in ISDN. In B-ISDN, calls and connections may be controlled separately. A connection is point-to-point or multipoint, symmetric or asymmetric, and characterized by a specific QOS class and throughput. A call may consist of multiple connections, and any connection can be established, modified, or terminated during a call. A user may have multiple signaling entities communicating with the network through different VC connections. Calls can be reconfigured dynamically by adding or dropping connections or parties during the call.

The control plane is also layered and shares the same physical and ATM layers with the user plane. This implies that signaling cells are transported in the ATM layer in the same manner as user data cells. However, unlike user data cells, signaling cells will be processed by ATM switches. The structure of the control plane is shown specifically for the UNI and NNI in Figure 3.3. At the UNI, *signaling AAL* (SAAL) functions support the exchange of variable-length signaling messages above the ATM layer [3–5]. The SAAL adapts high-layer signaling information into signaling ATM cells. The high-layer access signaling protocol is the ITU-T standard Q.2931 (formerly Q.93B) [6]. The ATM Forum has specified a version that contains a subset of Q.2931 and additional messages for point-to-multipoint connections [7]; a new version is being drafted in closer alignment with Q.2931.

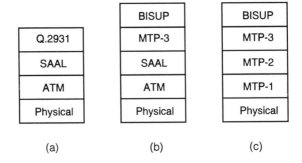

(a)   (b)   (c)

Figure 3.3 Protocol stacks for (a) access signaling, (b) interoffice signaling over ATM, and (c) interoffice signaling over SS7 lower layers.

At the NNI, the high-layer interoffice signaling protocol is the ITU-T standard *broadband ISDN user part* (BISUP), which was derived from the ISUP of signaling system number 7 [8–12]. There are two possibilities for supporting BISUP. Figure 3.3(b) shows BISUP supported over ATM through SAAL and MTP-3 (the SS7 network layer *message transfer part level* 3). Alternatively, Figure 3.3(c) shows BISUP over the existing SS7 network (MTP levels 1–3) [13,14]. Instead of BISUP, it should be noted that the ATM Forum has specified Q.2931 for the private NNI.

This section describes the signaling cells, SAAL, and high-layer signaling protocols. The emphasis here is on the ATM layer. These topics will be revisited in Chapter 9, where the main interest will be the processing involved in the SAAL and high-layer signaling protocols.

3.3.1 Signaling Cells

As mentioned, signaling information is carried in the ATM layer in the form of signaling cells. Signaling cells are carried in signaling virtual channels and identified by their VCI fields. Pre-assigned VCI codes for signaling cells at the UNI and NNI are listed in Tables 2.2 and 2.3. For point-to-point signaling, a signaling VC is allocated in each direction to each signaling entity. At the UNI and NNI, VCI = 5 is reserved for the point-to-point signaling virtual channel (the VPI/VCI values are the same in both directions). Network-provided signaling (between the user and network) utilizes the signaling VC within the virtual path VPI = 0 to establish, modify, and release VCCs for end-to-end user data transfer. User-provided signaling (between users) can use the signaling VC in any virtual path other than VPI = 0 to control VCCs within that pre-established VPC.

Point-to-multipoint signaling configurations are supported at the UNI; e.g., when multiple users share a single UNI. A general broadcast signaling VC may be used for call offering in the point-to-multipoint direction. The general broadcast signaling VC is indicated by VCI = 4 in any VP, and it is activated when metasignaling is used in this VP.

In a point-to-multipoint signaling configuration, signaling entities may require their own signaling VCs. Metasignaling is then used to assign and remove individual signaling VCs [2]. A permanent metasignaling VC between the user and the network is indicated by the pre-assigned values VPI = 0, VCI = 1. A metasignaling VC between users, identified by VCI = 1 in any virtual path (other than VPI = 0), can be used to establish and manage signaling VCs within that VP. In requesting a signaling VC, the metasignaling message identifies a service profile (if service profiles are implemented by the network provider). A service profile is a collection of information maintained by the network characterizing a set of services provided to the user, e.g., subscription parameters, directory numbers, interface configuration. The service profile associates a level of service with the requested signaling VC.

3.3.2 Signaling AAL

SAAL consists of a common part and a *service-specific convergence sublayer* (SSCS) [3]. The SAAL common part is the AAL5 common part (described in Appendix C). The SSCS is further divided into *service-specific coordination functions* (SSCF) and a *service-specific connection-oriented protocol* (SSCOP). Strictly speaking, SSCF and SSCOP are not protocol sublayers (in the OSI sense) but a separation of functions.

There are two versions of SSCF for the UNI [5] and the NNI [15]. In general, SSCF was designed to allow the exchange of messages between high-layer signaling entities by using the services of the lower SSCOP. It provides for establishment and release of two types of connections to the signaling entities: *assured* and *unacknowledged*. For assured connections, variable-length signaling messages (up to 4,096 bytes) are carried with protection from loss, misinsertion, corruption, and disordering. For unacknowledged connections, signaling messages are not protected from possible loss, misinsertion, and disordering.

These connections are provided by specified procedures for invoking the services of SSCOP. There is no communication between peer SSCF entities; i.e., SSCF does not add or remove AAL information to the signaling messages. The only actions of SSCF are passing data between the higher layer signaling entity (Q.2931 or BISUP) and SSCOP, and invoking the services of SSCOP. Thus, SSCF is merely a coordination function that maps SSCOP services to the needs of the higher layer signaling entities. To invoke SSCOP services, it follows procedures and state-transition diagrams whose details are specified in [5,15].

SSCOP uses the unguaranteed delivery service of the AAL5 common part to provide a reliable transport service of variable-length data units up to 65,527 bytes between its users [4]. SSCOP relies on error detection in AAL5 and adds loss-recovery and error-control functions above the AAL5 common part. Additional functions include connection control (establishment and release) and flow control. These functions are performed by means of messages (SSCOP PDUs) between peer SSCOP entities. Specific messages are discussed in Chapter 9.

3.3.3 Higher Layer Signaling

B-ISDN signaling is based on modifications of the ISDN access signaling protocol Q.931 and interoffice signaling protocol ISUP (ISDN User Part). Q.931 is a 1988 Blue Book Recommendation describing the messages, protocols, and features for user-network signaling across the ISDN UNI via the D channel. ISUP is the higher layers of SS7 for control of circuit-switched connections between ISDN switches. Modified for B-ISDN, the access signaling protocol is Q.2931 and the interoffice signaling protocol is BISUP (broadband ISDN user part). The current versions of Q.2931 and BISUP will be gradually enhanced for sophisticated services, separate call/connection control, multipoint connections, and multimedia calls.

The set of Q.2931 messages for call and connection control are listed in Table 3.1 [6,16]. Additional messages for point-to-multipoint connections are included [7]. Every message contains the information elements shown in Figure 3.4, including:

- *Protocol discriminator* (1 byte): to identify messages for user-network call control or other purposes;
- *Call reference value* (4 bytes): to identify the call at the local UNI to which the message applies;
- *Message type* (2 bytes): to indicate the message function (see Table 3.1);
- *Message length* (2 bytes): to indicate the number of bytes in the message;
- *Message-specific information elements* (variable length).

Table 3.1
Access Signaling Messages for Call/Connection Control

Message	Function
Alerting	Sent by destination to network or by network to originator to indicate destination alerting has been initiated
Call proceeding	Sent by destination to network or by network to originator to indicate call setup has been initiated and more call setup information is not needed
Connect	Sent by destination to network or by network to originator to indicate call acceptance by destination
Connect acknowledge	Sent by network to destination to indicate that the call has been successfully awarded
Progress*	Sent by user or by network to indicate progress of a call
Setup	Sent by user to network and by network to destination to initiate call/connection establishment
Setup acknowledge*	Sent by network to originator or by destination to network to indicate that call establishment initiated by additional information may be required
Release	Sent by user to request connection clearing or by network to indicate that connection is cleared and user should release the connection identifier and call reference after sending *release complete*
Release complete	Sent by user or by network to indicate that equipment has released call reference and connection identifier

Table 3.1 (continued)

Message	Function
Information*	Sent by user or by network to provide further information
Notify	Sent by user or by network to indicate information pertaining to a call/connection
Status	Sent by user or by network to respond to *status enquiry* or report certain error conditions at any time
Status enquiry	Sent by user or by network to solicit *status*
Add party[+]	Sent by user or by network to add a party to the existing connection
Add party acknowledge[+]	Sent by user or by network to confirm that *add party* request was successful
Add party reject[+]	Sent by user or by network to indicate that *add party* request was not successful
Drop party[+]	Sent by user or by network to clear a party from existing point-to-multipoint connection
Drop party acknowledge[+]	Sent by user or by network to confirm that *drop party* request was successful

* Additional messages included to support interworking with narrowband ISDN.
† Additional messages for point-to-multipoint connections specified by ATM Forum.

Protocol discrim- inator	Call refer- ence	Msg type	Msg length	Optional
bytes: 1	4	2	2	variable

Figure 3.4 Q.2931 message format.

The set of BISUP messages for call and connection control are listed in Table 3.2 [8–12]. As shown in Figure 3.5, all BISUP messages consist of these fields:

- *Routing label* (4 or 7 bytes): to specify origination and destination points;
- *Message type code* (1 byte): to define the function and the format of the message;
- *Message length* (1 or 2 bytes): the number of bytes of the message content;
- *Message compatibility information* (1 byte): to differentiate between different protocol versions;
- *Message content* (variable length): message-specific parameters.

Table 3.2
BISUP Messages for Call/Connection Control

Message	Function
Address complete (ACM)	Returned by destination switch to acknowledge that call is proceeding to the called user and to indicate the called user's status
Answer (ANM)	Returned by destination switch to indicate that the called user has accepted the call and information transfer can begin
Call progress (CPG)	Sent in either direction to indicate that an event of significance to originating or terminating access has occurred
Initial address (IAM)	Sent by originating switch to propagate call request to destination switch
IAM acknowledgment (IAA)	Returned by a switch to acknowledge receipt of IAM message
IAM reject (IAR)	Returned by a switch to reject IAM message
Release (REL)	Request to terminate connection and release connection identifier and call reference
Release complete (RLC)	Response to *release* message to acknowledge the release of call reference and connection identifier
Resume (RES)	Request to resume communication after a temporary suspension (used only in interworking with ISDN)
Subsequent address (SAM)	Sent by originating switch following IAM to convey additional called-party number information
Suspend (SUS)	Request for temporary suspension of communication without releasing call

Routing label	Msg type code	Msg length	Msg compat- ibility	Msg content
bytes: 4 or 7	1	1 or 2	1	variable

Figure 3.5 BISUP message format.

Chapter 9 will explain the Q.2931 and BISUP protocols in more detail. It should be noted that signaling is actively undergoing development in the standards. Working documents from the standards organizations and the ATM Forum may have discernible differences in this area, but it should be expected that all versions will be aligned eventually.

3.4 MANAGEMENT PLANE

To sustain the desired QOS for connections, it is necessary to monitor and control the ATM network to ensure the continued and correct operation of facilities and the efficient utilization of network resources. The management plane in Figure 3.1 represents network monitoring and control functions, primarily operations and maintenance at each level and supervision of the network on a system level [1]. The management plane is subdivided into plane management and layer management.

Plane management is responsible for functions related to the network as a whole and coordination between all planes of the protocol reference model; therefore, it is not layered. Consistent with the conventional domains of network management, specific functions of plane management have been identified as:

- Fault management to dynamically detect, isolate, and correct failures;
- Performance management to continually monitor, report, and evaluate the behavior of network elements;
- Configuration management to initialize facilities into service and check or change their service status;
- Accounting management to collect, process, and report information on resource usage for billing;
- Security management to regulate the access to and control of network elements' databases.

Layer management consists of management functions particular to specific layers. This section is concerned primarily with the ATM-layer management, which includes ATM-layer operations and maintenance (OAM) and metasignaling. Metasignaling was described earlier in Section 3.3.1. The discussion below summarizes the information flows related to the currently defined functions of ATM-layer OAM [17,18].

3.4.1 ATM-Layer Operations and Maintenance

OAM in the physical and ATM layers depends on the exchange of management information, which are referred to as OAM flows [19–22]. The OAM flows in the physical layer are designated as F1 to F3 OAM flows corresponding to the regenerator section, digital section, and transmission path levels, respectively. Chapter 6 will describe how physical-layer OAM information is carried in the SONET section, line, and path overhead.

The ATM layer depends on the bidirectional exchanges of cells carrying OAM information related to specific VPCs and VCCs. At the VP and VC levels, they are called F4 and F5 OAM flows, respectively. F4 OAM cells have the same VPI value as user data cells of the same VPC but are distinguished by the following pre-assigned VCI values: VCI = 3 for segment OAM (i.e., cells communicated within the bounds of a VPC segment only) and VCI = 4 for end-to-end OAM (cells communicated from VPC endpoint to endpoint). F5 OAM cells have the same VPI/VCI values as the user data cells of the same VCC but are identified by these pre-assigned PT field values: PT = 4 for segment OAM and PT = 5 for end-to-end OAM. Notice that F5 OAM cells share the same VCC as user data cells, but the VCC of F4 OAM cells excludes user data cells.

F4 and F5 OAM flows are initiated during or after connection establishment. OAM cells for both directions of the F4 and F5 flows must follow the same physical route so that any connecting points can monitor the OAM information from both directions. Both endpoints and connecting points can generate, insert, monitor (non-intrusively), and process OAM cells for that virtual connection; only endpoints of a flow can extract and terminate OAM cells.

All OAM cells will have the format shown in Figure 3.6. The OAM cell-type field indicates the type of management function as listed in Table 3.3: fault management, performance management, or activation/deactivation. The function-type field indicates the specific function performed by that cell. The EDC field is a CRC-10 error detection code using the generating polynomial $x^{10} + x^9 + x^5 + x^4 + x + 1$.

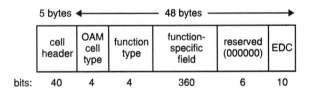

Figure 3.6   OAM cell format.

Table 3.3
Field Codes of OAM Cells

OAM Cell Type	Value	Function Type	Value
Fault management	0001	Alarm indication signal (AIS)	0000

Table 3.3 (continued)

OAM Cell Type	Value	Function Type	Value
		Remote defect indicator (RDI)	0001
		Continuity check	0100
		Cell loopback	1000
Performance management	0010	Forward monitoring	0000
		Backward reporting	0001
		Monitoring & reporting	0010
Activation/deactivation	1000	Performance monitoring	0000
		Continuity check	0001

3.4.1.1   Fault Management

In general, fault management concerns the detection and analysis of failures within the network. Typical functions include alarm surveillance, fault localization, and diagnostic testing. The objective of fault management in the ATM layer is to monitor and test the status of VPCs and VCCs. This is performed by:

- Alarm surveillance and reporting;
- Continuity checks;
- Loopback cells.

The procedures are illustrated in Figure 3.7. The format of fault-management cells is shown in Figure 3.8.

If the physical layer indicates a failure (e.g., loss of signal, loss of cell synchronization), a VPC/VCC failure will be reported in the ATM layer with two types of cells: *alarm indication signal* (AIS) and *remote defect indicator* (RDI). AIS cells flow in the same direction (downstream) as user data cells, whereas RDI cells flow in the opposite direction (upstream). Both will contain fields to specify the type of failure (1 byte) and its location (15 bytes).

Upon receiving a failure indication from the physical layer, the detecting VPC/VCC connecting point will wait a short time for the physical-layer automatic protection switching. If the failure indication persists, the detecting VPC/VCC connecting point will issue an AIS cell to notify downstream nodes of connection unavailability. AIS cells will continue to be generated at regular intervals until the fault is cleared. After receiving a certain number of AIS cells, the VPC/VCC endpoint will begin to send RDI cells upstream to notify the

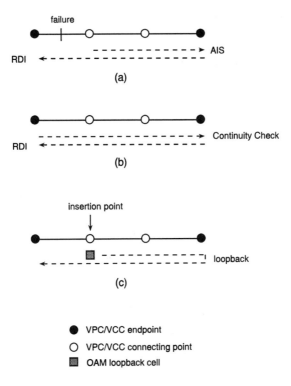

Figure 3.7 Fault-monitoring procedures: (a) alarm surveillance, (b) continuity check, and (c) cell loopback.

source VPC/VCC endpoint of the downstream failure. Fault localization and recovery actions are then initiated.

Continuity checking is not currently standardized but may be adopted in the future. If a VPC/VCC failure has not been indicated from the physical layer but no user data cells have been sent downstream by a VPC/VCC endpoint for a certain length of time, it will send a continuity check cell downstream. The purpose of the continuity-check cell is to confirm that an inactive connection is still alive. If the destination VPC/VCC endpoint does not receive any cell within a certain time in which a continuity check cell was expected, it assumes that connectivity has been lost and will send a RDI cell to the source VPC/VCC endpoint. The same procedure is carried out in the reverse direction as well.

Although alarms and continuity checks are useful for fault detection, a means to test VPC/VCC connectivity on demand will be useful to locate faults. The OAM cell-loopback capability will allow an OAM cell to be inserted into a VPC/VCC and looped back (i.e., returned in the reverse OAM flow). The loopback capability might also allow the measurement of round-trip cell transfer delays. Fields in the OAM loopback cell include:

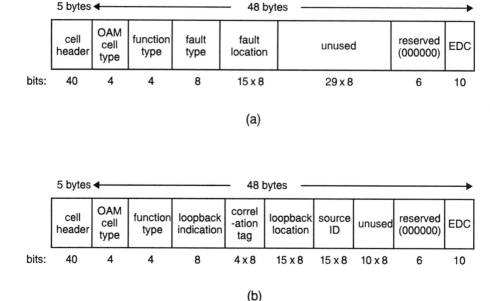

Figure 3.8 Formats of OAM fault management cells: (a) AIS/RDI cells, and (b) loopback cells.

- *Loopback indication* (1 byte): to signify whether loopback has occurred;
- *Correlation tag* (4 bytes): to uniquely identify the cell, possibly by a timestamp;
- *Loopback location* (15 bytes): to indicate the points for loopback;
- *Source ID* (15 bytes): to allow the originator to recognize its own cells.

3.4.1.2 Performance Management

While acute failure conditions will be detected by fault monitoring, intermittent or low-level error conditions due to malfunctions may cause a subtle deterioration in network performance. The continuous collection of performance data to detect such deterioration is the responsibility of performance management. In the ATM layer, performance management depends on the monitoring of the QOS of VPCs and VCCs.

The performance-monitoring procedure involves the insertion of OAM performance-monitoring cells between blocks of user data cells. The OAM cells contain information about the preceding block to the downstream VPC/VCC endpoint. A request to insert a monitoring cell is raised after every N user cells, where the block size N may be 128, 256, 512, or 1,024. The monitoring cell is inserted in the next unassigned cell slot such that the actual block size may vary from N by 50% (the monitoring cell may eventually be forced in). At the downstream VPC/VCC endpoint, the block of user data cells is examined, and the results are compared with the contents of the subsequent OAM monitoring cell. Monitoring results are reported backwards using the reverse OAM flow.

The performance monitoring procedure is illustrated in Figure 3.9. In forward monitoring, the source VPC/VCC endpoint performs an even parity BIP-16 error-detection code calculation over the information field of a block of N user data cells. The result, along with the block size N, is sent in an OAM performance-monitoring cell immediately following the user data block. At the destination node, the same error check is calculated over the block of user cells and compared with the contents of the following OAM cell. The number of errored BIP-16 parity bits detected and the count of lost/misinserted cells are communicated to ATM-layer management and reported back to the source node using the reverse OAM flow. Intermediate connecting points have the option of monitoring the procedure and results.

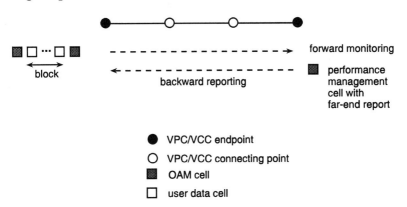

Figure 3.9 Performance-monitoring procedure.

The performance-management cell format is shown in Figure 3.10. It includes fields for:

- *Monitoring cell sequence number* (1 byte): to indicate the sequential identity of the cell;
- *Total-user cell number* (2 bytes): to indicate the user block size N;
- *Block error-detection code* (2 bytes): even parity BIP-16 computed over the information fields of the block;
- *Timestamp* (4 bytes): to indicate the time of origination;
- *Block error results* (1 byte): for backward reporting of the number of errored BIP-16 parity bits observed at the destination;

- *Lost/misinserted cell count* (2 bytes): for backward reporting of the number of lost/misinserted cells observed at the destination.

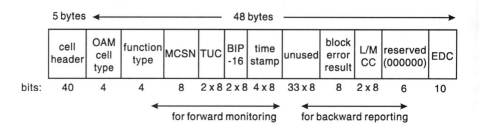

Figure 3.10   Format of OAM performance-management cell.

The user or the network management can initiate or terminate the performance-monitoring procedure for VPCs/VCCs through the use of activation/deactivation OAM cells that are exchanged between the two VPC/VCC endpoints. The cell format shown in Figure 3.11 includes these fields:

- *Message ID* (6 bits): to indicate the message function as listed in Table 3.4;
- *Directions of actions* (2 bits): to specify the direction of monitoring;
- *Correlation tag* (8 bits): to uniquely identify the cell;
- *PM block sizes A-B* (4 bits): block size chosen for the direction away from the activator/deactivator;
- *PM block sizes B-A* (4 bits): block size chosen for the direction toward the activator/deactivator.

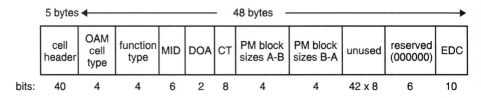

Figure 3.11   Format of OAM activation/deactivation cell.

3.4.2   Interim Local Management

While further details of the management plane functions continue to be studied by the ITU-T, the ATM Forum has defined an interim local management interface (ILMI) [7]. Based on the *simple network management protocol* (SNMP) and a standard ATM UNI *management information base* (MIB), it allows the ATM user to obtain status and control information about VPCs/VCCs at its UNI.

SNMP is a protocol designed by the Internet Engineering Task Force to centrally manage large heterogeneous networks [23]. It has become the de facto standard for managing local area networks (LANs) and multivendor TCP/IP (transmission control protocol/Internet protocol) networks. Based on a client-server architecture, it specifies a connectionless protocol for the exchange of a small set of messages between *agents* and a centralized management station. An agent resides in each network element to monitor objects that are defined in a MIB. Objects can be hardware, software, or a connection.

According to the ILMI specification, each ATM user device has a *UNI management entity* (UME) that supports ILMI functions for that UNI. Bidirectional ILMI communications take place between adjacent ATM UMEs through the exchange of SNMP messages encapsulated into ILMI cells using AAL5. ILMI cells are identified at the UNI by the pre-assigned values VPI = 0 and VCI = 16. By means of SNMP, an UME can access the UNI MIB information associated with an adjacent UME. The ATM UNI MIB contains information about the physical layer, ATM layer, ATM-layer statistics, and VPCs/VCCs [7]. SNMP and the ATM MIB will be discussed further in Chapter 10.

3.5 CONCLUSIONS

ATM switching systems can be viewed as network elements that relay, store, generate, and process all the types of information flowing in the network. This chapter pointed out that different types of ATM cells are implied by the three planes of the B-ISDN protocol reference model. Besides user data cells, other types of cells include signaling cells, OAM cells, and ILMI cells. All cells are routed in the same manner through the network according to the ATM protocol information contained in the cell headers. The main purpose of the cell header is identification of the virtual path and virtual channel connection. Other header fields allow identification of the payload type, forward congestion indication, cell loss priority, and header error control. The information fields of user data cells are carried transparently, but the payloads of the other types of cells may require processing by the network.

Signaling cells convey Q.2931 messages across the UNI or BISUP messages across the NNI. The network must interpret these signaling messages using SAAL and carry out the high-layer signaling protocol. The implications of the ATM switch are examined in Chapter 9.

OAM cells carry network information within the information fields. The network must process these cells and follow the appropriate OAM procedures. For example, the network must handle AIS, RDI, and loopback cells in fault-management procedures. It must handle performance-management cells in performance-monitoring and reporting procedures.

ILMI cells convey SNMP messages across the UNI. The network must interpret these messages in accordance with the SNMP protocol. The implications are investigated in Chapter 10.

It should be remarked that the control plane and management plane are still in the process of development in the standards. In the future, there may well be other types of information flows that must be handled by ATM switches.

References

[1]   ITU-T Rec. I.321, *B-ISDN Protocol Reference Model and Its Applications*, Geneva, April 5, 1991.

[2]   ITU-T Rec. I.311, *B-ISDN General Network Aspects*, Helsinki, March 1–12, 1993.

[3]   ITU-T Draft Rec. Q.2100, *B-ISDN Signaling ATM Adaptation Layer Overview Description*, Geneva, Nov. 29–Dec. 17, 1993.

[4]   ITU-T Draft Rec. Q.2110, *B-ISDN ATM Adaptation Layer—Service Specific Connection Oriented Protocol (SSCOP)*, Geneva, Nov. 29–Dec. 17, 1993.

[5]   ITU-T Draft Rec. Q.2130, *B-ISDN Signaling ATM Adaptation Layer—Service Specific Coordination Function for Support of Signaling at the User-to-Network Interface (SSCF at UNI)*, Geneva, Nov. 29–Dec. 17, 1993.

[6]   ITU-T Draft Rec. Q.2931, *B-ISDN Access Signaling System DSS2 (Digital Subscriber Signaling System No. 2)*, Geneva, Dec. 1993.

[7]   ATM Forum, *ATM User-Network Interface Specification Version 3.0*, Sept. 10, 1993.

[8]   Bellcore, *Broadband Switching System SS7 Requirements Using the Broadband Integrated Services Digital Network User Part (BISUP)*, GR-1417-CORE, Issue 1, Feb. 1994.

[9]   ITU-T Draft Rec. Q.2761, *BISUP—Functional Description*, Geneva, Dec. 1993.

[10] ITU-T Draft Rec. Q.2762, *BISUP—General Functions of Messages and Signals*, Geneva, Dec. 1993.

[11] ITU-T Draft Rec. Q.2763, *BISUP—Formats and Codes*, Geneva, Dec. 1993.

[12] ITU-T Draft Rec. Q.2764, *BISUP—Basic Call Procedures*, Geneva, May 1993.

[13] Jabbari, B., "Common Channel Signaling System Number 7 for ISDN and Intelligent Networks," *Proc. of the IEEE*, Vol. 79, Feb. 1991, pp. 155–169.

[14] Modarressi, A., and R. Skoog, "An Overview of Signaling System No. 7," *Proc. of the IEEE*, Vol. 80, April 1992, pp. 590–606.

[15] ITU-T Draft Rec. Q.2140, *B-ISDN Signaling ATM Adaptation Layer—Service Specific Coordination Function for Support of Signaling at the Network-Node Interface (SSCF at NNI)*, Geneva, Nov. 29–Dec. 17, 1993.

[16] Bellcore, *B-ISDN Access Signaling Generic Requirements*, TA-NWT-001111, Issue 1, Aug. 1993.

[17] Bellcore, *Generic Requirements for Operations of Broadband Switching Systems*, TA-NWT-001248, Issue 2, Oct. 1993.

[18] ITU-T Rec. I.610, *B-ISDN Operation and Maintenance Principles and Functions*, Helsinki, March 1–12, 1993.

[19] Anderson, J., and M. Nguyen, "ATM-Layer OAM Implementation Issues," *IEEE Communications Mag.*, vol. 29, Sept. 1991, pp. 79–81.

[20] Breuer, H-J., "ATM-Layer OAM: Principles and Open Issues," *IEEE Communications Mag.*, Vol. 29, Sept. 1991, pp. 75–78.

[21] Farkouh, S., "Managing ATM-Based Broadband Networks," *IEEE Communications Mag.*, Vol. 31, May 1993, pp. 82–86.

[22] Yoneda, S., "Broadband ISDN ATM-Layer Management: Operations, Administration, and Maintenance Considerations," *IEEE Network,* Vol. 4, May 1990, pp. 31–35.

[23] Case, J., et al., "Simple Network Management Protocol," *Internet Working Group Request for Comments 1157*, Network Information Center, SRI International, Menlo Park, CA, May 1990.

Traffic Control and Resource Management

4

4.1 INTRODUCTION

The previous chapters presented an introduction to the ATM concept, whereby all information is carried through the network in the common form of ATM cells. Chapter 3 described the planes of the B-ISDN protocol reference model, which represent the three types of information flows in ATM networks: user data, signaling, and management. This background material is essential because the main function of ATM switching systems is to store, process, and forward these information flows.

Before proceeding to the design of ATM switching systems beginning in the next chapter, however, it is necessary to complete the discussion of the ATM technique with the present chapter on *traffic control* and *resource management*. Traffic control is a practical issue arising in the implementation of ATM. In any type of communication network with shared resources, including ATM networks, the capability to monitor and regulate traffic flows is crucial. Without traffic control, it is well-known that unrestricted demands for shared network resources (e.g., buffers, bandwidth, or processors) can seriously degrade network throughput and efficiency. Traffic control is necessary to both protect the quality of services perceived by users and ensure the efficient utilization of network resources. Traffic-control mechanisms must be implemented within the switching systems and the higher network protocol layers.

The problem of traffic control in ATM networks has been widely recognized for a long time. Over the past few years, a consensus on the basic principles of traffic control has slowly emerged within the industry. ITU-T Recommendation I.371 was an attempt to formulate a general outline of traffic-control principles and functions. Work is continuing on the details of specific control mechanisms and procedures. Recognizing the importance of traffic control, traffic management is one of the working groups in the ATM Forum. The group is currently focusing on the definition of a new *available bit-rate* (ABR) service and a related traffic-control scheme.

Much of this chapter is based on ITU-T Recommendation I.371 and current ATM Forum specifications. It is not intended to be a comprehensive survey because the body of literature on the subject is boundless. The objective of this chapter is to complete the background information on ATM, which will be applied to the study of ATM switching systems in the remainder of the book. Chapter 5 will outline a general functional switch architecture model that will be investigated in more detail throughout the following chapters.

4.2 GENERAL PRINCIPLES

While the specific details of some procedures have not yet been resolved, a consensus has coalesced more or less on the general framework of traffic-control principles. The basic principles described are centered around these notions:

- Quality of service;
- Statistical sharing versus isolation;
- Levels of control;
- Reactive and preventive controls.

The principles surrounding these ideas are described below. Later, in Sections 4.3 through 4.5, we discuss the specific traffic-control functions of:

- Connection admission control;
- Usage/network parameter control;
- Congestion control.

Connection admission control will be treated in more depth in Chapter 9.

4.2.1 Quality of Service

As mentioned in Chapter 2, the basic service provided by ATM networks is end-to-end sequential cell transport. The service is initiated by a user request for a virtual connection, which is either admitted or rejected by the network. Grade of service (GOS) pertains to the *offered* traffic in terms of the blocking probability at the level of connection admissions and rejections. After a connection is accepted, carried cells may experience two basic types of impairments within the network: delay and loss. Quality of service (QOS) refers to the set of parameters such as cell delays, delay variation, and cell loss rate that pertain to the impairments experienced by *carried* traffic [1,2]. These parameters are concerned with the user's perception of a network service. The network is responsible for maintaining a level of QOS expected by its users.

For the diverse mix of services in B-ISDN, ATM networks will support a number of specified QOS classes:

- *Class A*: for circuit emulation and CBR services;
- *Class B*: for VBR video and speech;
- *Class C*: for connection-oriented data (e.g., frame relay);
- *Class D*: for connectionless data.

Each QOS class is characterized by specific QOS requirements. For instance, class A connections will require tightly bounded cell delays and delay variation [3]. Additional QOS classes may be defined later. In fact, a new ABR service is being defined with probably a low (or zero) cell loss rate and unconstrained cell delay variation. Furthermore, an unspecified QOS class with no specific cell delay or cell loss requirements may be supported by an ATM network [2]. Without traffic differentiation into QOS classes, the network would be required to support the most stringent QOS requirements for all traffic. In principle, traffic differentiation benefits the network provider by allowing the relaxation of appropriate QOS requirements.

Related to QOS, network performance refers to the set of parameters that measures the ability of the network to provide its services between users [1]. While QOS is meaningful from the perspective of users at the point of service access, network performance is defined from the viewpoint of the network provider at points within the network. At the call level, network performance parameters may include connection set-up delay, connection release delay, and blocking probability. At the cell level, network performance parameters may include cell error rate, cell loss rate, cell misinsertion rate, end-to-end cell delay, and cell delay variation. In general, network performance will be higher than necessary to satisfy the QOS requirements of a service.

In ATM, network performance may be impaired by congestion caused by contention for limited resources (i.e., buffers, bandwidth, and processors). The consequences of uncontrolled congestion are shown in Figure 4.1. Congestion is exhibited in both circuit-switched and packet-switched networks when the offered traffic load exceeds the network's designed capacity. Because ATM is connection-oriented and packet-oriented, ATM networks may exhibit congestion at both levels of connections and cells. At the level of connections, call processors will become preoccupied with unsuccessful call attempts. At the level of cells, transmission links will become saturated with traffic, and buffers will overflow with cells. Thus, uncontrolled congestion will be manifested by a dramatic increase in call blocking, cell delays, and cell loss rate. Congestion control attempts to detect and react to congestion to minimize its intensity, spread, and duration.

4.2.2 Statistical Sharing versus Isolation

Traffic control in ATM is difficult because of a fundamental dilemma between conflicting objectives: *statistical sharing of resources* for efficiency and *isola-*

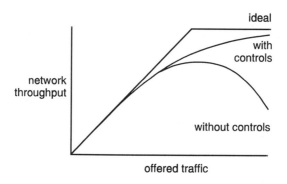

Figure 4.1 Effect of congestion without traffic controls.

tion between traffic flows for QOS protection. A gain in efficiency can be achieved by statistically multiplexing VBR connections whose total peak rate exceeds the physical transmission link rate (while the total average rate is less than the link rate, of course). If the traffic streams are numerous and independent, then the probability that their instantaneous total rate will exceed the link rate (i.e., when many sources are active at their peak rates simultaneously) will be small. This behavior is described by the well-known Law of Large Numbers, which states that the total rate will approach the total average rate with a probability of one when the number of independent streams becomes very large. To realize the statistical multiplexing gain (the ratio of the total peak rate to the link rate), it is desirable to maintain a high utilization factor and to maximize the degree of statistical sharing of network resources.

An undesirable consequence of statistical multiplexing is the possibility that the QOS of one connection may be adversely affected by traffic in the other connections [4–10]. For instance, a burst in one stream could fill up the multiplexer buffer and thereby increase cell delays for all streams. Many traffic streams could burst simultaneously and cause a buffer overflow. The probability of buffer overflow and excessive queuing delays (symptoms of congestion) is greater at higher loads. Therefore, it is desirable to maintain a low utilization factor (which may not be economically feasible) or otherwise provide isolation between traffic streams to reduce the effect of burstiness in one stream on the QOS of another stream (e.g., so-called fair queuing [11]). Unfortunately, these approaches conflict with the objective of statistical multiplexing.

Priorities are a useful mechanism to isolate or modify the mutual effects between traffic streams. Delay priorities prescribe the order in which queued cells are scheduled for transmission on a shared link; loss priorities specify the preferential occupation of shared buffer space. For example, cells with high delay priority will be given preference for transmission over low delay priority cells. The effect of low-priority traffic on the delays of high-priority traffic is thereby reduced. However, the high-priority traffic obviously has a great effect on the delays of low-priority traffic. This example points out that priorities only specify the preferential treatment of one traffic class relative to another. One traffic class benefits at the expense of another class. The discussion of priorities will be continued later in Section 4.5.1.

The network will necessarily operate at some compromise point between high and low utilization, depending on the relative importance of efficient utilization versus QOS protection. The operating point will also depend on the burstiness and predictability of the traffic flows. Bursty and unpredictable traffic incurs a higher risk of congestion and compels a lower utilization factor. Unfortunately, many traffic sources have unpredictable or unknown statistics, such as image retrieval or high-speed data [12]. Most likely, the network will operate initially at a conservatively low utilization. As traffic characteristics are understood better through experience, it is likely that a higher utilization factor and efficiency can be achieved.

4.2.3 Levels of Control

Traffic flows in ATM can be viewed at different levels, which are identified by different traffic entities [1,8,13–18]:

- Calls (possibly consisting of multiple connections);
- Virtual path connections;
- Virtual channel connections;
- Bursts (consisting of consecutive cells);
- Individual cells.

Traffic control consists of a set of control mechanisms that can be exercised on the different traffic entities at each level. A complete set will eventually be necessary to handle the diverse and unpredictable traffic types in B-ISDN.

Each control mechanism has a characteristic timescale. A classification of traffic-control mechanisms according to timescales is shown in Figure 4.2. Mechanisms operating on individual cells are the most instantaneous because the control decisions depend only on the local conditions within a switch. For example, selective cell discarding depends on the level of congestion in the switch buffers. In contrast, other mechanisms operate across the network on the timescale of end-to-end propagation delays. These mechanisms involve the one-way passage of information between two points along a virtual connection. For instance, in *explicit forward congestion indication* (EFCI), the detection of congestion is carried within the headers of cells traveling downstream in a VPC/VCC. Still other mechanisms operate on an even longer timescale involving a bidirectional exchange of messages and responses. An example of this is CAC, where the establishment of a new connection is attempted by means of signaling messages, and nodes along the route can either accept or block the request.

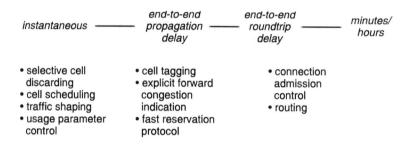

Figure 4.2 Timescales of traffic-control mechanisms.

4.2.4 Preventive and Reactive Controls

Since ATM is a packet-oriented technique, it might be thought that traditional feedback-based flow-control mechanisms used in conventional data networks (e.g., window-based flow control or source throttling [19]) will be applicable in ATM networks. However, two arguments have been made against the use of feedback-based control. First, it is not appropriate for real-time sources, which generally cannot be expected to be controllable by the network. Second, the effectiveness of feedback-based control is fundamentally limited by the propagation delay. The time to transmit a cell is much shorter than the time to detect congestion and notify the source to react [13]. High-speed sources in ATM are capable of sending too many cells into the network before feedback information can propagate through the network to control them [20].

Hence there is a consensus that feedback-based control, and more generally *reactive* controls, will have limited usefulness in high-speed ATM networks (except for specialized services such as the ABR service). It is widely believed that ATM networks will rely primarily on *preventive* methods (or rate-based methods) rather than reactive methods [13,17,20–22]. Preventive methods attempt to avoid congestion by ensuring that each connection remains within the bounds that the network used to allocate network resources during connection set-up. Preventive methods consist primarily of two functions: connection admission control and *usage parameter control* (UPC, sometimes called input policing) to regulate the amount of traffic entering the network. Reactive methods include selective cell discarding, explicit forward congestion indication, and dynamic route reconfiguration, which react to the detected onset of congestion.

4.3 CONNECTION ADMISSION CONTROL

ATM was chosen to be connection-oriented because connections are natural for real-time conversational services (e.g., voice or video). Connections are also advantageous for the network provider because routing decisions per cell are simplified to a table look-up, and reassembly of the original user data is simpler when the cell sequence is preserved.

Consequently, CAC is a fundamental part of traffic control in ATM. CAC and UPC are the main functions of preventive traffic control. As in the circuit-switched telephone network, CAC consists of:

- Negotiating a new connection request with the users;
- Deciding on admission or rejection of the new connection;
- Allocating the appropriate network resources.

Some of the important issues are:

- The characterization of source traffic and QOS requirements (see Section 4.3.1);
- Routing;
- The connection admission/rejection policy (see Section 4.3.2).

Routing (or path computation) attempts to maximize the long-term network throughput by uniformly distributing traffic to utilize the network efficiently, while minimizing end-to-end delays. Although routing is an important part of CAC, it is not discussed here because there has been little research completed at this point.

A B-ISDN call may involve one or more virtual connections (e.g., for multimedia or multiparty services) [23]. If multiple connections are required, admission or rejection is determined for each virtual connection. Connection requests (and renegotiation of connection parameters) are made through the exchange of signaling information (see Section 3.3). CAC uses the connection request to determine:

- An estimation of the resulting QOS if the new connection is accepted;
- Traffic parameters for UPC;
- The required network resources to be allocated along a route.

A new connection is admitted by the network only if it is estimated that the new connection can be established with the required QOS while maintaining the guaranteed QOS of existing connections.

The connection request is passed along the route. Each node decides whether it can allocate the necessary resources. The new request is accepted only if it is accepted at each node. Acceptance of the new connection implies agreement on a traffic contract specifying the obligations between the user and network. Once established, the parameters of a virtual connection may be changed only through renegotiation between the user and network.

4.3.1 Traffic Contract

The starting point of the traffic contract is a traffic description. An *ATM traffic descriptor* is a set of traffic parameters that can be used to characterize an ATM connection, such as peak rate, average rate, and maximum burst length at peak rate. A *source-traffic descriptor* is a subset of the ATM traffic descriptor that is used during connection set-up to characterize a requested connection. A *connection-traffic descriptor* characterizes a connection at the UNI. It consists of:

- Source traffic descriptor;
- Cell delay variation tolerance;
- Conformance definition.

The connection-traffic descriptor is used by the network during connection set-up to allocate network resources and derive parameters for UPC. The conformance definition is used by the UPC to distinguish conforming and nonconforming cells without ambiguity (see Section 4.4).

If the network admits a new connection, it implies agreement on a traffic contract specifying the obligations between the user and network [2]. A traffic contract consists of:

- Connection traffic descriptor;
- Requested QOS class;
- Definition of a compliant connection.

A compliant connection is determined by the network provider and differs from the conformance definition, which applies to individual cells. For example, a compliant connection might allow for a certain number of nonconforming cells.

An important issue is the set of traffic parameters to include in the source-traffic descriptor. All parameters should be simple to be determinable by the user, interpretable for billing, useful to CAC for resource allocation, and enforceable by UPC. The set should be small but sufficient for the diverse types of traffic in B-ISDN. CBR connections may be described simply by the rate. The situation for VBR connections is much more complicated. The main issue is how to characterize the burstiness of a VBR source (e.g., ratio of peak to average rate or mean burst length). VBR connections will clearly require more parameters than the peak rate to indicate their degree of burstiness; and two source-traffic descriptors may be used to separately specify the high loss priority CLP = 0 and low loss priority CLP = 1 flows.

Some examples of traffic parameters that have been proposed for the source-traffic descriptor are:

- Peak cell rate and cell delay variation tolerance [2,24];
- Sustainable cell rate and burst tolerance [2];
- Minimum cell interarrival time [25];
- Minimum of average cell interarrival time over a specified interval [25];
- Average rate [24];
- Mean and maximum burst length [24].

4.3.2 Peak Cell Rate and Cell Delay Variation

Two necessary parameters are the peak cell rate and the cell delay variation tolerance [2]. The peak cell rate is not simply the reciprocal of the minimum interarrival time between consecutively transmitted cells. Consider the example of a slotted transmission link where cells may be transmitted only within fixed time slots at the rate of N bps. With the simple definition of peak rate, the only possible peak rates would be N, $N/2$, $N/3$, and so on. This suggests that the simple intuitive definition of peak rate is too limited. A different definition has been proposed by the ATM Forum in terms of the generic cell rate algorithm below.

4.3.2.1 Generic Cell Rate Algorithm

The so-called *generic cell rate algorithm* (GCRA) has been proposed as a reference model to define certain parameters of a cell stream [2]. These parameters are useful for connection set-up as well as rate enforcement in UPC. The GCRA involves two parameters, an increment I and a limit L, and the algorithm is thus denoted as $GCRA(I,L)$. It can be explained by either of two equivalent versions: a virtual scheduling algorithm or a continuous-state leaky bucket algorithm. The virtual scheduling algorithm is explained here; the leaky bucket and its variations are discussed later in Section 4.4.

In the virtual scheduling algorithm in Figure 4.3, the actual arrival time of the nth cell, $t(n)$, is compared with its theoretical arrival time $T(n)$, which is the expected arrival time under the assumption that cells are all spaced equally in time with distance I. The algorithm is intended to ensure that the cell rate is not greater than I^{-1} on the average, with some tolerance dependent on L; that is, cells will not arrive too much earlier than their theoretical arrival times. The cell is deemed to be conforming if $t(n) > T(n) - L$; otherwise it is nonconforming (too early). The theoretical arrival time for the next cell, $T(n + 1)$, is calculated as a function of $t(n)$. If the nth cell is conforming and $t(n) < T(n)$, then the next theoretical arrival time is set to $T(n + 1) = T(n) + I$. If the cell is conforming and $t(n) \geq T(n)$, then the next theoretical arrival time is set to $T(n + 1) = t(n) + I$. Nonconforming cells are not counted in the update of the theoretical arrival times.

The GCRA will be revisited in Section 4.4.4, which will discuss its use to enforce traffic parameters in UPC.

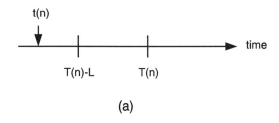

(a)

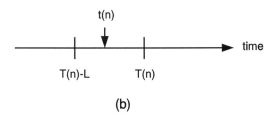

(b)

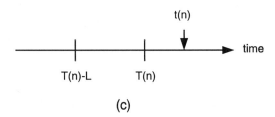

(c)

Figure 4.3 Virtual scheduling algorithm: (a) cell is too early and nonconforming; (b) cell is early but conforming, and $T(n + 1) = T(n) + I$; (c) cell is conforming, and $T(n + 1) = t(n) + I$.

4.3.2.2 Equivalent Terminal

The peak cell rate and the cell delay variation tolerance are defined using the GCRA and an equivalent terminal model [2]. Figure 4.4 shows the functions in an equivalent terminal, which is a conceptual model for representing the generation of a cell stream from the user (the user premises equipment may be much more complicated in actuality). It does not mean that the user terminal actually performs these functions, only that the cell stream crossing the UNI appears *as if* it were generated from an equivalent terminal. Conceptually, cells are generated in the ATM layer and shaped (i.e., buffered to separate them in time) such that they conform to a $GCRA(I_p, 0)$ at the physical-layer service access point (denoted as PL-SAP). This is a conceptual point where cells from the ATM layer are presented to the physical layer for transmission. The peak cell rate is defined as the inverse, $R_p = 1/I_p$.

Equivalent terminal

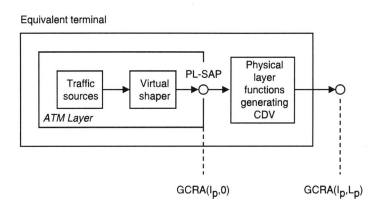

Figure 4.4 Equivalent terminal model for peak cell rate and cell delay variation tolerance.

The cell delay variation tolerance is closely associated with the peak cell rate. After the ATM layer presents cells at the PL-SAP for transmission, some randomness is introduced into the spacings of the cell stream (e.g., due to multiplexing, addition of physical-layer overhead, insertion of OAM cells, or waiting for time slots). Thus, the cell stream may no longer conform to a $GCRA(I_p, 0)$. The upper bound on the distortion in the cell stream is the cell delay variation tolerance. If this tolerance is denoted as L_p, the cell stream generated by the equivalent terminal conforms to a $GCRA(I_p, L_p)$ at the terminal output. Clearly, larger values of L_p will allow greater deviation from the idealized cell stream in which cells are spaced exactly apart by time intervals of I_p. This permits greater *cell clumping*, or groups of consecutive cells.

4.3.3 Sustainable Cell Rate and Burst Tolerance

For a CBR source, the peak cell rate and the cell delay variation tolerance are sufficient parameters to be useful for resource allocation. However, they are not sufficient parameters for VBR sources because they do not indicate any measure of burstiness. For VBR sources, it is desirable to also specify the average rate (if known), which is an important parameter for resource allocation.

The sustainable cell rate and burst tolerance are upper bounds on the average rate and allowable deviation from this average rate (according to [2] but not yet adopted in standards). As before, these parameters can be defined using the conceptual equivalent terminal model shown in Figure 4.5. In the ATM layer, cells are generated and passed to the physical layer at equal intervals of I_s. The sustainable cell rate is defined as $R_s = 1/I_s$. Naturally, I_s is meaningful only if it is greater than I_p. At the PL-SAP, the cell stream is conforming to a $GCRA(I_s,0)$.

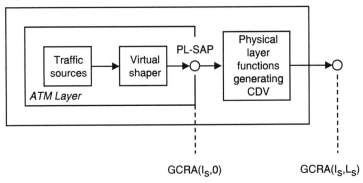

Figure 4.5 Equivalent terminal model for sustainable cell rate and burst tolerance.

Before transmission, operations in the physical layer will introduce deviations in the spacings of the cell stream (e.g., due to multiplexing, the addition of physical-layer overhead, the insertion of OAM cells, or waiting for time slots). The upper bound on these deviations is the burst tolerance. If the burst tolerance is L_s, the cell stream generated at the output of the equivalent terminal conforms to a $GCRA(I_s,L_s)$.

The sustainable cell rate and burst tolerance constrain the maximum length of a burst at the peak cell rate. It is a straightforward exercise to demonstrate that

$$maximum\ burst\ length = 1 + \left\lfloor \frac{L_s}{I_s - I_p} \right\rfloor$$

where $\lfloor x \rfloor$ is the floor function denoting the greatest integer less than or equal to x.

4.3.4 Resource Allocation

Although traffic parameters will be subject to standardization, network providers will implement their own resource-allocation methods and connection-admission policies. Resource allocation is a complicated problem in B-ISDN because there will be connections with widely different characteristics and network-performance requirements. It is unclear how to determine acceptance or rejection of connections among different services on a fair and equitable basis [26,27]. For instance, acceptance of a high-bandwidth connection could result in the blocking of a number of low-bandwidth connections. It might be preferable to reject the high-bandwidth connection in favor of the low-bandwidth connections (which affects more users). Calls involving multiple parties and multiple connections complicate the problem further [23].

Another complicated issue is resource allocation for statistically multiplexed VBR connections (see Section 4.2.2). A conservative admission policy for VBR connections based on only peak rates may result in low network utilization. If a higher network utilization is desired by taking advantage of statistical multiplexing, there will be a probability that peak-rate bursts could cause buffer overflows or excessive queuing delays. The desired operating point will be a compromise between efficient utilization and QOS protection, which will be better understood only through practical experience gained from the operation of actual ATM networks.

Some examples of proposed connection-admission policies will be surveyed in Chapter 9, where the focus is more on design and implementation.

4.3.4.1 Role of Virtual Paths

The use of virtual paths in resource management is expected to be important, at least initially, for a number of reasons [28–32]. First, by maintaining excess capacity on VPCs in anticipation of future VCCs, the amount of processing required to set up new VCCs can be reduced. VCCs can be established by making simple connection-admission decisions at VPC endpoints, and no processing at VPC connecting points is required. The decision simply depends on whether the existing VPC has sufficient unused capacity. If so, no time is required to set up a new VPC for every requested VCC.

Second, VPCs allow a way to logically segregate QOS classes while allowing VCCs to be statistically multiplexed. VCCs with similar QOS requirements can be grouped in the same VPCs. Third, VPCs allow a group of VCCs to be managed and policed more simply. This reduces management and control costs. Finally, dynamic routing control at the level of virtual paths allows a simple method for adaptive network reconfiguration. Path routing can be changed simply by modifying routing information at VPC connecting points.

Strategies for the reservation of capacity on VPCs will involve a trade-off between capacity costs and control costs. Network providers will determine their own strategies for using VPCs in resource management. Some strategies will be outlined in Chapter 9.

4.3.4.2   Fast Reservation Protocol

For some data applications, such as bursty LAN-to-LAN data transfers, the source traffic is characterized by bursts at peak rate separated by periods of inactivity. The peak rate is the only known parameter, and other traffic parameters are not meaningful. For this type of traffic, it should not be necessary to follow a lengthy connection set-up procedure to negotiate a detailed traffic contract. A better approach may be to negotiate the rate at the beginning of each burst, following a simplified set-up procedure called *fast reservation protocol* [17,18,33,34]. It is not a part of ATM traffic-control standards but might be included in the future.

A special cell precedes the burst to request the network resources. Each burst may be admitted or blocked. If admitted, the resources are released immediately after the burst. This procedure reduces the signaling time and ensures reliable transport of correlated cells belonging to a larger data unit. It is an alternative suitable for services that do not require a guaranteed QOS, that are more sensitive to cell loss than delay, and that have unpredictable traffic characteristics.

4.4   USAGE/NETWORK PARAMETER CONTROL

Usage parameter control is necessary to monitor and regulate incoming traffic flows at the UNI to ensure compliance with agreed traffic contracts. At the NNI, the policing function is called *network parameter control* (NPC). The objective is protection of the network from intentional or unintentional deviations from the negotiated traffic parameters that can adversely effect the QOS of other (compliant) connections. Specific tasks are checking the validity of VPI/VCI values and checking that the rates of incoming traffic from active VPCs/VCCs are conforming to agreed parameters.

If cell loss priority is used, UPC will be operated separately on the CLP = 0 and CLP = 1 components of a VPC/VCC, or on the CLP = 0 and CLP = 0 + 1 flows [2]. If cell tagging is exercised, UPC is applied to the CLP = 0 flow first. A CLP = 0 cell may be tagged by changing its loss priority to CLP = 1 (see Section 4.4.1); then tagged cells (now with CLP = 1) will be combined with the other CLP = 1 cells before entering the UPC mechanism for the CLP = 1 or CLP = 0 + 1 flow.

A UPC/NPC mechanism should have these features:

- Be simple to implement and understandable by the user;
- Respond quickly to violations;
- Allow for a margin of tolerance due to practical uncertainties;
- Appear transparent if the source is conforming.

In addition, UPC/NPC should minimize these two types of errors:

- *False alarm*: taking actions on cells when the source is conforming;
- *Late alarm*: failing to take actions when the source is not conforming to the traffic contract.

An issue is how strictly UPC/NPC should be performed [35]. Due to practical uncertainties, some laxity is necessary (e.g., a user may be uncertain about the average source rate to declare during connection set-up). Another issue is the difficulty of policing the average rate [36]. If the average rate is unknown, it can be estimated from a short sample of traffic, but this involves a certain risk of incorrect policing. Estimation from a longer sample of traffic may be more accurate but increases the reaction time to violations.

A particular UPC/NPC mechanism has not been standardized, although the ATM Forum has specified a leaky-bucket algorithm called the GCRA (see Section 4.3.2). The adoption of the GCRA does not imply a particular implementation, although the GCRA is functionally equivalent to a continuous-state leaky-bucket algorithm (see Section 4.4.3). Besides the GCRA, some previously proposed UPC/NPC mechanisms include: rectangular sliding window [37,38], triangular sliding window [37], jumping window [36], and exponentially weighted moving average [36,37].

4.4.1 Cell Tagging

It is the responsibility of the user to conform to the parameters in the traffic contract. For cells in violation of the traffic contract, the UPC can tag or mark cells with high loss priority by changing their loss priority to CLP = 1, or the UPC can discard cells. If the tagging option is exercised, tagged cells (now with CLP = 1) are merged with other CLP = 1 cells before they enter the UPC mechanism for the CLP = 1 or CLP = 0 + 1 flow. Within the network, CLP = 1 cells are discarded first if congestion occurs.

Cell tagging may be desirable when there is a significant probability that tagged traffic may be carried through the network without adversely affecting network performance (e.g., when the network load is light). It may be especially appropriate for services without stringent QOS requirements. If tagged traffic can be carried successfully, it is advantageous to both users and the network provider to do so.

If the probability of successfully carrying tagged traffic is low (e.g., there is a heavy network load), cell tagging is not desirable because tagged cells will use valuable network resources and increase the congestion level for no useful purpose. It would then be better to discard the excess traffic at the UPC to avoid wasting network resources.

4.4.2 Traffic Shaping

Traffic shaping may be performed by the user before entrance into the network or by the network immediately after the UPC mechanism. The purpose of traffic shaping by the user is to ensure conformance to the traffic contract and avoid cell loss in the UPC. The purpose of traffic shaping by the network is to reduce the peak cell rate or burstiness of VBR source traffic by spacing out cells. This reduces the queuing (and, hence, cell delays and cell loss) within the network at the expense of additional buffering delays at the network edge. The idea of the traffic shaper has appeared under different names, e.g., throughput-burstiness filter [39], spacer-controller [40], and regulator [41].

If traffic shaping is done within the network, it is not subject to standardization. It is implemented and performed at the discretion of the network provider. A common example of a traffic shaper is the leaky-bucket algorithm [39–41].

4.4.3 Leaky-Bucket Algorithm

The leaky-bucket algorithm has been used for a long time to regulate overloads in the controls of stored program-controlled switching systems [42]. It was the first algorithm proposed for UPC in ATM [43] and has received a great deal of attention, mainly due to its implementation simplicity [13,20,37,39,42,44–46]. It is also noteworthy because the GCRA adopted by the ATM Forum is functionally equivalent to a continuous-state leaky-bucket algorithm.

The basic leaky bucket is shown in Figure 4.6 as a token-queuing scheme. A buffer (or token bucket) of size B containing tokens is drained at a constant leak rate R. An arriving cell attempts to add a token into the buffer, and the cell is allowed to pass if the token bucket is not full. If the bucket is full, the arriving cell is discarded. Conceptually, the tokens can be viewed as arrivals to a finite-capacity, single-server queue with deterministic service times. It is readily apparent that the leaky bucket enforces the average rate R and allows temporary bursts above the rate R depending on the bucket size B. The implementation requires a simple up/down counter to reflect the contents of the token bucket.

A number of variations of the basic leaky bucket are possible. Instead of discarding cells when the token bucket is full, arriving cells may be allowed to queue in an input buffer. Also, instead of discarding cells, it is an option to tag cells (lower their loss priority) and pass them for possible later discarding. A cell spacer at the output is a traffic-shaping option to smooth out the cell interdeparture times.

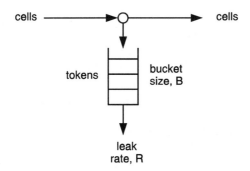

Figure 4.6 Basic leaky-bucket algorithm.

It has been proposed to use multiple leaky buckets to enforce different parameters. For example, the dual leaky bucket shown in Figure 4.7 can be used to enforce the peak rate at the first leaky bucket and the average rate at the second leaky bucket [42]. The bucket sizes and can be dimensioned for the desired tolerances for cell delay variation and bursts. This can be used for UPC when the traffic contract involves peak cell rate, cell delay variation tolerance, sustainable cell rate, and burst tolerance (see Section 4.3).

The effectiveness of the leaky bucket has been raised as an issue. In the basic scheme in Figure 4.7, the only adjustable parameters are R and B. If B is small, there is little tolerance for variations in the cell interarrival times, and conforming cells may be mistakenly discarded. On the other hand, if B is too large, it becomes ineffective as a policing mechanism because it allows more deviation from R [42].

4.4.4 GCRA Revisited

As stated earlier in Section 4.3, a $GCRA(I,L)$ is functionally equivalent to a continuous-state leaky bucket. The bucket drains continuously at a rate of 1 per unit time and is filled by the increment I for each conforming cell arrival. An

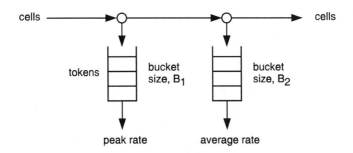

Figure 4.7 Example of dual leaky bucket.

arriving cell is deemed to be conforming only if the bucket contents are less than the limit L upon arrival; otherwise, it is nonconforming. The capacity of the bucket is $L + I$.

Multiple GCRAs may be used in combination to monitor different sets of parameters [2]. For example, if there are CLP = 0 and CLP = 1 components of a VPC/VCC cell stream, UPC for peak rate is applied to the high loss priority CLP = 0 cell stream and also applied to the total CLP = 0 + 1 cell stream. Thus, the component cell streams must conform to a $GCRA(I_0,L)$ and a $GCRA(I_{0+1},L)$, where I_0 is the peak rate of the CLP = 0 component, I_{0+1} is the peak rate of the total CLP = 0 + 1 stream, and L is the cell delay variation tolerance. Cells are conforming if and only if they conform to both GCRA stages; nonconforming cells are discarded unless tagging is exercised. With tagging, CLP = 0 cells not conforming to the $GCRA(I_0,L)$ will be changed to CLP = 1. At the $GCRA(I_{0+1},L)$, nonconforming cells are discarded.

If sustainable cell rate and burst tolerance are used as parameters for the CLP = 0 flow, a $GCRA(I_{0+1},L)$ enforces the peak cell rate and cell delay variation tolerance of the total CLP = 0 + 1 stream. A $GCRA(I_{s0},L + b_0)$ enforces the sustainable cell rate and burst tolerance of the CLP = 0 component, where I_{s0} is the sustainable cell rate of the CLP = 0 flow and b_0 is the burst tolerance for the CLP = 0 flow. If cell tagging is exercised, nonconforming cells at the $GCRA(I_{s0},L + b_0)$ are tagged by changing their loss priority to CLP = 1 and nonconforming cells at the $GCRA(I_{0+1},L)$ are discarded.

4.5 CONGESTION CONTROL

While CAC and UPC are functions to prevent congestion, there may still be a small probability of congestion caused by temporary overload of buffers within the network. The purpose of congestion control is detection of congestion and reaction to minimize the speed, effects, and duration of congestion. For simplicity and speed, the ATM protocol does not include conventional link-level flow controls, which are appropriate only for delay-tolerant traffic. In ATM, congestion control actions include selective cell discarding and *explicit forward congestion indication* (EFCI). Other congestion-control functions, such as feedback control for ABR connections, are under study.

4.5.1 Delay and Loss Priorities

Selective cell discarding is an action dependent on cell loss priorities (refer to Section 4.2.2). ATM allows loss priorities to be assigned explicitly to individual cells using the CLP bit in the header. When congestion occurs and cell loss is unavoidable, low priority CLP = 1 cells are subject to discarding before CLP = 0 cells. The CLP = 1 cells are either nonconforming to the traffic contract (if tagged by the network) or contain expendable user data (if tagged by the user). Loss priorities can reduce the loss of critical information, for example, by using layered coding of video or voice [47–51]. Some believe it is a means primarily for making the network more robust to bursty traffic, which is not achievable by any practical overdimensioning [14,52].

Two implementation approaches to selective cell discarding have been considered in [52]. In the push-out scheme, an arriving CLP = 0 cell can join a full queue by discarding a queued CLP = 1 cell; arriving CLP = 1 cells cannot join a full queue. In the partial-buffer-sharing scheme, when the queue reaches a specified threshold, only CLP = 0 cells are admitted; arriving CLP = 1 cells are rejected. It is observed that the push-out scheme has the optimal performance, but the partial-buffer-sharing scheme can have a close performance and a much simpler implementation.

Delay priorities are useful to reduce the end-to-end delays and delay jitter of time-critical traffic [24]. ATM allows delay priorities to be assigned implicitly per VPC/VCC; i.e., cells of the same VPC/VCC will have the same delay priority associated with their VPI/VCI in a look-up table.

Delay priorities affect the order in which buffered cells are scheduled for transmission on a shared link. Cell scheduling can be decided on the basis of individual cells or cycles. In scheduling by cells, the earliest-due-date (or earliest-deadline-first) policy has been shown to have optimal properties. Consider a queue containing cells with deadlines. Cells not transmitted by their deadlines are discarded. The policy of choosing the cell with the earliest (but not expired) deadline will minimize the number of discarded cells [53].

In scheduling by cycles, the scheduling decisions are made only at the start of each cycle. An example is the asynchronous time-sharing scheme [54]. In each cycle, time slots are first given to the minimum number of queued real-time cells that cannot be delayed until the next cycle to still make their deadlines. The remainder of the cycle is filled with nonreal-time cells.

Another example of scheduling by cycles is proposed in [55]. At the start of each cycle, a list of priority assignment weights is determined. These specify the relative ratio of time slots in the cycle that are assigned with highest priority to each traffic class. If no cells of the assigned highest priority are waiting, then any cell may use that slot.

There have not been many studies considering both delay and loss priorities simultaneously. Two classes of traffic, cells requiring either low loss (e.g., data) or low delay (e.g., voice or video), are assumed in [56]. It is proposed that these two classes can be supported by a so-called LDOLL (low delay or low loss) queue, which gives service priority to low-delay cells and space priority to low-loss cells. If a buffer is full, an arriving low-loss cell can push out the low-delay cell that has waited the longest. If the number of low-loss cells in the queue is less than a threshold, then service is given to low-delay cells; otherwise low-loss cells are serviced.

4.5.2   Explicit Forward Congestion Indication

While delay and loss priorities are used for traffic-control actions within a switch, EFCI is a mechanism for the communication of congestion information from the network to the user to enable end-to-end control actions. If a network node experiences congestion, it can inform downstream nodes and the destination user by changing the PT field in the cell headers (see Table 2.4). The destination user will read the congestion indications and tell the appropriate source to adjust its rate (for traffic that can be flow-controlled or -adjusted) [17]. Naturally this depends on the cooperation of the end users to respond appropriately to the congestion indication. This mechanism can not be expected to prevent congestion or increase utilization, but it may help to mitigate the cell loss rate during persistent congestion periods (with duration at least an order of magnitude longer than the propagation delay [17]). The method by which a network node monitors its internal operation and classifies its congestion state is considered to be dependent on implementation and not subject to standardization (see Chapter 10).

It has been proposed that nodes use a set of thresholds to trigger EFCI [14]. At the first threshold, EFCI is activated using only CLP = 1 cells. The next threshold triggers selective cell discarding of CLP = 1 cells. At the final threshold, EFCI is activated using CLP = 0 cells as well as CLP = 1 cells. The downstream endpoint can infer the level of congestion by detecting the received CLP = 1 cells with congestion indicated, the loss of CLP = 1 cells, and the received CLP = 0 cells with congestion indicated.

A natural complement would be explicit backward congestion notification where a congestion message is sent upstream (in the backward direction of a VPC/VCC) directly to the source for appropriate action. This may be more complicated to implement than EFCI and the need for it in addition to EFCI is uncertain.

4.6   CONCLUSIONS

Traffic control in ATM has been established on a framework of general principles. First, virtual connections will be differentiated into multiple QOS classes defined by cell delay and cell loss rate requirements, which will be supported by the ATM network. Second, the network will operate at a compromise point between the conflicting objectives of statistical multiplexing for efficient utilization versus isolation between traffic flows for QOS protection. Third, traffic control consists of a set of mechanisms exercised at different levels on different traffic entities. Each mechanism has a characteristic timescale, and a complete set of controls will be eventually necessary to handle the diverse and unpredictable traffic types in B-ISDN. Finally, ATM networks will rely primarily on preventive control methods, although reactive controls will also be necessary to control the intensity, spread, and duration of congestion. Preventive control functions are mainly CAC and UPC, which are responsible for the regulation and enforcement of input traffic into the network at the levels of connections. Congestion control, including selective cell discarding and EFCI, is responsible for actions to react to temporary congestion.

The traffic controls discussed in this chapter must be considered in the study of ATM switch architectures because they must be supported and implemented within an ATM switch. First, a switch must contain functions related to CAC—they must support signaling, process connection requests, and allocate resources. While some aspects of CAC will be covered by standards (e.g., signaling and QOS parameters), other aspects may be implemented at the discretion of the network provider (e.g., routing algorithm and connection-admission policy). Chapter 9 will be devoted to the topic of CAC functions within the ATM switching system.

Second, a switch must contain UPC/NPC functions for every VPC/VCC to be policed. The UPC will require implementation of a GCRA or multiple GCRAs in some combination. If the network provider chooses to exercise cell tagging and traffic shaping, these options must also be implemented in the UPC/NPC mechanism. UPC/NPC will be revisited in Chapter 6.

Finally, the switch architecture must consider the implementation of congestion-control functions, such as selective cell discarding and EFCI. Selective cell discarding is part of the buffer management strategy within a switch, which may also include a cell-scheduling policy using delay priorities. To support EFCI, a switch must monitor its internal operation and classify its congestion state. The implementation of congestion-control functions will depend on the network provider. Congestion control is discussed further in Chapters 8 and 10.

From considerations of traffic control, it is clear that ATM switching systems must be responsible for much more than buffering and relaying ATM cells. Traffic-control functions will have a substantial impact on the switch architecture. This will be evident in the next chapter, which presents a general functional switch architecture model that will be studied in more detail in later chapters.

References

[1] Anagnostou, M., et al., "Quality of Service Requirements in ATM-Based B-ISDNs," *Computer Communications*, vol. 14, May 1991, pp. 197–204.

[2] ATM Forum, *ATM User-Network Interface Specification Version 3.0*, Sept. 10, 1993.

[3] Ferrari, D., "Client Requirements for Real-Time Communication Services," *IEEE Communications Mag.*, Vol. 28, Nov. 1990, pp. 65–72.

[4] Baiocchi, A., et al., "Loss Performance Analysis of an ATM Multiplexer Loaded with High-Speed ON-OFF Sources," *IEEE J. on Selected Areas in Communications*, Vol. 9, April 1991, pp. 388–393.

[5]   Hashida, O., et al., "Switched Batch Bernoulli Process (SBBP) and the Discrete-Time SBBP/G/1 Queue with Application to Statistical Multiplexer Performance," *IEEE J. on Selected Areas in Communications*, Vol. 9, April 1991, pp. 394–401.

[6]   Lampe, D., "Traffic Studies of a Multiplexer in an ATM Network and Applications to the Future Broadband ISDN," *Int. J. of Digital and Analog Cabled Systems*, Vol. 2, 1989, pp. 237–245.

[7]   Murata, M., et al., "Analysis of a Discrete-Time Single-Server Queue with Bursty Inputs for Traffic Control in ATM Networks," *IEEE J. on Selected Areas in Communications*, Vol. 8, April 1990, pp. 447–458.

[8]   Saito, H., et al., "An Analysis of Statistical Multiplexing in an ATM Transport Network," *IEEE J. on Selected Areas in Communications*, Vol. 9, April 1991, pp. 359–367.

[9]   Sato, Y., and K. Sato, "Evaluation of Statistical Cell Multiplexing Effects and Path Capacity Design in ATM Networks," *IEICE Trans. on Communications*, Vol. E75-B, July 1992, pp. 642–648.

[10] Sykas, E., et al., "Performance Evaluation of Statistical Multiplexing Schemes in ATM Networks," *Computer Communications*, Vol. 14, June 1991, pp. 273–286.

[11] Demers, A., et al., "Analysis and Simulation of a Fair Queuing Algorithm," *Internet Research & Experience*, Vol. 1, Sept. 1990, pp. 3–26.

[12] Roberts, J., "Variable Bit-Rate Traffic Control in B-ISDN," *IEEE Communications Mag.*, Vol. 29, Sept. 1991, pp. 50–56.

[13] Cidon, I., et al., "Bandwidth Management and Congestion Control in plaNET," *IEEE Communications Mag.*, Vol. 29, Oct. 1991, pp. 54–64.

[14] Eckberg, A., et al., "Controlling Congestion in B-ISDN/ATM: Issues and Strategies," *IEEE Communications Mag.*, Vol. 29, Sept. 1991, pp. 64–70.

[15] Filipiak, J., "M-Architecture: A Structural Model of Traffic Management and Control in Broadband ISDNs," *IEEE Communications Mag.*, Vol. 27, May 1989, pp. 25–31.

[16] Gallassi, G., et al., "Resource Management and Dimensioning in ATM Networks," *IEEE Network*, Vol. 4, May 1990, pp. 8–17.

[17] Gilbert, H., et al., "Developing a Cohesive Traffic Management Strategy for ATM Networks," *IEEE Communications Mag.*, Vol. 29, Oct. 1991, pp. 36–45.

[18] Hui, J., "Resource Allocation for Broadband Networks," *IEEE J. on Selected Areas in Communications*, Vol. 6, Dec. 1988, pp. 1,598–1,608.

[19] Gerla, M., and L. Kleinrock, "Flow Control: a Comparative Survey," *IEEE Trans. on Communications*, Vol. COM-28, April 1980, pp. 289–310.

[20] Bae, J., and T. Suda, "Survey of Traffic Control Schemes and Protocols in ATM Networks," *Proc. of the IEEE*, Vol. 79, Feb. 1991, pp. 170–189.

[21] Saito, H., et al., "Traffic Control Technologies in ATM Networks," *IEICE Trans.*, Vol. E74, April 1991, pp. 761–771.

[22] Woodruff, G., and R. Kositpaiboon, "Multimedia Traffic Management Principles for Guaranteed ATM Network Performance," *IEEE J. on Selected Areas in Communications*, vol. 8, April 1990, pp. 437–446.

[23] Crutcher, L., and A. Waters, "Connection Management for an ATM Network," *IEEE Network*, Vol. 6, Nov. 1992, pp. 42–55.

[24] Vakil, F., and H. Saito, "On Congestion Control in ATM Networks," *IEEE LTS*, Vol. 2, Aug. 1991, pp. 55–65.

[25] Ferrari, D., and D. Verma, "A Scheme for Real-Time Channel Establishment in Wide-Area Networks," *IEEE J. on Selected Areas in Communications*, Vol. 8, April 1990, pp. 368–379.

[26] Cooper, C., and K. Park, "Toward a Broadband Congestion Control Strategy," *IEEE Network*, Vol. 4, May 1990, pp. 18–23.

[27] Hong, D., and T. Suda, "Congestion Control And Prevention in ATM Networks," *IEEE Network*, Vol. 5, July 1991, pp. 10–16.

[28] Burgin, J., and D. Dorman, "Broadband ISDN Resource Management: The Role of Virtual Paths," *IEEE Communications Mag.*, Vol. 29, Sept. 1991, pp. 44–48.

29] Habib, I., and T. Saadawi, "Controlling Flow and Avoiding Congestion in Broadband Networks," *IEEE Communications Mag.*, Vol. 29, Oct. 1991, pp. 46–53.

30] Ohta, S., and K. Sato, "Dynamic Bandwidth Control of the Virtual Path in an Asynchronous Transfer Mode Network," *IEEE Trans. on Communications*, Vol. 40, July 1992, pp. 1,239–1,247.

31] Sato, K., et al., "Broadband ATM Network Architecture Based on Virtual Paths," *IEEE Trans. on Communications*, Vol. 38, Aug. 1990, pp. 1,212–1,222.

32] Sato, K., et al., "The Role of Virtual Path Crossconnections," *IEEE LTS*, Vol. 2, Aug. 1991, pp. 44–54.

33] Boyer, P., and D. Tranchier, "A Reservation Principle with Applications to the ATM Traffic Control," *Computer Networks and ISDN Systems*, Vol. 24, 1992, pp. 321–334.

34] Ohnishi, H., et al., "Flow Control Schemes and Delay/Loss Tradeoff in ATM Networks," *IEEE J. on Selected Areas in Communications*, Vol. 6, Dec. 1988, pp. 1,609–1,616.

35] Okada, T., et al., "Traffic Control in Asynchronous Transfer Mode," *IEEE Communications Mag.*, Vol. 29, Sept. 1991, pp. 58–62.

36] Rathgeb, E., "Modeling and Performance Comparison of Policing Mechanisms for ATM Networks," *IEEE J. on Selected Areas in Communications*, Vol. 9, April 1991, pp. 325–334.

37] Dittmann, L., et al., "Flow Enforcement Algorithms for ATM Networks," *IEEE J. on Selected Areas in Communications*, Vol. 9, April 1991, pp. 343–350.

38] Yamanaka, N., et al., "Precise UPC Schemes and Bandwidth Allocation Methods for ATM-Based B-ISDN Characterized by Wide-Ranging Traffic Parameter Values," *Int. J. of Digital and Analog Communication Systems*, Vol. 5, Oct.-Nov. 1992, pp. 203–215.

39] Eckberg, A., et al., "Bandwidth Management: A Congestion Control Strategy for Broadband Packet Networks—Characterizing the Throughput-Burstiness Filter," *Computer Networks and ISDN Systems*, Vol. 20, 1990, pp. 415–423.

40] Boyer, P., et al., "Spacing Cells Protects and Enhances Utilization of ATM Network Links," *IEEE Network*, Vol. 6, Sept. 1992, pp. 38–49.

41] Cruz, R., "A Calculus for Network Delay," *IEEE Trans. on Information Theory*, Vol. 37, Jan. 1991, pp. 114–141.

42] Niestegge, G., "The 'Leaky Bucket' Policing Method in the ATM (Asynchronous Transfer Mode) Network," *Int. J. of Digital and Analog Communication Systems*, Vol. 3, 1990, pp. 187–197.

43] Turner, J., "New Directions in Communications (or Which Way to the Information Age?)," *IEEE Communications Mag.*, Vol. 25, Oct. 1986, pp. 8–15.

44] Butto, M., et al., "Effectiveness of the 'Leaky Bucket' Policing Mechanism in ATM Networks," *IEEE J. on Selected Areas in Communications*, Vol. 9, April 1991, pp. 335–342.

45] Sidi, M., et al., "Congestion Control Through Input Rate Regulation," *IEEE Trans. on Communications*, Vol. 41, March 1993, pp. 471–477.

46] Yamanaka, N., et al., "Performance Limitation of Leaky Bucket Algorithm for Usage Parameter Control and Bandwidth Allocation Methods," *IEICE Trans. on Communications*, Vol. E75-B, Feb. 1992, pp. 82–86.

47] Ghanbari, M., "Two-Layer Coding of Video Signals for VBR Networks," *IEEE J. on Selected Areas in Communications*, Vol. 7, June 1989, pp. 771–781.

48] Goodman, D., "Embedded DPCM for Variable Bit Rate Transmission," *IEEE Trans. on Communications*, Vol. COM-28, July 1980, pp. 1,040–1,046.

49] Kishino, F., et al., "Variable Bit-Rate Coding of Video Signals for ATM Networks," *IEEE J. on Selected Areas in Communications*, Vol. 7, June 1989, pp. 801–806.

50] Petr, D., et al., "Priority Discarding of Speech in Integrated Packet Networks," *IEEE J. on Selected Areas in Communications*, Vol. 7, June 1989, pp. 644–659.

51] Verbiest, W., et al., "The Impact of the ATM Concept on Video Coding," *IEEE J. on Selected Areas in Communications*, Vol. 6, Dec. 1988, pp. 1,623–1,632.

52] Kroner, H., et al., "Priority Management in ATM Switching Nodes," *IEEE J. on Selected Areas in Communications*, Vol. 9, April 1991, pp. 418–427.

[53] Saito, H., "Optimal Queuing Discipline for Real-Time Traffic at ATM Switching Nodes," *IEEE Trans. on Communications*, Vol. 38, Dec. 1990, pp. 2,131–2,136.

[54] Hyman, J., et al., "Real-Time Scheduling with Quality of Service Constraints," *IEEE J. on Selected Areas in Communications*, Vol. 9, Sept. 1991, pp. 1,052–1,063.

[55] Takagi, Y., et al., "Priority Assignment Control of ATM Line Buffers with Multiple QOS Classes," *IEEE J. on Selected Areas in Communications*, Vol. 9, Sept. 1991, pp. 1,078–1,092.

[56] Awater, G., and F. Schoute, "Optimal Queuing Policies for Fast Packet Switching of Mixed Traffic," *IEEE J. on Selected Areas in Communications*, Vol. 9, April 1991, pp. 458–467.

ATM Switching System Architectures

5

5.1 INTRODUCTION

The previous chapters have reviewed the current state of ATM standards and industry agreements as preparation for this chapter on ATM switching system architectures. Chapters 1 and 2 covered the fundamentals of the ATM technique. Chapter 3 described the different types of information flows in ATM networks: user data, control, and management. An overview of traffic-control functions was presented in Chapter 4.

The objective of this chapter is to apply the preceding background information towards the development of a general functional architecture model of an ATM switching system. This architecture model specifies only the *functional* requirements of a switching system and a possible, logical arrangement of those functions within the system. The purpose of the model is to facilitate the future study of switch design, complexity, and performance. Although the model will have implications about switch design, it is not intended to prescribe any particular implementation.

It may already be apparent that ATM switches are *switching systems* and much more than a fabric that simply routes and buffers cells (as it is usually meant by *ATM switch* [1]). In addition to relaying cells, switching systems must contain the functions represented by the control plane and management plane in the B-ISDN protocol reference model discussed in Chapter 3. Furthermore, switching systems must support and implement a set of traffic-control functions as delineated in Chapter 4. We refer to the distribution of all of these functions within the system as the *switch architecture*. In this chapter, the functions are identified and partitioned into a few major functional blocks. The remainder of the book will investigate each functional block in more detail.

5.2 FUNCTIONAL REQUIREMENTS

In the broad sense, an ATM switch has a set of input ports and output ports through which the switch is interconnected to users, other switches, and other network elements. The switch is assumed to provide only a cell relay service and it supports the necessary control and management functions related to the service.

In practice, the switch may also perform interworking functions to support various service-specific interfaces for narrowband circuits, frame relay [2] switched multimegabit data service (SMDS) [3,4], or other services [5]. For the purposes of this study, it is assumed that the switch interfaces are the standardized framed (SONET/SDH) ATM UNI or NNI. Important as they are, the topics of interworking and service-specific interfaces will not be covered here.

In addition to the input and output ports, the switch may have other interfaces for exchanging control and management information with special-purpose networks such as the intelligent network [6] and telecommunications management network [7].

We will begin by revisiting the three planes of the B-ISDN protocol reference model. The corresponding types of information flows—user data, control (signaling), and management—have different purposes in the ATM network and suggest different functional requirements within the switch. We will then consider the additional requirements imposed in the switch by traffic-control functions. These requirements are examined below to identify the major functional blocks of the ATM switch architecture. Each functional block will be defined in more detail in Section 5.3.

5.2.1 User Plane Considerations

As represented by the ATM layer of the B-ISDN protocol reference model, the main function of an ATM switch is to relay user data cells from its input ports to the appropriate output ports. The flow of user data traffic through the switch is shown in Figure 5.1. The information within the cell payloads is carried transparently by the ATM network, and therefore the switch processes only the cell headers. The headers are processed when the cells are received at the input ports. The VPI/VCI information derived from the cell headers is used to route the cells through the switch to the appropriate output ports. The cells are prepared for physical-layer transmission at the switch output ports.

The cell relay service involves three distinct functions that are represented by the functional blocks in Figure 5.1. First, cells are received by *input modules* (IMs) at the switch input ports and prepared for routing through the switch. The routing is performed by a *cell switch fabric* (CSF). Finally, the cells are prepared for transmission by *output modules* (OMs) at the switch output ports. The input modules, output modules, and cell switch fabric together perform the basic cell routing and buffering functions required in ATM switching. The same func-

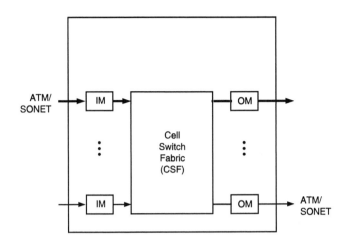

Figure 5.1 Flow of user data traffic.

tional blocks, with additional processing, will also be used to handle the flows of control and management information related to the ATM layer.

5.2.2 Control Plane Considerations

As discussed in Section 3.3, the control plane in the B-ISDN protocol reference model represents functions related to the establishment and control of switched VPCs/VCCs. The control plane consists of a signaling AAL above the ATM layer and physical layer. Connection-control information is carried in signaling cells identified by their VPI/VCI fields. Unlike user data cells, the information contained in the payloads of signaling cells is not transparent to the network; the signaling information must be processed and interpreted by the ATM switch. Therefore, the switch must identify incoming signaling cells, separate them from user data cells, and perform the AAL functions to interpret the signaling information. If the switch generates control information, it encapsulates the information into signaling cells that are mixed with the outgoing user data cell traffic.

The flow of signaling information is shown in Figure 5.2(a). Because signaling cells use the same ATM-layer transport as do user data cells, they flow through the input modules, the output modules, and the cell switch fabric. However, in addition, the signaling information is processed by a functional block shown as CAC. In Figure 5.2(a), it is assumed that the signaling information is routed to and from the CAC by the cell switch fabric, but it is not necessary to use the CSF. For example, in Figure 5.2(b), the signaling information may be passed directly from the input modules to the CAC to the output modules.

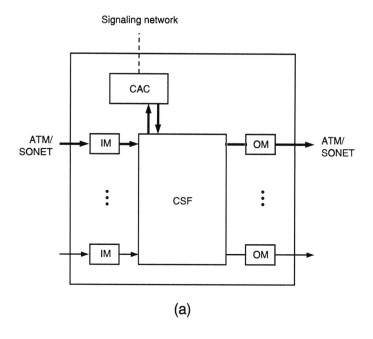

(a)

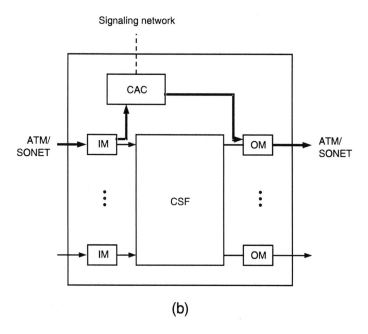

(b)

Figure 5.2 Flow of control information (a) using CSF, and (b) without using CSF.

Alternatively, control information may be exchanged through a signaling network such as an SS7 network (recall Section 1.3.3). In this case, the CAC has an interface to the signaling network as shown in Figure 5.2. The CAC may also use the signaling network to communicate with the intelligent network (see Section 1.4.4).

5.2.3 Management Plane Considerations

Recall from Section 3.4 that the management plane in the B-ISDN protocol reference model represents the functions that monitor and control the ATM network to ensure its correct and efficient operation. The management plane consists of plane management and ATM-layer management, which are not completely defined in standards yet. From the existing standards and work in progress [8], the management functions required in ATM switching systems can be broadly identified as:

- *Fault management*: to detect, isolate, and report failures in the switch;
- *Performance management*: to continually monitor, evaluate, and report the behavior of switch components;
- *Configuration management*: to activate or deactivate switch components into or out of service;
- *Security management*: to regulate the access to and control of the switch database;
- *Accounting management*: to measure usage of switch resources for customer billing;
- *Traffic management*: to monitor and regulate traffic to prevent and control congestion.

These functions are the responsibility of a functional block shown as *system management* (SM) in Figure 5.3.

A major responsibility of the SM is support of the ATM-layer OAM procedures defined for fault management and performance management (see Section 3.4.1). The procedures involve the flows of OAM cells identified by their VPI/VCI or PT fields. Like signaling cells, the information contained in the payloads of OAM cells may be recognized and processed by the ATM switch. The switch must identify incoming OAM cells, separate them from other cells (if appropriate), and perform the necessary processing functions to support the ATM-layer OAM procedures. In the OAM procedures, the switch may generate OAM cells and mix them into the outgoing user data cell streams.

The flow of OAM information is shown in Figure 5.3(a). Along with user data cells and signaling cells, OAM cells flow through the input modules, output modules, and cell switch fabric. The processing of OAM cells is performed by the SM. Here it is assumed that the OAM cells are routed to and from

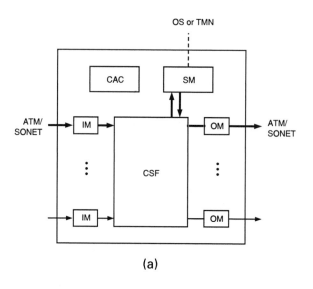

(a)

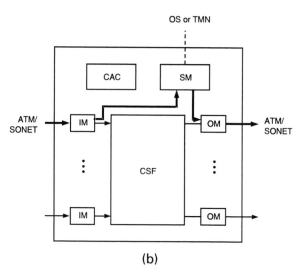

(b)

Figure 5.3 Flow of management information (a) using CSF, and (b) without using CSF.

the SM by the cell switch fabric, but it is not necessary to use the CSF. For example in Figure 5.3(b), the OAM cells may be passed directly from the input modules to the SM to the output modules.

Another major responsibility of the SM is support of the *interim local management interface* (ILMI) for each UNI (see Section 3.4.2). The ILMI allows users to obtain status and control information about VPCs/VCCs across their UNI. For each UNI, the SM contains a *UNI management entity* (UME) that monitors the objects described in a standardized ATM UNI management information base. Each ATM user device also contains a UME. Adjacent UMEs can communicate with each other across the UNI by means of SNMP messages carried in ILMI cells, which are identified by their VPI/VCI fields (see Table 2.2).

Again, the ILMI cells follow the flow through input modules, CSF, output modules, and SM in Figure 5.3(a). Here, the cell switch fabric routes ILMI cells to and from the SM, where the UME interprets and responds to the encapsulated SNMP messages. Alternatively, ILMI cells may be passed to and from the SM without going through the cell switch fabric as shown in Figure 5.3(b).

Finally, the SM should support network-wide operations, administration, maintenance, and provisioning (OAM&P) functions, which will likely be proprietary to the network provider. As shown in Figure 5.3, the SM may exchange network-management information with an operations system (OS) through a direct interface or through a TMN [7].

5.2.4 Traffic Control Considerations

As described in Chapter 4, traffic control functions must be supported in ATM switching systems. These functions include connection admission control, usage/network parameter control, and congestion control. CAC has been covered earlier in Section 5.2.2. UPC/NPC functions must be performed at the ingress points to the switch; therefore, they are handled by the input modules. Congestion-control functions are regarded here as part of the SM, which is generally responsible for the management of all operations within the switch, including buffer management. Specific actions of buffer management, under the supervision of the SM, are carried out in the cell switch fabric where the buffers are located.

5.3 SWITCH ARCHITECTURE MODEL OVERVIEW

The previous section has identified the need for these broadly defined functional blocks:

- *Input modules:* to receive incoming cells and prepare them for routing through the CSF;
- *Output modules:* to prepare outgoing cells for transmission;
- *Cell switch fabric:* to route user data cells from input to output ports and possibly route signaling and management cells between the other functional blocks in the switch;
- *Connection admission control:* to process and interpret signaling information and decide about connection admission or rejection;
- *System management:* to perform all management and traffic-control functions to ensure the correct and efficient operation of the switch.

An overview of each functional block is presented below.

Two points are noteworthy here. First, these functional blocks are all service independent. Second, the partitioning of functions into these particular functional blocks is more or less consistent with other related studies such as [8,9], and it is certainly not unique. Other partitioning may be possible and equally valid as a reference architecture model. It will also be seen later that the partitioning does not always have precisely defined boundaries between functional blocks. For instance, some CAC and SM functions may reside in the input modules and output modules. However, we do not believe that the usefulness of the model or the partitioning exercise is diminished.

5.3.1 Input Modules

At each input port, the first function of an input module is termination of the incoming SONET signal and extraction of the ATM cell stream. Basically, this involves:

- Conversion of the optical signal into an electrical one;
- Recovery of the digital bitstream;
- Processing of the SONET overhead;
- Cell delineation;
- Cell rate decoupling (discarding empty cells).

The cells must then be prepared for routing through the cell switch fabric. This requires a number of functions on each cell:

- Error checking in the cell header using the HEC field;
- Validation and translation of the VPI/VCI values;
- Determination of the destination output port;
- Possible sorting of signaling cells and routing to CAC;
- Possible sorting of management cells and routing to SM;
- Usage/network parameter control for each VPC/VCC to be policed;
- Addition of an internal tag.

An internal tag may be added to each cell at the input modules and removed at the output modules. It might contain two types of information: internal routing and housekeeping. For internal routing, the tag could contain fields related to destination output port, loss tolerance, delay priority, timestamp, maximum-delay bound, delay-variation tolerance, or broadcast/multicast connection identifier. For housekeeping purposes (i.e., internal performance monitoring), the tag might contain fields for source-user identifier, cell sequence number, cell type, or error check for the cell payload. Of course, other

ıseful fields can be conceived as well. Since the internal tag exists only within
he switch, its contents are determined entirely by the switch designer.

The input modules will be the subject of Chapter 6.

i.3.2 Output Modules

"he output modules perform many of the reverse functions of the input mod-
ıle. However, the OMs are considerably simpler than the IMs because their
nain responsibility is to prepare ATM cell streams for physical transmission.
ıpecific functions may include:

- Removal and processing of the internal tag from each cell;
- Possible translation of the VPI/VCI values;
- HEC field generation and inclusion into the cell headers;
- Possible mixing of signaling cells from CAC and management cells from
  SM with outgoing user data cells streams;
- Cell rate decoupling (adding empty cells);
- Mapping cells into SONET payloads;
- Generation of SONET overhead;
- Conversion of the digital bitstream into an optical signal.

Chapter 7 will cover the output modules in more detail.

5.3.3 Cell Switch Fabric

n general, the cell switch fabric is primarily responsible for transferring cells
)etween the other functional blocks in the switch. In particular, user data cells
nust be routed from the input modules to output modules. It is feasible to use
he cell switch fabric to route signaling cells and management cells to the CAC
)r SM through special ports on the fabric. However, it is not necessary to use
:he CSF if the input and output modules have direct data paths to the CAC and
ıM; then the input modules (rather than the CSF) have the responsibility to sort
)ut signaling cells and management cells and send them to the CAC or SM.

Besides routing, a number of other possible functions of the cell switch
fabric are important to consider:

- Cell buffering;
- Traffic concentration and multiplexing;
- Redundancy for fault tolerance;
- Multicasting or broadcasting;
- Cell scheduling based on delay priorities;
- Selective cell discarding based on loss priorities;
- Congestion monitoring and activation of EFCI.

The cell switch fabric will be treated in more depth in Chapter 8.

5.3.4 Connection Admission Control

The CAC performs all functions related to the establishment, modification, and termination of connections at the levels of virtual paths and virtual channels. More specifically, the CAC may be responsible for:

- High-layer signaling protocols;
- Signaling AAL functions to interpret or generate signaling cells;
- Interface with a signaling network;
- Negotiation of traffic contracts with users requesting new VPCs/VCCs;
- Renegotiation with users to change established VPCs/VCCs;
- Allocation of switch resources for VPCs/VCCs, including route selection;
- Admission/rejection decisions for requested VPCs/VCCs;
- Generation of UPC/NPC parameters.

CAC will be the subject of Chapter 9.

5.3.5 System Management

The SM is complex because it has many important responsibilities:

- Physical-layer OAM;
- ATM-layer OAM;
- Configuration management of switch components;
- Security control for the switch database;
- Usage measurements of switch resources for customer billing;
- Traffic management;
- Administration of a management information base;
- Customer-network management;
- Interface with operations systems or TMN;
- Support of network management.

Because each listed item involves more specific functions, further details of the SM are postponed to Chapter 10.

5.4 DISTRIBUTION OF FUNCTIONS

The switch architecture model shown in Figure 5.3 assumes that the CAC and SM functions are centralized. It is possible, and perhaps advantageous, to distribute the CAC and SM functions within the system. The degree of distribution of functions and its effect on the switch performance are fundamental issues. In this section, some preliminary considerations are introduced. The issue of distribution will be revisited several times in the following chapters as each functional block is discussed in detail.

5.4.1 Distribution of CAC

A centralized CAC, as depicted in Figure 5.2, implies that a single processing unit receives signaling cells from the input modules, interprets the signaling information, and performs the admission decisions and resource allocation for all connections in the switch. The input modules, output modules, and cell switch fabric only sort out signaling cells to the CAC and receive signaling cells from the CAC.

The CAC functions may be distributed to blocks of input modules as shown in Figure 5.4. Within each block, the input modules recognize signaling cells and pass them to the associated CAC. The distributed CACs have the same control and processing functions as before, only for a much smaller number of input ports.

The centralized approach of Figure 5.2 is simpler to implement, but connection control processing could become a performance bottleneck for large switch sizes if the CAC becomes overloaded. The distributed approach of

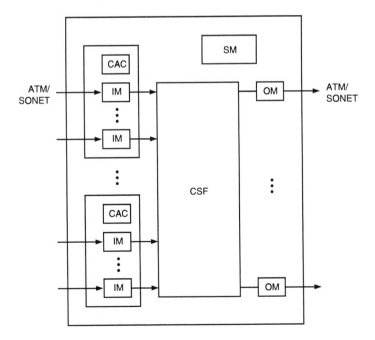

Figure 5.4 CAC functions distributed to blocks of input modules.

Figure 5.4 eliminates the bottleneck by dividing the connection-control processing among multiple parallel CACs. However, the distributed implementation is likely to be more complicated. To allocate resources to a new connection, for example, each CAC must have knowledge of all established connections through the cell switch fabric. The information about the state of connections and available resources must be communicated and coordinated among the distributed CACs.

These blocks of input modules, each with an associated CAC, are called front-end processing modules in Hitachi's hyper-distributed ATM switching system [10] and broadband line modules in NEC's experimental ATM switching system [11]. Their approaches go further than distribution of only CAC; both Hitachi's front-end processing modules and NEC's broadband line modules also contain a small ATM routing fabric, and they are designed to operate independently as small stand-alone ATM switches. In terms of our model, it means that part of the CSF functions are also distributed among the blocks of input modules as in Figure 5.5.

Returning to Figure 5.4, it is possible to further distribute portions of the CAC functions to each input module and output module. This approach is illustrated in Figure 5.6, where the distributed CAC functions within each input

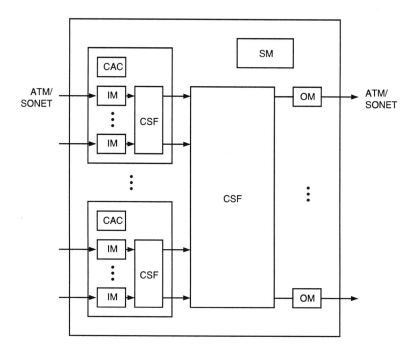

Figure 5.5 CAC and CSF functions distributed to blocks of input modules.

module and output module are designated as *IM-CACs* and *OM-CACs*, respectively. The IM-CACs could handle extraction and preprocessing of signaling cells (e.g., signaling AAL functions) and pass high-layer control information to the central CAC for decision-making. This would relieve some of the processing demands on the central CAC. The OM-CACs might handle encapsulation of high-layer control information into outgoing signaling cells.

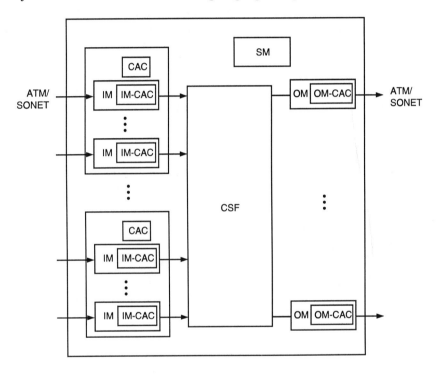

Figure 5.6 CAC functions distributed to blocks of inputs, each input module, and each output module.

5.4.2 Distribution of SM

SM functions are assumed to be centralized in Figure 5.3. The centralized SM responsible for managing the entire switching system is a potential bottleneck if it can be overloaded with processing demands. It is possible to distribute SM functions to blocks of input modules in a manner similar to the distribution of CAC in Figure 5.4. The distributed approach may avoid a processing bottleneck, but some care is required to properly coordinate the actions of the distributed SMs. The distributed SM approach may be necessary in the approach of

Figure 5.5, where each block of input modules is designed to be capable of operating as an independent stand-alone switch; each block should then contain its own CAC and SM functions.

It is probably desirable to distribute part of the SM functions to each input module. In Figure 5.7, the distributed parts of the SM functions within each input module are referred to as *IM-SMs*. The IM-SMs are capable of directly monitoring the incoming user data cell streams. This capability is necessary, for example, for ATM-layer OAM performance monitoring, which involves an error check calculated over blocks of user data cells (recall Section 3.4.1). Direct measurements of the incoming cell streams may also be necessary for accounting-management purposes. For another example, it makes sense to perform physical-layer OAM within each input module where the physical layer is terminated. These are three examples of functions—OAM performance monitoring, traffic measurements for accounting, and physical-layer OAM—that are natural to be included in the IM-SMs.

Likewise, SM functions may also be partially distributed to each output module; these functions within each output module are designated as *OM-SMs*. The OM-SMs may be capable of monitoring the outgoing cell streams (e.g., for accounting management) and generating outgoing management information

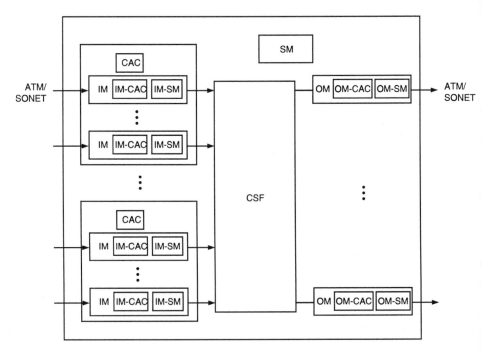

Figure 5.7 In addition to distributed CAC, SM functions are distributed to each input module and output module.

(e.g., as part of physical-layer OAM and ATM-layer OAM). The distribution of SM functions to the input module and output module is covered in Chapter 10.

5.5 CONCLUSIONS

In this chapter, we have considered the functional requirements implied by the B-ISDN protocol reference model and traffic-control functions, and we've developed the basic functional blocks of a switch architecture model. This model provides a possible, logical partitioning of functions into broadly defined blocks: input modules, output modules, cell switch fabric, CAC, and system management.

It is possible, and perhaps advantageous, to distribute the CAC and SM functions through the system. For example, they may be partially distributed to IM-CACs and IM-SMs within each input module, and to OM-CACs and OM-SMs within each output module. Distribution of functions could help to relieve a potential bottleneck due to centralized processing. The degree of distribution of functions and its effect on the switch performance are fundamental issues. Some preliminary considerations were introduced in this chapter. The issue of distribution will be revisited repeatedly throughout the rest of the chapters as each functional block is discussed in detail.

References

[1]   Tobagi, F., "Fast Packet Switch Architectures for Broadband Integrated Services Digital Networks," *Proc. of the IEEE*, Vol. 78, Jan. 1990, pp. 133–178.

[2]   ANSI, *American National Standard for Telecommunications—Frame Relay Bearer Service—Architectural Framework and Service Description*, T1.606, 1990.

[3]   Bellcore, *Generic System Requirements in Support of Switched Multi-megabit Data Service*, TR-TSV-000772, Issue 2, May 1991.

[4]   Bellcore, *Generic Requirements for SMDS Networking*, TA-TSV-001059, Issue 2, Aug. 1992.

[5]   Bellcore, *Broadband ISDN Switching System Generic Requirements*, TA-NWT-001110, Issue 2, Aug. 1993.

[6]   Robrock II, R., "The Intelligent Network—Changing the Face of Telecommunications," *Proc. of the IEEE*, Vol. 79, Jan. 1991, pp. 7–20.

[7]   ITU-T Rec. M.3010, *Principles for a Telecommunications Management Network*, Geneva, Oct. 5, 1992.

[8]   Bellcore, *Generic Requirements for Operations of Broadband Switching Systems*, TA-NWT-001248, Issue 2, Oct. 1993.

[9]   Helstern, T., and M. Izzo, "Functional Architecture for a Next Generation Switching System," *INFOCOM'90*, pp. 790–795.

[10] Sakurai, Y., et al., "ATM Switching System for B-ISDN," *Hitachi Review*, Vol. 40, 1991, pp. 193–198.

[11] Suzuki, K., et al., "An ATM Switching System—Development and Evaluation," *NEC Research & Development*, Vol. 32, April 1991, pp. 242–251.

Input Module 6

6.1 INTRODUCTION

In the previous chapter, a general functional architecture model of an ATM switching system was outlined. The model represents a partition of functions into five major functional blocks: input modules, output modules, cell switch fabric, CAC, and system management. Each functional block will be studied in the following chapters, beginning with this chapter on the input module.

The input module (IM) is especially important because it is the entry point of traffic into an ATM switching system. Several tasks must be performed there. First, the physical-layer (SONET) signal must be terminated and ATM cells must be extracted. As we will see in this chapter, SONET overhead requires considerable processing. Second, the IM must process the cell headers and prepare the user data cells for routing through the cell switch fabric. Third, cells containing signaling and management information must be recognized and, if appropriate, sorted out from user data cells. Unlike user data cells, signaling and management cells may need to be routed to the CAC and SM functional blocks for processing. Finally, the IM may support some CAC and SM functions. The portions of CAC and SM functions distributed to each IM are referred to as IM-CAC and IM-SM, respectively. The precise degree of distribution of CAC and SM functions is a design issue.

Since the IM is rather complicated and detailed, an overview is presented in Section 6.2. Section 6.3 is a review of the SONET standard. Much of this chapter is spent on SONET because it is a topic as broad as ATM. Section 6.4 covers cell delineation. The processing of ATM cell headers is described in Section 6.5. Sections 6.6 and 6.7 discuss the support of CAC and SM functions.

6.2 OVERVIEW OF FUNCTIONS

This section presents a functional overview of the IM. The earlier discussion suggests that the functions within the IM can be categorized into: physical layer, ATM layer, CAC, and system management. As shown in Figure 6.1, the input module consists of six major functional blocks:

- SONET functions;
- Cell delineation and header-error control (HEC);
- UPC/NPC;
- Cell processing;
- IM-CAC;
- IM-SM.

The SONET and cell delineation blocks provide the physical-layer functions. The ATM-layer functions are provided by the UPC/NPC and cell-processing blocks. As mentioned earlier, the IM-CAC and IM-SM blocks are portions of the CAC and SM functions that reside in the input modules.

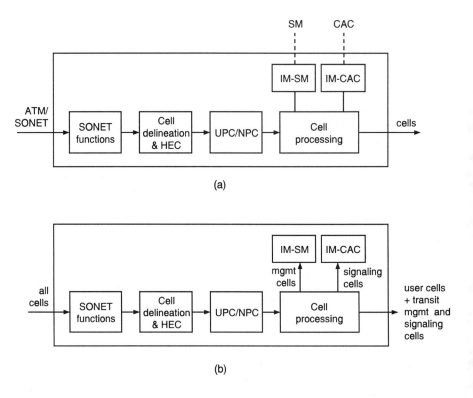

(a)

(b)

Figure 6.1 (a) Functional diagram of the input module; and (b) flows of user cells, signaling cells, and management cells.

6.2.1 Physical-Layer Functions

Recall that the interfaces of the ATM switching system are assumed to be the standardized B-ISDN UNI or NNI. The public UNI and NNI are both based on SONET/SDH, DS1/DS3, and unframed or cell-based physical-layer specifications [1,2]. (For the private UNI, a 100-Mbps multimode fiber and a 155-Mbps multimode fiber or shielded twisted pair physical interface has been specified by the ATM Forum [3].) As mentioned earlier, the SONET-based UNIs/NNIs are assumed here. For cell-based UNIs/NNIs, the input module would not be required to perform SONET-related functions but would use idle cells for cell delineation.

SONET physical-layer functions can be divided into two sublayers: *physical medium sublayer* (PM) and *transmission convergence sublayer* (TC). The PM sublayer deals with medium-dependent transmission characteristics such as bit timing and line coding. The TC sublayer handles physical-layer aspects that are independent of the transmission medium characteristics. These include SONET frame generation/recovery, payload mapping, multiplexing, frequency justification/pointer processing, cell delineation, cell rate decoupling, and header-error control.

6.2.2 ATM-Layer Functions

After the ATM cells are extracted from the incoming SONET signals, the input modules process the ATM protocol information contained in the cell headers. Based on the header information, the IMs determine the destination of each cell and prepare them for routing through the cell switch fabric by attaching an internal tag. Signaling and management cells might be sent directly to the CAC and SM. Specific ATM-layer functions include:

- Generic flow control (for UNIs);
- Validating and translating VPI/VCI values;
- Usage parameter control (for UNIs) and network parameter control (for NNIs);
- Traffic shaping (optional);
- Sorting out signaling and management cells;
- Adding an internal tag to each cell.

6.2.3 IM-CAC

As discussed in Chapter 5, connection admission control can be performed by a centralized CAC functional block (see Figure 5.2). The input modules recognize incoming signaling cells and route them to the CAC (either directly or through a special port in the cell switch fabric). The CAC performs SAAL functions on the signaling cells, processes the high-layer signaling messages, and makes re-source allocation decisions.

To alleviate a possible performance bottleneck caused by centralized processing, CAC functions can be distributed to the input modules. Figure 5.4 shows a separate CAC responsible for call processing for blocks of input ports. The input modules are unchanged. The only difference is that the input modules route signaling cells to the CAC associated with that block of input ports, instead of a centralized CAC.

Figure 5.6 shows a further distribution of CAC functions into each input module. The IM-CACs alleviate some of the processing burden from the CAC. For example, the IM-CACs might handle SAAL processing of incoming signaling cells. The CAC functional blocks are still responsible for interpretation of high-layer signaling messages and making resource-allocation decisions. The precise distribution of CAC functions to the IM-CACs is a design issue. This is investigated further in Chapter 9 on connection admission control.

6.2.4   IM-SM

As discussed in Chapter 5, the SM functional block is responsible for all management and control functions to ensure the correct and efficient operation of the switch. It performs specific functions related to performance management, fault management, configuration management, security management, accounting management, and traffic management. It also supports network management between the switch and network managers or customers.

Figure 5.3 shows a centralized SM functional block. The input modules recognize incoming cells containing management information and route them to the SM (either directly or through a special port in the cell switch fabric).

It might be argued that some SM functions reside naturally within the input modules. For example, the input modules handle physical-layer OAM when the SONET overhead is processed. Also, ATM protocol monitoring is done when the input modules process the cell headers. For these functions, the precise boundary between the input modules and the SM is a matter of judgment.

To alleviate the possible performance bottleneck due to centralized processing, it might be desirable to distribute more SM functions to the input modules. Figure 5.7 shows a portion of SM functions distributed to each input module. The IM-SMs alleviate some of the processing burden from the central SM. The precise amount of distribution of SM functions to the input modules is a design issue. This topic is covered more fully in Chapter 10.

6.3   SONET STANDARD

As mentioned in Section 1.4, the *synchronous optical network* (SONET) standard is a modular family of rates and formats for interfaces used in fiber-optic transmission systems [4–8]. SONET is the North American version of the ITU-T standard *synchronous digital hierarchy* (SDH) [9–12]. SONET and SDH are mostly—but not entirely—compatible. The basic STS-1 rate of SONET is 51.84 Mbps, whereas the basic STM-1 rate of SDH is 155.52 Mbps.

Compared to the existing T-carrier transmission system (in North America) and E-carrier system (in Europe), SONET offers these features:

- *Standardized optical interface:* The SONET interface uses standard optical signals that eliminate existing proprietary conversions between optical and electrical signals. This enables fiber terminals to evolve from multistage, multimodule architectures to single-stage, single-module architectures.
- *Enhanced OAM&P:* Using dedicated overhead channels, SONET supports self-diagnostics, fault analysis, alarm generation, performance monitoring, and protection switching in a real-time fashion. SONET operations, administration, maintenance, and provisioning (OAM&P) capabilities are useful for survivable network architectures.
- *Flexible frame format:* The SONET frame format is designed to carry a wide range of signals, including all existing T-carrier and E-carrier signals at rates of 150 Mbps and higher. SONET encompasses rates of 51.84 Mbps to 2.488 Gbps, extendible up to 13 Gbps. Thus, SONET is capable of supporting future broadband services.
- *Connectivity:* As an international standard, SONET will be the transport technology of choice for the global communications infrastructure. Furthermore, SONET provides seamless interconnectivity with numerous current and emerging services such as B-ISDN and SMDS.
- *Synchronous mode of multiplexing:* SONET supports a synchronous mode of multiplexing, which allows one-step adding and dropping of signals without bringing all signals down to the DS-1 level. This greatly reduces the requirements for multiplexing/demultiplexing equipment and enables more efficient switching and network management.

The remainder of this section is a concise review of the SONET frame format, payload mapping, and OAM&P. Interested readers are referred to the standards and references for more details.

6.3.1 SONET Frame Format

As shown in Figure 6.2, SONET is structured in four layers: physical layer, section layer, line layer, and path layer (the top layer). Consistent with OSI layering principles, each layer relies on services provided by the layer below and in turn provides services to the layer above. The layering scheme clearly reflects the processing sequence done in SONET network elements and forms

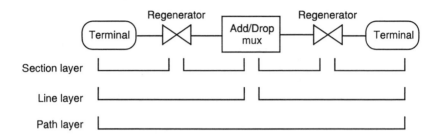

Figure 6.2   SONET layering concept.

the basis of the SONET frame format. Each layer, except the physical layer, is associated with a set of overhead information for embedded operation support.

The physical layer governs the transmission of electrical or optical signals across the physical medium. Although SONET signals can be either electrical or optical, electrical transmission is limited to short distances for low bit-rates. Characteristics of this layer are optical parameters, pulse shapes, power, wavelength, line coding, and bit-rates.

The section layer is responsible for reliable communication between adjacent SONET network elements. A SONET network element is any equipment (within or outside an ATM switching system) that terminates at least the section layer of a SONET interface. Regenerators are one example of a SONET network element. Overhead information at this layer includes framing, scrambling, order wire communication, error checking, and *data communication channel* (DCC).

The line layer establishes reliable communication between SONET line terminating equipment where SONET signals are multiplexed or demultiplexed. This layer provides synchronization, multiplexing, pointer processing for frequency justification, and automatic protection switching. Overhead information is used for line-error monitoring, protection switching, pointer maintenance, and express orderwire functions. Future use of *embedded operation channels* (EOC) in this layer will support integrated network management.

The path layer terminates end-to-end communications. The path overhead provides signal labeling, path maintenance and control, and sub-rates (rates below DS-3) payload mapping. This layer carries both user information and OAM&P messages through the entire network in support of end-to-end network management.

6.3.1.1   SONET Basic Frame

The basic building block of the SONET signal is the *synchronous transport signal-level 1* (STS-1). STS-1 refers to an electrical signal; the optical equivalent is *optical carrier 1* (OC-1). Figure 6.3(a) represents the STS-1 frame structure as a 9-row by 90-column matrix of bytes. The order of transmission of an STS frame is row-by-row, from left to right. In each byte, the most significant bit is transmitted first. STS-1 frames are 125 µs in length, resulting in a basic rate of 51.84 Mbps. Each byte in the STS-1 frame can be regarded as a 64-Kbps clear channel.

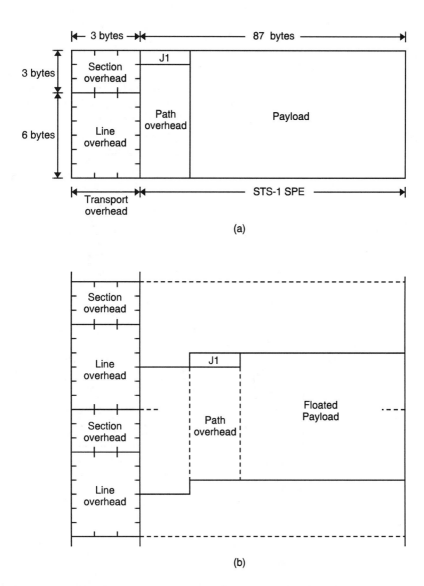

Figure 6.3 (a) Static STS-1 frame format, and (b) STS-1 frame format with floated SPE.

An STS-1 frame consists of two parts: the *synchronous payload envelope* (SPE) and transport overhead. The SPE is the part of the signal that can be structured to efficiently carry user signals of various bit-rates and formats. For instance, an STS-1 SPE can be structured to transport DS-1, DS-2, or DS-3 signals. A unique feature of SONET is that the SPE is allowed to float within the STS frame, as shown in Figure 6.3(b), to account for the phase difference between an STS frame and the SPE. Notice that the path overhead is part of the STS-1 payload because it is accessed only by SONET STS-1 path terminating equipment.

Transport overhead is the other part within the basic signal. The overhead consists of section overhead and line overhead as illustrated in Figure 6.3(a). The contents of these overhead fields are shown in Figure 6.4. By structuring the overhead in this manner, SONET network elements need only access the information necessary for its functions, simplifying the design of some network elements because not all of the overhead must be processed.

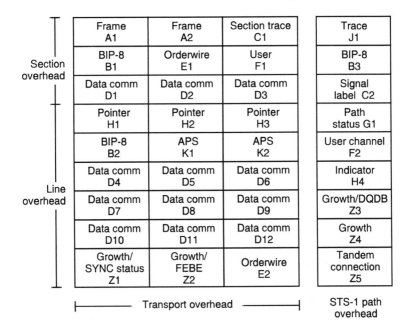

Figure 6.4 SONET overhead.

6.3.1.2 SONET Multiplexing

Higher rate SONET signals can be obtained by byte-interleaving N frame-aligned STS-1s to form an STS-N signal. Depending on the choice of N, a wide range of bit-rates from 150 Mbps to 2.4 Gbps can be realized for the STS-N signal. Typical values of N and the corresponding bit-rates are summarized in Table 6.1. The STS-N frame format is shown in Figure 6.5 (the subscript n on the overhead byte denotes the nth STS-1 signal). When forming an STS-N signal, the transport overhead of individual STS-1 signals need to be frame-aligned before interleaving. The STS-1 SPEs are not required to be aligned because each STS-1 has a unique payload pointer to mark the location of its SPE. Figure 6.6 illustrates an example of two-stage multiplexing of 12 STS-1 signals to form an STS-12 signal.

Table 6.1
Bit Rates for Allowed OC-N Signals

OC-N	Bit Rate (Mbps)
OC-1	51.84
OC-3	155.52
OC-12	622.08
OC-24	1,244.16
OC-48	2,488.32

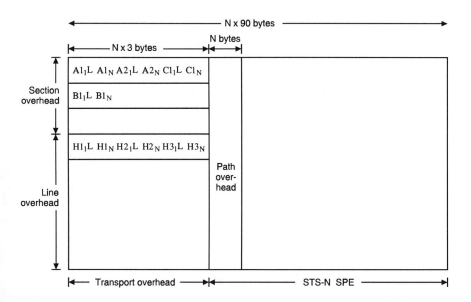

Figure 6.5 STS-N frame format.

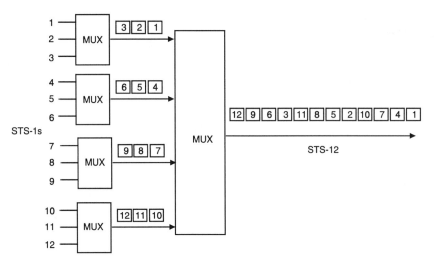

Figure 6.6 An STS-12 generated by two-stage multiplexing.

6.3.1.3   SONET Concatenation

High bandwidth services such as ATM usually require a single payload at a bit-rate that is a multiple of the STS-1 rate. To support such services, SONET employs a mechanism that allows a number of basic signals (e.g., STS-1) to be linked together to form a concatenated signal. Concatenation means that the linked signals are processed and transported as a single entity through the network. Concatenated signals are designated by STS-Nc where N is the equivalent number of STS-1 signals providing the required rate (the optical equivalent is OC-Nc).

Figure 6.7 depicts the STS-3c frame format as an example. The transport overhead is (3×3) columns by 9 rows and the SPE is (3×87) columns by 9 rows. The period of a frame is still 125 µs. The first STS-1 within an STS-Nc has regular transport overhead values. The overhead in all subsequent STS-1s are either undefined or set to special patterns to indicate that the STS-1s are part of an STS-Nc. Only one set of path overhead is required in the STS-Nc SPE. The path overhead always appears in the first of the STS-1s that make up the STS-Nc. ATM standards specify two access rates for the B-ISDN UNI: 155.52 Mbps and 622.08 Mbps [1,2]. These rates can be achieved by STS-3c and STS-12c, respectively.

6.3.1.4   SONET Payload Scrambling

To maintain the stability of SONET clock recovery circuitry, each SONET frame (SPE and transport overhead) will be scrambled by the generating polynomial

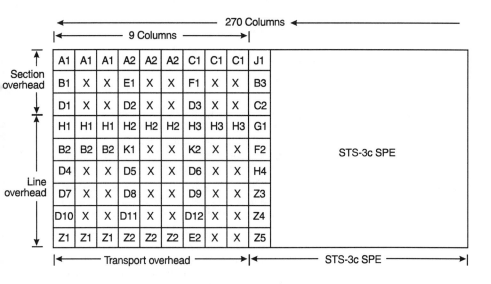

Figure 6.7 STS-3c frame format.

$1 + x^6 + x^7$ in real time. For obvious reasons, the framing bytes A1, A2, and the STS-1 identification byte C1 in an STS-1 frame are not scrambled. In an STS-N signal, all A1, A2, and C1 bytes from the component STS-1s are not scrambled.

6.3.1.5 SONET Overhead Bytes

The SONET overhead bytes serve a variety of functions. Each overhead byte is associated with a layer and is processed or created by the SONET network element that terminates that layer. In the description below, overhead bytes are identified by the names used in Figure 6.4.

Nine bytes of the overhead are devoted to the section layer. Section overhead provides frame alignment, section trace, section-error monitoring, orderwire, user channel, and data communication channel. Specific section overhead bytes are listed in Table 6.2.

Table 6.2
SONET Section Overhead

Section Overhead Bytes	Description
A1, A2 (Framing bytes)	Each STS-1 frame begins with reserved bit patterns A1 = 11110110, A2 = 00101000. SONET network elements use a framing algorithm to extract framing patterns from SONET signals and check for frame alignments. A1 and A2 are provided in all STS-1 signals within an STS-N signal.
C1 (Section trace)	C1 in the first STS-1 in an STS-N frame is reserved for section trace; all other C1 bytes are undefined. Detail of section trace is under study; it replaces STS-1 identification function.
B1 (Section BIP-8)	B1 is allocated in each STS-1 for section-error monitoring by even-parity checksum calculated over all bits of the previous STS-N frame after scrambling. Newly computed BIP-8 is placed in the B1 byte of current STS-1 before scrambling. In an STS-N frame, B1 is defined only for the first STS-1.
E1 (Orderwire)	E1 is reserved for a voice channel between regenerators, hubs, and remote terminals. It is defined only for the first STS-1 in an STS-N signal.
F1 (Section user channel)	F1 provides a 64-Kbps clear channel for the network provider. It is defined only for the first STS-1 of an STS-N signal.
D1, D2, D3 (Section data communication channel)	D1, D2, and D3 form a 192-Kbps message-based data communication channel for alarms, maintenance, control, monitoring, administration, and other communication needs between section terminating equipment. They are defined only for the first STS-1 of an STS-N signal.

SONET line overhead consists of nine bytes that support the transport of the STS path layer payload and its overhead across the physical medium. Line overhead is responsible for line maintenance, error monitoring, protection switching, and data communication for management functions. Specific functions of line overhead bytes, except the H1 and H2 bytes, are summarized in Table 6.3. The H1 and H2 bytes have been assigned to the following three functions:

- *Payload pointer:* The H1 and H2 bytes can be viewed as one 16-bit word as shown in Figure 6.8. Bits 1 through 4 carry a new data flag (NDF) which allows a new pointer value to be assigned when a change occurs in STS payloads. The pattern NDF = 0110 indicates normal operation and NDF = 1001 signals a new payload in the STS frame. Bits 7 through 16 carry a pointer value between the range of 0 to 782, which indicates the offset in bytes between the pointer action byte H3 and the first byte of the STS SPE (not counting transport overhead bytes). The STS payload pointer is a method for allowing flexible and dynamic alignment of the SPE within the STS frame. Thus, the pointer is able to accommodate differences not only in the phases of the STS SPE and the transport overhead, but in the frame rates as well. When the rate of the STS SPE is less than the SONET frame rate, the SPE will periodically slip back in time and the pointer is incremented by one. This is indicated by inverting bits 7, 9, 11, 13, and 15 (I-bits) of the pointer word. In the frame containing inverted I-bits, a positive stuff byte is placed immediately after the H3 byte. Subsequent pointers contain the new offset. Figure 6.9 illustrates the positive pointer justification. When the rate of the STS SPE is greater than SONET frame rate, the SPE will periodically advance in time and the pointer is decremented by one. This is indicated by inverting bits 8, 10, 12, 14, and 16 (D-bits) of the pointer word. In the frame containing inverted D-bits, the extra SPE byte replaces the H3 byte. Subsequent pointers contain the new offset. Figure 6.10 illustrates the negative pointer justification.

- *Concatenation indicator:* In an STS-Nc signal, except for the first STS-1, the H1 and H2 bytes associated with the other STS-1s are set to H1 = 10010011, H2 = 11111111 to indicate that the STS-1s are part of the STS-Nc.
- *Path alarm indication signal (Path AIS):* An all-ones pattern in bytes H1 and H2 is an indication to path terminating equipment that a failure has been detected upstream.

Table 6.3
SONET Line Overhead

Line Overhead Bytes	Description
H1, H2	H1 and H2 are multifunctional and are used as payload pointers, concatenation indicators, and path AIS (see Section 6.3.1.5).
H3 (Pointer action byte)	H3 is assigned for SPE justification. It carries the extra SPE byte when a negative justification occurs in pointer operation. H3 is required in all STS-1 signals in an STS-N signal.

Table 6.3 (continued)

Line Overhead Bytes	Description
B2 (Line BIP-8)	B2 is allocated in each STS-1 for line-error monitoring by even-parity checksum calculated over all bits of the line overhead and the STS-1 payload of the previous STS-1 frame before scrambling. Newly computed BIP-8 is placed in the B2 byte of current STS-1 before scrambling. B2 is required in all STS-1 signals within an STS-N signal.
K1, K2 (APS channel)	K1 and K2 are allocated for automatic protection switch signaling between line terminating equipment. In an STS-N signal, these are only defined for the first STS-1. Bits 6, 7, and 8 of K2 byte are used by line terminating equipment to signal line AIS (111) downstream and to issue line RDI (110) upstream.
D4-D12 (Line data communication channel)	D4-D12 form a 576 Kbps message-based data communication channel for alarms, maintenance, control, monitoring, administration, and other communication needs between line terminating equipment. They are defined only for the first STS-1 of an STS-N signal.
Z1 (Synchronous status message/growth)	Z1 is partially defined. Bits 5–8 of the first STS-1 in an STS-N frame are allocated to convey the synchronous status of the network element.
Z2 (Line FEBE/growth)	Z2 is partially defined. In an STS-Nc signal, Z2 of the third STS-1 is used for a line layer far-end block error (FEBE) function. Bits 5–8 are set to the count of interleaved bit blocks detected in error by the B2 bytes. The count has a range between 0 to 8N.
E2 (Orderwire)	E2 is reserved for an express orderwire channel between line terminating equipment. It is defined only for the first STS-1 of an STS-N signal.

Finally, path overhead will be created for each STS SPE at its origin and remain with the SPE until the SPE is terminated by a path terminating network element. In an STS-Nc signal, only one set of path overheads is defined and is contained in the first STS-1. The STS path overhead consists of nine bytes to support four classes of functions:

- *Payload-independent overhead functions*: J1, B3, C2, and G1 bytes;
- *Mapping-dependent overhead functions*: H4 byte;
- *Application-specific overhead functions*: F2, Z3, and Z5 bytes;
- *Undefined overhead functions for future use*: Z4 byte.

Specific functions of the path overhead bytes are summarized in Table 6.4.

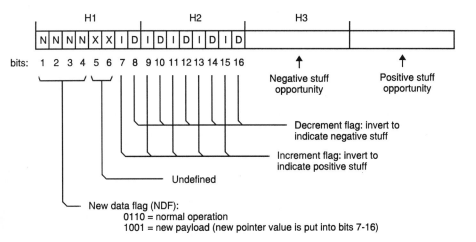

Figure 6.8 Coding for payload pointers H1 and H2 in an STS-1.

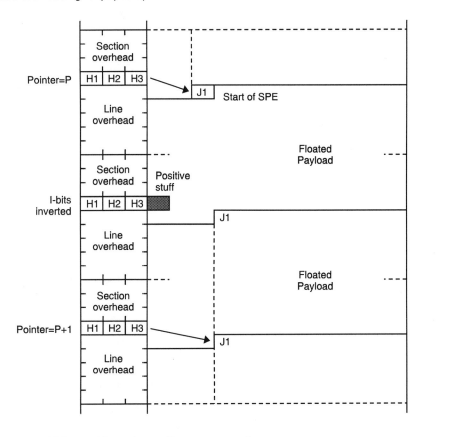

Figure 6.9 STS-1 positive pointer adjustment operation.

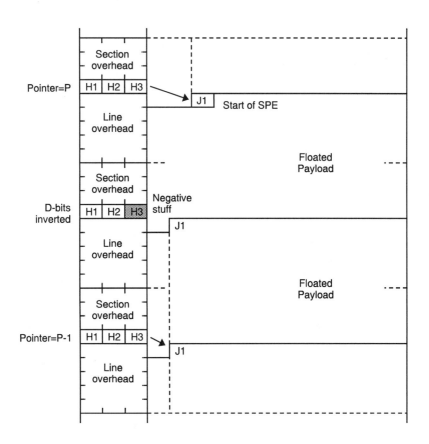

Figure 6.10 STS-1 negative pointer adjustment operation.

Table 6.4
SONET Path Overhead

Path Overhead Bytes	Description
J1 (STS path trace)	J1 is used to repetitively transmit a user-selectable 64-byte string to enable path terminating equipment to verify its continued connection to the intended transmitter.
B3 (Path BIP-8)	B3 is allocated for path-error monitoring by even-parity checksum calculated over all bits of the previous STS SPE before scrambling. Newly computed path BIP-8 is placed in the B3 byte of current STS SPE before scrambling.

Path Overhead Bytes	Description
C2 (Path signal label)	C2 is allocated to indicate the construction of the STS SPE. Eight values are defined. For examples, C2 = 0 indicates "STS SPE unequipped," meaning the path-terminating equipment is present but the path connection is not active; C2=1 indicates "STS SPE equipped—nonspecific payload;" and C2 = 2 represents floating VT mode.
G1 (Path status)	G1 is allocated to convey the path-terminating status and performance back to the originating path-terminating equipment. Four most significant bits carry a FEBE count representing the number of interleaved-bit blocks that have been detected in error by the path BIP-8 byte. The fifth bit is allocated to an STS path RDI signal.
H4 (Indicator byte)	H4 is a multi-purpose indicator used in certain payload mappings.
F2 (Path user channel)	F2 is allocated for network provider communications between path-terminating equipment, except when used for DQDB layer management.
F2, Z3 (DQDB layer management)	In a DQDB application, F2 and Z3 are used to convey DQDB layer management information.
Z4 (Growth)	Undefined.
Z5 (Tandem connection)	Allocated for tandem-connection monitoring in a network.

6.3.2 SONET Payload Mapping

An important benefit of SONET is its flexible frame format, which can be structured to accommodate existing narrowband and future broadband services. This section gives an overview of the mappings of network services into STS SPEs, followed by a discussion of the mapping of ATM cells into STS-3c SPEs for B-ISDN services.

Depending on its bit-rate, a network service can be mapped into one of three possible payload structures: virtual tributaries (VTs), which are subdivisions within an STS-1 payload; STS-1 SPE; or STS-Nc SPE.

6.3.2.1 Sub-STS-1 Services

The VT structures are designed to transport services of rates below STS-1. Four different VT sizes have been defined: VT1.5 (1.728 Mbps), VT2 (2.304 Mbps), VT3 (3.456 Mbps), and VT6 (6.912 Mbps). For each VT size, Table 6.5 lists the corresponding bit-rate, service, and the number of columns occupied in the 9-row STS-1 SPE structure.

Table 6.5
Virtual Tributaries

VT Level	Line Rate (Mbps)	Service	Columns
VT1.5	1.728	DS-1	3
VT2	2.304	CEPT-1	4
VT3	3.456	DS-1C	6
VT6	6.912	DS-2	12

To allow an efficient mixing of VTs of different sizes in an STS-1 SPE, the SPE is divided into seven VT groups. Each VT group occupies 12 columns of the 9-row structure and may contain four VT1.5s, three VT2s, two VT3s, or one VT6. Each VT group is allowed to contain only VTs of one size; however, within an STS-1 SPE, different VT groups may contain different VT sizes.

The SONET standard has further defined a floating mode VT construction. Detailed descriptions of the mappings of synchronous DS-1 and asynchronous DS-1C/DS-2 into floating mode VTs can be found in [12].

6.3.2.2 STS-1 Services

There are high bit-rate services that would occupy an entire STS-1 SPE. The mapping of ATM cells into an STS-1 SPE is described in [7].

6.3.2.3 Super Rate Services

Broadband services of bit-rates higher than the STS-1 rate would require an STS-Nc for transport over SONET networks. The mappings of four such services (DS-4, FDDI, ATM, and MAN) into STS-3c have been defined [7]. Of the four services, only the mapping for ATM is discussed here, due to its relevance to ATM switch design.

ATM cells traversing a B-ISDN UNI/NNI are mapped into an STS-3c SPE, as shown in Figure 6.11. The ATM cells are located horizontally (by row) in the STS-3c SPE, with the cell boundaries aligned with the STS-3c byte boundaries. Because the STS-3c payload capacity is not an integer multiple of the ATM cell length, a cell is allowed to cross the SPE boundary. To ensure that cells are properly extracted from SONET SPEs, a cell delineation algorithm has been defined (see Section 6.4).

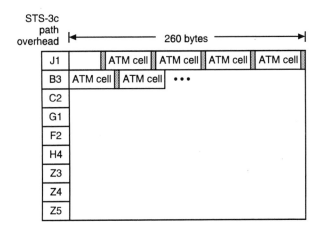

Figure 6.11 STS-3c mapping for ATM cells.

To provide security against payload information replicating the frame synchronous scrambling sequence used at the section layer, the 48-byte information fields of ATM cells are scrambled before STS-3c framing. A self-synchronous scrambler with the generator polynomial $1 + x^{43}$ is specified for this purpose. The scrambler operates for the duration of the 48-byte information field in every cell.

6.3.3 SONET OAM&P

Beyond signal formats and interfaces, SONET includes a set of standard management capabilities to monitor, control, and reconfigure a digital transmission network. A significant portion of the overhead channels in the STS-1 frame are assigned as embedded operation channels (EOCs) for the transport of OAM&P information between SONET network elements. EOCs may be bit-oriented or message-oriented. The former includes the fields in the overhead that are coded binary numbers designated for management functions, such as APS (K1 and K2 bytes) and path trace (J1 byte). The latter consists of the section (D1, D2, and D3 bytes) and line data communication channels (D4 to D12 bytes) that are dedicated for network operations and management.

The EOCs provide a considerable amount of bandwidth for carrying management messages between operations systems and SONET network equipment. Using sophisticated protocols on message-oriented EOCs, an operations system can access the status of all network equipment. The full implementation of SONET OAM&P capabilities could allow network providers to significantly reduce the time and cost required to operate and maintain optical-fiber net works. Three aspects of SONET OAM&P with direct relevance to the input modules in the ATM switch are alarm surveillance, performance monitoring and testing. To take advantages of SONET OAM&P features, an ATM switching system with SONET interfaces is required to implement the OAM&P proce dures described in this section. In particular, the alarm surveillance, perform ance monitoring, and testing functions need to be implemented in the input modules where the incoming SONET signals are terminated.

6.3.3.1 Alarm Surveillance

SONET alarm surveillance involves the detection and reporting of certain de fect conditions in the network. It also specifies the responses of SONET equip ment to the defects. Associated with each defect condition is a failure state which is invoked by a SONET network element if the defect persists for a period of time. Upon entering a failure state, the network element will set a local failure indication and send a notification to an operations system (the system-management functional block will handle this in an ATM switch) Currently, there are eight defect conditions that should be detected:

- *Loss of signal (LOS)*: All incoming SONET signals are monitored for LOS before descrambling by detecting an all-zeros pattern, which corresponds to the absence of light pulses for OC-N interfaces or the absence of voltage transitions for STS-N interfaces. An LOS defect is detected when an all-ze ros pattern on the incoming SONET signal lasts 100 µs or longer. When the LOS defect persists for 2.5 (±0.5) seconds, a SONET network element declares an LOS failure, sets an LOS failure indication, and sends an alarm message to system management. The LOS defect condition is terminated when two consecutive valid frame patterns have been detected and, dur ing the intervening time, no all-zeros pattern qualifying as an LOS defect exists. An LOS failure is cleared when the LOS defect is absent for 10 seconds. After clearing the failure, the SONET network element clears the failure indication and sends a clear message to system management.
- *Loss of frame (LOF)*: When a persistent *severely errored framing* signal is observed for a period of 3 ms, an LOF defect may have occurred and should be confirmed. A severely errored framing signal is an indication that a SONET network element has received at least four consecutive errored framing patterns. When an LOF defect persists for 2.5 seconds, an LOF failure state is declared. Upon declaring the LOF failure, an LOF failure indication is set, and an alarm message is sent to system manage ment. The LOF defect is terminated within 3 ms of a continuous in-frame condition on the incoming signal. The LOF failure will be cleared when the LOF defect is absent for 10 seconds or when an LOS failure is de

clared. The clearing of an LOF failure will be followed by resetting the failure indication and sending a clear message to system management.

- *Loss of pointer (LOP)*: A SONET network element that interprets pointers should detect a loss of pointer (LOP-P) defect on an STS if a valid pointer is not found in *N* consecutive frames or if *N* consecutive new data flags are detected, where *N* is in the range between eight and ten. A similar procedure is used to detect LOP on VT superframes (LOP-V). The declaration of an LOP-P (or LOP-V) failure is made when the LOP-P (or LOP-V) defect persists for 2.5 seconds. Two conditions that terminate the LOP-P (or LOP-V) defect are: the STS (or VT) signal has a valid pointer with normal new data flag in three consecutive STS frames (VT superframes), and a SONET path (or VT) alarm indication signal is received in the STS (or VT) signal. The clearing of an LOP failure is handled in the same way as the LOF/LOS failure.

- *Equipment failure*: Certain equipment failures should be detected and reported as alarms to system management. Equipment to be monitored could be processors, synchronization equipment, protection switch equipment, power circuitry, cross-connect switch fabric, backup memory, and DCC equipment. Upon detecting an equipment failure, a network element should switch to duplex or standby equipment (if available), set a local failure indication, and send an alarm message to system management. Upon clearing an equipment failure, a network element should clear the local failure indication and send a message to system management to clear the alarm.

- *Loss of synchronization*: The quality of primary and secondary timing signals are monitored by SONET network elements. Any degradation or loss of these timing signals are detected and reported as alarms to system management.

- *Troubles on APS channel:* A SONET network element supporting linear *automatic protection switching* (APS) will monitor three failure conditions on the APS channel: protection switching byte failure, channel match failure, and APS mode mismatch failure. The handling of each of these failure conditions is described in [7].

- *DCC failure:* A SONET network element will be able to detect a DCC failure defect, which is defined as either a DCC hardware failure or failure of the line carrying the DCC. Upon declaring a DCC failure, a switch is made to standby DCC equipment. A DCC failure indication is set and a notification is sent to system management.

- *Signal label mismatch (SLM) failure:* This failure occurs when a received STS or VT signal label (C2 byte in path overhead) does not match either the locally provisioned label value or the label value of *nonspecific payload* code. Two types of signal label mismatches need to be monitored:

STS signal label mismatch and VT signal label mismatch. Details of these mismatch failures can be found in [7].

When a SONET network element detects any of the eight defects and their associated failures, it should issue maintenance signals to alert both downstream and upstream network elements of the local failure, in order to limit the effects of the failure. A set of maintenance signals have been defined in SONET: *alarm indication signal* (AIS), *remote defect indication* (RDI), and *remote failure indication* (RFI).

6.3.3.2   Downstream AIS

AIS is the maintenance signal used to alert downstream equipment that an upstream defect has been detected. SONET standards support four types of AIS signals: line AIS, STS path AIS, VT path AIS, and DS-n AIS. The first three types of AIS are relevant to the IM and are discussed here.

- *Line AIS* (AIS-L) is generated by a section terminating equipment (STE) to notify the downstream line terminating equipment (LTE) that a defect has been detected on the incoming SONET section. Within 125 µs of detecting an LOS or LOF defect, an AIS-L is sent downstream by constructing an OC-N signal that contains valid section overhead and a scrambled all-ones pattern for the remainder of the SPE. A downstream LTE detects an AIS-L defect when all ones are observed in bits 6, 7, and 8 of the K2 byte in five consecutive frames. Upon detection, the LTE can initiate protection switching if linear APS is supported in the LTE. An AIS-L defect lasting for 2.5 (±0.5) seconds will cause the LTE to declare an AIS-L failure followed by the setting of a local AIS-L failure indication. If a failure report is required, the LTE will send an AIS-L alarm message to system management. The upstream STE will stop generating AIS-L within 125 µs of terminating the defect that caused the AIS-L signal to be sent downstream. In turn, the downstream LTE will cancel the AIS-L defect when five consecutive frames are received with bits 6, 7, and 8 of the K2 bytes holding any patterns other than "111." An AIS-L failure will be cleared by the LTE after the AIS-L defect is absent for 10 (±0.5) seconds. Upon clearing the failure, the LTE will clear the corresponding failure indication and send an alarm clearing message to system management.
- *STS path AIS* (AIS-P) is sent by an LTE to the downstream path terminating equipment (PTE) on each constituent STS path. The LTE will generate an AIS-P within 125 µs of detecting an LOS, LOF, AIS-L, or LOP-P defect in its incoming signals. An AIS-P signal is a scrambled all-ones signal in bytes H1, H2, and H3, as well as in the entire STS SPE. The downstream PTE detects an AIS-P defect by observing an all-ones pattern in bytes H1

and H2 for three consecutive frames. An AIS-P defect lasting for 2.5 (±0.5) seconds will cause the PTE to declare an AIS-P failure, followed by the setting of a local AIS-P failure indication. If required, the PTE will send an AIS-P alarm message to system management. The upstream LTE will stop generating AIS-P within 125 µs of terminating the defect that caused the AIS-P signal to be sent downstream. In turn, the downstream PTE will cancel the AIS-P defect when three consecutive frames are received with the H1 and H2 bytes containing a valid STS pointer and a new data flag set to "1001," or a valid identical STS pointer with a normal new data flag. An AIS-P failure will be cleared by the PTE after the AIS-P defect is absent for 10 (±0.5) seconds. Upon clearing the failure, the PTE will reset the corresponding failure indication and send an alarm clearing message to system management.

- *VT path AIS* (AIS-V) is generated by a PTE to alert the downstream VT PTE that a defect has been detected in the upstream STS path containing the VT. Within 500 µs of detecting an LOS, LOF, AIS-L, AIS-P, LOP-P, LOP-V, or an STS path SLM (signal label mismatch) defect, a PTE will generate a downstream AIS-V signal for each VT in the affected STS path. An AIS-V signal is constructed by placing a scrambled all-ones code in the entire VT, including VT path overhead bytes. A VT PTE will declare an AIS-V failure if an AIS-V defect persists for 2.5 (±0.5) seconds. The procedure involved in deactivating an AIS-V defect and removing an AIS-V failure is similar to the procedure for AIS-P defect and failure except that the VT pointer and a timing parameter of 500 µs are specified.

6.3.3.3 Upstream RDI and RFI

Before SONET, digital transmission facilities used yellow signals to alert upstream network elements of a downstream failure. In order to achieve higher efficiency in alarm surveillance, SONET adopts a layered maintenance strategy that employs three types of upstream maintenance signals: RDI (formerly far-end-receiver-failure or FERF), RFI, and yellow signals. The RDI and RFI signals are used to isolate troubled SONET sections. Separate RDI signals are defined for SONET line, STS path, and VT path layers. The persistence of an incoming RDI defect will cause a corresponding RFI failure to be declared in the upstream SONET network element.

The procedures involved in the generation and removal of RDI defects and RFI failures on each SONET layer are similar to each other. The procedure for line RDI (RDI-L) defect and line RFI (RFI-L) failure is given here as an example of the typical handling of upstream maintenance signals. Detailed discussions on RDI, RFI, and yellow signals can be found in [7].

An LTE will generate an RDI-L signal upstream within 125 µs of detecting an LOS, LOF, or AIS-L defect. The RDI-L signal is constructed by inserting the code *110* in bits 6, 7, and 8 of the K2 byte. An upstream LTE detects an RDI-L defect when it observes the *110* pattern in the K2 byte for five consecutive frames. The upstream LTE will declare a RFI-L failure when the RDI-L defect persists for 2.5 (±0.5) seconds. Upon declaring an RFI-L failure, the LTE will set an RFI-L failure indication for the line and send a message to system management. The upstream LTE will terminate the RDI-L defect when bits 6, 7, and 8 of the K2 byte contain any pattern other than *110* in five consecutive frames. The RFI-L failure will be cleared when the RDI-L defect is absent for 10 (±0.5) seconds. Upon clearing the failure, the LTE will clear the failure indication and send a clear message to system management.

The association between downstream AIS and upstream RDI/RFI signals in each SONET layer is illustrated in Figure 6.12. In order to eliminate redundant failure reporting, a SONET network element should not report a failure that is caused by a previous failure declared at the network element. The reporting hierarchy of failures related to downstream maintenance signals is: LOS, LOF, AIS-L, LOP-P, AIS-P, SLM-P, LOP-V, AIS-V, and SLM-V. The reporting hierarchy of failures related to upstream maintenance signals is: RFI-L, RFI-P, and RFI-V. For example, when an SLM-P failure is declared, the forthcoming LOP-V, AIS-V, and SLM-V failures on the same incoming SONET signal should not be reported by the network element. For each type of SONET equipment, Table 6.6 summarizes the relationship between SONET defects and upstream/downstream maintenance signals.

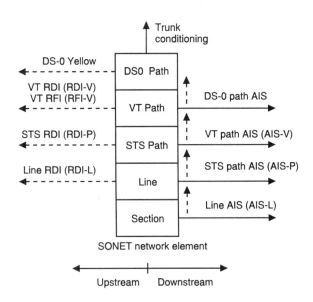

Figure 6.12 SONET maintenance signals at each layer.

Table 6.6
Relationship Between SONET Equipment, Defects, and Maintenance Signals

Equipment	Defects in Incoming Signal	Downstream Signal Sent	Upstream Signal Sent
STE	LOS or LOF	AIS-L	None
LTE	LOS, LOF, or AIS-L	AIS-P	RDI-L
	LOP-P	AIS-P	None
	RDI-L	None	None
PTE	LOS, LOF, or AIS-L	AIS-V	RDI-L and RDI-P
	LOP-V	AIS-V	None
	LOP-P or AIS-P	AIS-V	RDI-P
	SLM-P	AIS-V	RDI-P
	RDI-L or RDI-P	None	None

Notes:
1. STE, LTE, and PTE are section-, line-, and path-terminating equipment, respectively.
2. AIS-L, AIS-P, and AIS-V are terminated by downstream LTE, PTE, and VT termination equipment, respectively.
3. RDI-L and RDI-P are terminated by upstream LTE and PTE, respectively.

6.3.3.4 SONET Performance Monitoring

The SONET functional blocks in the input module are responsible for carrying out SONET-related performance-monitoring functions that include the collection of performance data based on overhead bits in the section, line, and path layers, and for providing in-service monitoring of transmission quality. The four basic tasks performed by performance monitoring are:

- Detection of transmission degradation;
- Derivation of performance parameters from the detected degradation;
- Comparison of performance parameters with associated thresholds;
- Communication of threshold crossings to an operations system (through system management).

Various performance parameters should be monitored and recorded over different specified time intervals. For each line and section layer parameter, there are four monitoring intervals: current 15-minute, current day, previous 15-minute, and previous day. For each path layer parameter, 35 monitoring intervals are defined: current 15-minute, current day, previous day, and 32 previous 15-minute intervals.

For some parameters, thresholds are set for the current 15-minute and/or current day monitoring interval. A notification of a threshold crossing will be sent to system management when these parameters exceed the thresholds during the monitoring intervals.

All SONET network elements should monitor these physical-layer parameters: laser bias current, optical power transmitted, and optical power received. These parameters should be continuously monitored, and threshold crossings should be reported to system management.

There are four section layer parameters to be monitored:

- *Severely errored framing second*: a second during which either out-of-frame (OOF) or change-of-frame-alignments (COFAs) occurred;
- *Section coding violations*: a count of BIP-8 (B1 byte) errors detected;
- *Section errored seconds*: a second during which at least one section coding violation or OOF/COFA event occurred;
- *Section severely errored seconds*: a second with K or more section coding violations or a second during which at least one OOF/COFA event has occurred.

Section severely errored seconds should be monitored and thresholded in all SONET network elements. The monitoring of other section layer parameters is optional.

There are six line layer parameters to be monitored:

- *Line coding violations*: the sum of the line BIP-8 (B2 byte) errors detected;
- *Line errored seconds*: a second during which at least one line coding violation event occurred;
- *Line severely errored seconds*: a second with K or more line coding violations on an OC-N line;
- *Protection switching counts*: the number of times that service has been switched from the monitored line to the protection line;
- *STS pointer justifications*: the difference between outgoing and incoming pointer justifications performed on an STS SPE that is not terminated;
- *Protection switching duration*: the number of seconds that service was removed from the line being monitored.

The first four parameters should be monitored and thresholded in all network elements. The monitoring of each of the other line-layer parameters is optional.

The following five near-end STS path layer parameters are for performance monitoring:

- *STS path coding violations*: similar to the line coding violations except that path BIP-8 (B3 byte) errors are considered;
- *STS path errored seconds*: similar to the line errored seconds except that the STS path coding violation events are considered;
- *STS path severely errored seconds*: similar to the line severely errored seconds except that the STS path coding violation events are considered;
- *VT pointer justifications*: the difference between outgoing and incoming pointer justifications performed on a VT SPE that is not terminated;
- *STS path unavailable seconds*: the number of seconds for which the STS path is declared unavailable at the onset of ten consecutive STS path severely errored seconds. (An STS path is also unavailable once the network element declares a red alarm or an AIS condition that affects the STS-path.)

Far-end STS path layer parameters can be derived from STS path far-end block error (FEBE) counts, i.e., bits 1 through 4 of STS path status byte G1.

STS path coding violations, errored seconds, and severely errored seconds should be monitored for 35 monitoring intervals and thresholded for current 15-minute and current day counts.

Four VT path layer parameters are specified in SONET: VT path coding violations, VT path errored seconds, VT path severely errored seconds, and VT path unavailable seconds. These parameters are similar to the STS path layer parameters except that the VT parameters are defined in the context of VT path layer overhead.

6.3.3.5 SONET Testing

SONET testing refers to the maintenance procedures to isolate failures to replaceable or repairable components. SONET specifies three maintenance functions that are required to support fault isolation in SONET equipment such as the input module: test access, diagnostics, and loopback.

Test access is the function that allows access to a SONET signal for the purposes of nonintrusive monitoring and intrusive testing. There are three categories of access for testing purposes:

- Fiber access for monitoring and testing of the optical signal and fiber;
- SONET signal access for monitoring and testing of the SONET format, mapping, and equipment specifications;
- Digital signal access to lower speed digital signals at the electrical level.

Diagnostic tools fall into two classes: internal troubleshooting and user testing. The former is used only by equipment manufacturers for equipment testing. User testing tools are functions that can be activated on demand to retrieve information from the overhead or operate special circuitry to support trouble analysis. The minimum requirements for diagnostic capabilities in SONET equipment are:

- Detection of equipment failures;
- Examination on demand of information received sequentially and repeatedly in the J1 byte by STS PTEs for connectivity verification;
- Examination at appropriate PTEs of the STS path and VT path signal labels to verify the construction of the STS or VT SPE;
- Counting at appropriate PTEs of STS path or VT path FEBE indications for a specified period of time.

Finally, the loopback function is needed to support preservice provisioning and in-service testing activities. Loopbacks may interrupt the flow of traffic and invoke exceptional operation procedures. There are two types of loopback: a facility loopback and a terminal loopback.

The facility loopback connects the incoming signal to the transmitter in the reverse direction. Because of the potential impact on the network, the use of facility loopback is discouraged and not required in SONET network elements.

A terminal loopback connects the signal about to be transmitted to the associated incoming receiver. The terminal loopback is strictly internal to a network element and is a self-checking tool to verify the integrity of the electronics associated with the receiver and the transmitted signal. All SONET network elements should support the terminal loopback.

6.3.4 SONET Block Interfaces

As shown in Figure 6.1, the SONET block in the input module interfaces to the cell-delineation block. Upon the completion of SONET path processing, the SONET block extracts the STS-3c/STS-12c payload and passes it to the cell-delineation block, where ATM cell boundaries are established and valid cells are collected for ATM-layer processing.

Physical-layer management is supervised by the SM (or the IM-SM if system management is distributed to the input modules). The SM receives SONET alarm reports and overhead information and coordinates testing of SONET functions. For example, all received AIS, RDI, and RFI signals are reported to the SM by the SONET block.

6.4 CELL DELINEATION AND HEADER-ERROR CONTROL

The cell-delineation functional block performs three major physical-layer functions: cell delineation, header-error control, and cell rate decoupling. As shown in Figure 2.3, the standardized ATM cell header includes a header-error control

(HEC) byte, which provides single bit-error correction and multiple bit-error detection over the 5-byte header in each cell.

For cells to be transmitted, the HEC field is generated after the first four bytes of the cell header are established. First, the HEC byte is set to zero, and the entire 5-byte header is converted into a code vector represented by a 39-degree polynomial. The code polynomial is divided (modulo 2) by the generator polynomial $x^8 + x^2 + x + 1$ to obtain an 8-bit remainder. To improve the cell-delineation performance during bit-slips, the 8-bit coset pattern "01010101" is added (modulo 2) to the remainder to form the HEC. The newly calculated HEC replaces the all-zeros HEC byte.

When a cell is received, the coset "01010101" is subtracted from the HEC field. The resulting HEC byte along with the other four header bytes form a 39-degree code polynomial. The code polynomial is divided by the generator polynomial to obtain an eight-bit remainder, also known as the syndrome. A zero syndrome is a strong indication that cell boundaries are correctly established and the cell header contains either no error or undetectable errors. On the other hand, a nonzero syndrome means one of three possibilities: cell boundaries are out of alignment, header fields contain errors, or both.

The HEC generated for a cell in this way is correlated to the contents of the cell header through the generator polynomial. The syndrome detects the existence of such a correlation between the first four bytes and the fifth byte in any 5-byte sequence. Since the syndrome indicates the validity of cell boundaries, the standardized cell delineation algorithm employs syndrome calculation as a means to establish and maintain cell boundaries [2].

Figure 6.13 shows the state diagram of the cell-delineation procedure. The procedure starts in a HUNT state in which the STS SPE is scanned bit-by-bit (or byte-by-byte) by a 5-byte sliding window. At each window position, the corresponding syndrome is calculated. If the syndrome is nonzero, the sliding window shifts one bit (or one byte) and a new syndrome is calculated and checked for zero. The process continues until a zero syndrome is obtained. At that point, it is assumed that one good header has been found, and the process enters the PRESYNC state.

In the PRESYNC state, the cell-delineation process enters the confirmation phase, in which the STS SPE is scanned on a cell-by-cell basis with the 5-byte window. If the next D consecutive cells all have zero syndromes, cell delineation is deemed to be firmly established and the process enters the SYNC state. Otherwise, the process returns to the HUNT state where the searching begins over again. During the HUNT and PRESYNC states, all cells are discarded.

In the SYNC state, the cell-delineation functional block performs three tasks:

- Identify cells with uncorrectable header errors and mark these cells for error analysis or discarding;

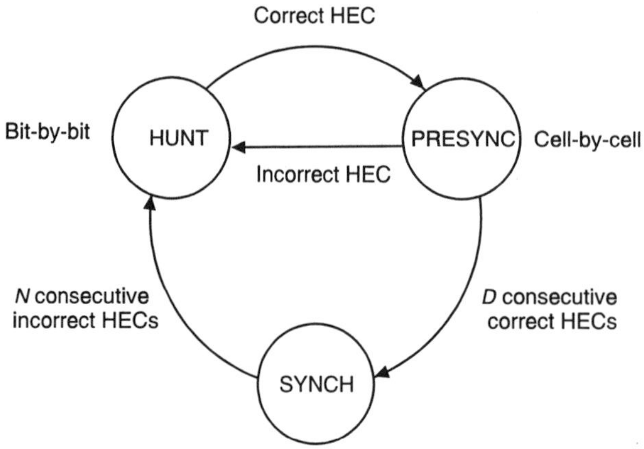

Correct HEC

Figure 6.13 Cell-delineation state diagram.

- Declare loss of cell delineation and return to the HUNT state when N consecutive cells with nonzero syndromes are received (in this case, only the first of the N cells is corrected, if possible, and the following N-1 cells are discarded);
- Pass all nonempty (assigned) cells received with zero syndromes to cell descramblers and discard all idle/unassigned cells.

Notice that cell rate decoupling is performed in the SYNC state and the cell-delineation block will descramble each successfully delineated cell before sending it to the UPC/NPC. The descrambling procedure is based on the self-synchronizing scrambler polynomial defined in [2].

The cell-delineation block will convey information about its status and performance to the SM (or the IM-SM). Information of interest would include the state information of the cell-delineation process, counts of errored cells, errored but corrected cells, and uncorrectable cells [13].

6.5 ATM-LAYER FUNCTIONS

After cell delineation, the incoming (assigned) cells are ready for ATM-layer processing. There are two blocks responsible for ATM-layer functions: UPC/NPC and cell processing. ATM-layer processing is common to all three types of ATM information flows: user cells, signaling cells, and management cells. These information flows are processed in sequence, first by the UPC/NPC and then the cell-processing block. At the cell-processing block, cells are diverted to different parts of the ATM switching system for appropriate processing, if required.

6.5.1 UPC/NPC

As described in Chapter 4, the UPC/NPC is responsible for performing usage parameter control and network parameter control for the UNI and NNI, respectively. They monitor and enforce the traffic rates across the interfaces according to some policing algorithm such as the leaky bucket. Figure 6.14 depicts the internal structure of the UPC/NPC, which consists of six components: UPC/NPC database, header-content check, UPC/NPC mechanism (e.g., shown as dual GCRAs), traffic shaping, header-error count, and nonconforming cell count.

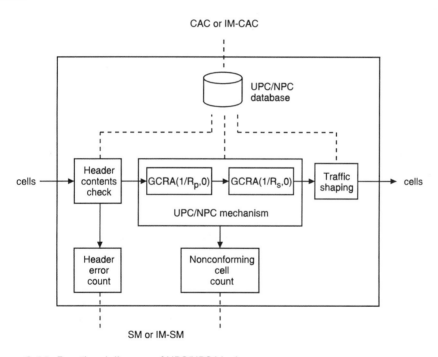

Figure 6.14 Functional diagram of UPC/NPC block.

The UPC/NPC database receives information from the central CAC or local IM-CAC about active VPCs/VCCs and their traffic parameters, e.g., peak cell rate, sustainable cell rate, burst tolerance, and thresholds. The VPCs/VCCs to be monitored are also identified (not every VPC/VCC may need to be monitored). The information in the database is necessary for proper enforcement of traffic rates for each monitored VPC/VCC.

The header-content check functional block examines all cell headers for valid field codes. Cells with invalid contents are extracted from the cell streams, counted, and recorded for analysis (discussed in greater detail later).

Typical examples of header-content errors might be invalid VPI/VCI values or undefined or invalid combinations of header field values (refer to Tables 2.2 and 2.3). Cells with invalid headers should be removed from the cell streams before the UPC/NPC mechanism. However, it is important that the header-content check should be simple so that the temporal characteristics of the cell stream are not changed significantly before the UPC/NPC.

Using parameters in the database, the UPC/NPC mechanism performs the actual traffic-rate monitoring and enforcement. In addition, it is natural for the UPC/NPC mechanism to keep counts of incoming cells in support of accounting management (if ingress cell counts are desired). Since UPC/NPC is defined for individual VPCs/VCCs, each active VPC or VCC may have a corresponding UPC/NPC mechanism. The mechanism will likely be a leaky-bucket algorithm; recall that the ATM Forum has specified the GCRA for the UPC [3]. Figure 6.14 includes an example of dual GCRAs in tandem to police the peak cell rate R_p and sustainable cell rate R_s (also shown in Figure 4.7 as dual leaky buckets). Nonconforming cells are either tagged or discarded (after being counted and recorded).

The optional traffic-shaping block smoothes the flows of traffic to the downstream parts of the switch, e.g., the cell-processing block and the cell switch fabric. The purpose of traffic shaping is to reduce the chance of traffic congestion that might occur inside a switch due to the burstiness of incoming traffic. The smoothed cell stream is sent to the cell-processing block.

The header-error count block receives cells with detected header errors (from the header-content check block). It counts the number of such cells per interface and stores the headers of errored cells for later analysis. This information may be requested by system management (or IM-SM) for the purposes of performance analysis. A notification may be sent to system management if the counts exceed some specified thresholds.

Likewise, nonconforming cells discarded by the UPC/NPC mechanism are counted per VPC/VCC and recorded for later analysis. This information may be requested by system management (or IM-SM) for the purposes of performance analysis. A notification may be sent to system management if the counts exceed some specified thresholds.

6.5.2 Cell Processing

The cell-processing functional block is where user cells, signaling cells, and management cells are first differentiated within the switch. After processing the ATM-protocol information in the cell headers, various actions are taken depending on the cell type. User data cells are prepared for routing through the cell switch fabric by translation of the VPI/VCI and the addition of an internal tag. Signaling cells and management cells may be extracted and diverted to the CAC (or IM-CAC) and SM (or IM-SM), respectively, for processing if required.

To carry out these functions, the cell-processing block consists of four components: VP/VC database, signaling-cells filter, management-cells filter, and
header translation. A functional diagram is shown in Figure 6.15.

The VP/VC database is essentially a lookup table with information about
the new VPI/VCI values and an output port for each active VPC/VCC. It includes information about pre-assigned VPIs/VCIs (see Tables 2.2 and 2.3) and
VPIs/VCIs assigned by CAC or network management.

Signaling cells will be recognized by their VPI/VCI values in the VP/VC
database. The signaling-cells filter will determine whether the signaling cells
need to be processed by the CAC (or IM-CAC). If processing is required, the
signaling cells are routed to the CAC directly or through a special output port
on the cell switch fabric. All other cells pass through the signaling-cells filter
transparently.

Similarly, management cells (e.g., ILMI and OAM cells) will be recognized
by their VPI/VCI values and PT codes. The management-cells filter will determine whether the management cells need to be processed by the SM (or IM-
SM). If processing is required, the management cells are routed to the SM
directly or through a special output port on the cell switch fabric.

Unlike the signaling-cells filter, user cells might not pass through the
management-cells filter transparently. The management-cells filter may need to
monitor user data cells. For example, the ATM-layer OAM performance-monitoring procedure requires that a count and error check be performed over blocks
of user cells. The management-cells filter will carry out these actions and report
the monitoring results to the SM (or IM-SM). The performance-monitoring
procedure will be activated or deactivated by request from the SM.

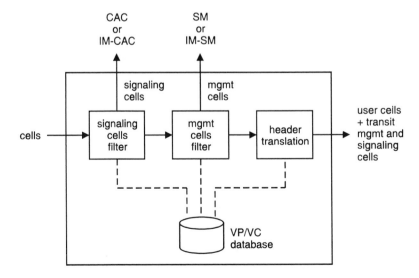

Figure 6.15 Functional diagram of cell-processing block.

From the VP/VC database, the header-translation block looks up the new VPI/VCI values and other information for each cell. The VPI/VCI values in each cell are translated to the new values. The other information about each cell could include:

- Source user;
- Destination user;
- Output port;
- Type of cell (user, control, or management);
- Cell-delay and cell-loss tolerances;
- Delay priority;
- Broadcast/multicast connection identifier.

This information can be included in an internal tag attached to each cell. The internal tag can be used for routing and housekeeping purposes. The routing information (e.g., output port, cell-delay and cell-loss tolerances, or delay priority) specifies how cells are handled in the cell switch fabric. The housekeeping information (e.g., source user or destination user) is useful for internal performance monitoring by system management. The header-translation block may generate additional housekeeping information (e.g., cell sequence number, error check for cell payload, or timestamp) to include in the internal tag. Since the tag exists only within the switch, the actual contents of the internal tag are determined by the switch designer.

6.6 IM-CAC

If the CAC is centralized in the switch, the input module must be capable of recognizing signaling cells (in the signaling-cells filter). Signaling cells are routed from the input module to the CAC directly or through a special port on the cell switch fabric. The centralized CAC interprets the signaling messages and sends outgoing signaling cells through the output modules.

As mentioned in Chapter 5, it may be desirable to distribute CAC functions to the input modules. For example, SAAL functions could be distributed to the IM-CACs to relieve the CAC from some processing. The precise distribution of CAC functions is a design issue. The distribution of CAC functions will be covered in Chapter 9.

6.7 IM-SM

If the SM is centralized in the switch, the input module must be capable of recognizing management cells (in the management-cells filter). Management cells are routed from the input module to the SM directly or through a special port on the cell switch fabric. However, there are reasons to distribute SM functions to the input modules. The input modules already carry out a number of functions that directly support system management; for example:

- Input modules naturally handle physical-layer OAM when processing SONET overhead;
- Input modules perform ATM protocol monitoring when processing cell headers;
- UPC/NPC makes ingress cell counts to support accounting management;
- Management-cells filter supports the ATM-layer OAM performance-monitoring procedure by making cell counts and error checks over blocks of user cells.

In fact, it might be argued that some SM functions are inherent in the input modules, depending on how the boundary between the IM and SM functions is drawn. A case could be made, for example, that the management-cells filter could be considered a part of the IM-SM because of its role in ATM-layer OAM.

Additional SM functions may be distributed to the input modules to relieve the SM of some processing burden. The precise distribution of SM functions is a design issue. Chapter 10 will discuss the distribution of SM functions in more detail.

6.8 CONCLUSIONS

This chapter has presented a functional partition of the input module. It is evident from the discussion that the input module carries out a considerable amount of SONET and ATM-layer processing. The input module is further complicated by the distribution of CAC and SM functions into the IM-CAC and IM-SM. Therefore, the design of the input module will be critical to the cost and performance of the ATM switching system. The design of the input module, and in particular the IM-CAC and IM-SM, should be studied further in order to better understand the cost-performance trade-offs.

References

[1]   ITU-T Rec. I.413, *B-ISDN User-Network Interface*, Helsinki, March 1–12, 1993.
[2]   ITU-T Rec. I.432, *B-ISDN User-Network Interface—Physical-Layer Specification*, Helsinki, March 1–12, 1993.
[3]   ATM Forum, *ATM User-Network Interface Specification Version 3.0*, Sept. 10, 1993.
[4]   ANSI, *American National Standard for Telecommunications—Digital Hierarchy Optical Rates and Formats Specifications*, T1.105-1988, 1988.

[5]   ANSI, *American National Standard for Telecommunications—Digital Hierarchy Optical Interface Specifications, Single Mode*, T1.106-1988, 1988.

[6]   Ballart, R., and Y-C. Ching, "SONET: Now It's the Standard Optical Network," *IEEE Communications Mag.,* Vol. 27, March 1989, pp. 8–15.

[7]   Bellcore, *Synchronous Optical Network (SONET) Transport Systems: Common Generic Criteria*, TA-NWT-000253, Issue 8, Oct. 1993.

[8]   Boehm, R., "Progress in Standardization of SONET," *IEEE LCS Mag.,* Vol. 1, May 1990, pp. 8–16.

[9]   ITU-T Rec. G.707, *Synchronous Digital Hierarchy Bit Rates*, Melbourne, Nov. 14–25, 1988.

[10] ITU-T Rec. G.708, *Network Node Interface for the Synchronous Digital Hierarchy*, Melbourne, Nov. 14–25, 1988.

[11] ITU-T Rec. G.709, *Synchronous Multiplexing Structure*, Melbourne, Nov. 14–25, 1988.

[12] Sexton, M., and A. Reid, *Transmission Networking: SONET and the Synchronous Digital Hierarchy*, Norwood, MA: Artech House, 1992.

[13] Bellcore, *Generic Requirements for Operations of Broadband Switching Systems*, TA-NWT-001248, Issue 2, Oct. 1993.

Output Module 7

7.1 INTRODUCTION

In Chapter 5, we introduced the five major functional blocks in the general ATM switch architecture model: input module, output module, cell switch fabric, connection admission control, and system management. It was natural to discuss the input module first, in Chapter 6, because it handles the entry of traffic into the switching system. The *output module* (OM) is the counterpart of the input module in the sense that it handles the departure of traffic from the switching system. The output module is the topic of the present chapter.

The primary responsibility of the output module is to receive cells from the cell switch fabric and prepare them for physical transmission on the output links. As might be expected, there is a significant degree of duality between the functions in the IM and OM. Many of the physical-layer and ATM-layer functions in the IM must be performed in reverse in the OM. For instance, the IM descrambles the payloads of incoming cells, while the OM scrambles the payloads of outgoing cells.

The background material in Chapter 6, in particular Section 6.3 on SONET and Section 6.4 on cell delineation, will be useful for this chapter. To avoid redundancy, the background material is not repeated in this chapter. Section 7.2 gives an overview of the functions required in the output module. Section 7.3 describes the ATM-layer processing for outgoing cells. Section 7.4 covers the transmission-convergence functions to map the ATM cells into the SONET payload. The physical transmission of SONET signals is discussed in Section 7.5. Finally, the distribution of CAC and SM functions into the output module is discussed in Sections 7.6 and 7.7, respectively.

7.2 OVERVIEW OF FUNCTIONS

The primary function of the output module is physical transmission of outgoing traffic on the output links. As in Chapter 6, it is assumed that the output modules support the B-ISDN UNI or NNI. The outgoing traffic consists of ATM cells mapped into SONET signals. Services above the ATM layer, such as frame relay and SMDS [1–4], may be supported by an ATM switching system in practice but are not covered here.

Similar to the IM, the output module contains physical-layer and ATM-layer functions. In addition, some portion of CAC and SM functions may be distributed to the output module. The distributed CAC and SM functions residing in the output module are referred to as OM-CAC and OM-SM, respectively.

A functional overview of the output module is shown in Figure 7.1. It consists of five basic functional blocks labeled as: cell processing, transmission convergence, SONET functions, OM-CAC, and OM-SM. The ATM-layer functions are supported by the cell-processing block. The SONET and transmission convergence blocks provide the physical-layer functions. As mentioned, the OM-CAC and OM-SM blocks refer to the distributed CAC and SM functions.

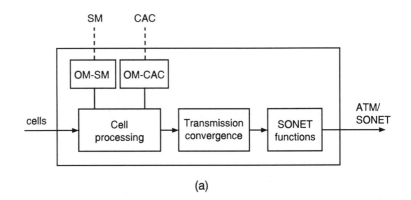

(a)

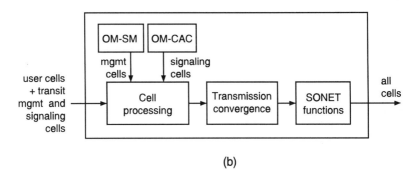

(b)

Figure 7.1 (a) Functional diagram of the output module; and (b) flows of user cells, signaling cells, and management cells.

7.2.1 Physical-Layer Functions

The output module prepares outgoing ATM cells for physical transmission. Recall from Chapter 6 that the physical layer consists of a transmission-convergence sublayer and physical-medium sublayer. The TC sublayer generates the SONET frame, generates the HEC, and maps ATM cells into the SONET payload. The PM sublayer handles the actual signal transmission depending on the physical medium.

7.2.2 ATM-Layer Functions

Compared to the input module, the ATM-layer functions in the output module are considerably simpler because most of the cell-header processing is done on incoming cells. However, some processing may be required for outgoing cells.

First, the internal tag must be removed from cells before transmission. As mentioned in Chapter 6, the IMs may attach an internal tag to each cell. Part of the tag is used for routing the cell through the cell switch fabric. The tag may also include information for internal housekeeping purposes (e.g., source user, destination user, cell sequence number, cell type, error check for cell payload, timestamp). The housekeeping information can be useful for system management to monitor the internal performance of the switch. For example, the timestamp could measure the time that a cell stays in the switch from arrival to departure. The output modules may record or process the housekeeping information for system management.

Second, the VPI/VCI values of broadcast/multicast cells may be translated at the output module. We have assumed that the cell switch fabric has the function of broadcasting or multicasting. That is, the input module identifies an incoming cell for multicast (and indicates the multicast connection in the internal tag), and the cell switch fabric duplicates the cell and routes the cells to the appropriate output ports. The VPI/VCI translation should not be done at the input modules because all duplicates end up with identical VPI/VCI values. For multicast cells, the new VPI/VCI values should be established after duplication in the cell switch fabric, i.e., in the output modules.

Third, the output module inserts signaling and management cells received from the CAC and SM into the outgoing cell stream. Recall that the input module extracts signaling and management cells from the incoming cell stream and diverts them to the CAC and SM for processing (if required). The CAC and SM will generate new signaling and management cells for transmission; they are sent to the output modules directly or through the cell switch fabric. If sent directly, the output module must mix the signaling and management cells into the outgoing cell stream.

Finally, the output module keeps counts of egress cells to support accounting management. It might be argued that egress cell counting can be regarded as a system-management function; it depends on how the boundary is drawn between OM and SM functions. In any case, it is natural to perform egress cell counting in the output modules. At the same time, as an option, the output module may exercise traffic shaping on the outgoing cell stream (if desired for traffic control).

7.2.3 OM-CAC

If CAC is centralized, the output module has a minimal supporting role. It will receive outgoing signaling cells from the CAC for transmission. It may supply traffic measurement information to the CAC, such as egress cell counts and link utilization.

To alleviate some processing from the CAC, it may be desirable to distribute some CAC functions to the output module. For example, the OM-CAC could handle the SAAL functions to encapsulate high-layer signaling messages into signaling cells. The precise degree of distribution of CAC functions to the output module is a design issue.

7.2.4 OM-SM

Like the input module, the output module might be considered to inherently contain some system-management functions. For example, the output module naturally does egress cell counts in support of accounting management. The output module also has the responsibility of SONET frame generation, which includes the generation of overhead for OAM&P. Thus, the output module naturally handles some physical-layer OAM (while the SM coordinates the physical-layer OAM activities in the IMs and OMs).

The distribution of additional system-management functions could be possible to alleviate the processing burden on the central SM. For example, rather than the SM, the OM-SM could handle the generation of new OAM cells. The precise amount of distribution of SM functions to the OM-SM is a design issue.

7.3 CELL PROCESSING

The cell-processing functional block receives outgoing user cells after they have routed through the cell switch fabric. Signaling cells may be received from the CAC either directly or through the cell switch fabric. Similarly, management cells may be received from the SM directly or through the CSF. The cell-processing block performs all ATM-layer processing required before the cells are ready for physical transmission.

As shown in Figure 7.2, the cell-processing block consists of four components: VP/VC database, signaling cells insertion, management cells insertion, and housekeeping and processing.

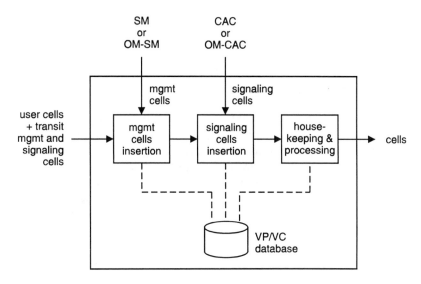

Figure 7.2 Functional diagram of cell-processing block.

7.3.1 VP/VC Database

The VP/VC database contains information about VP/VC connections—mainly new VPI/VCI values for multicast cells. As mentioned earlier, the VPI/VCI translation for multicast cells should not be done in the input modules because all duplicated cells, copied within the cell switch fabric, would end up with identical VPI/VCI values. For multicast cells, the VPI/VCI translation should be done after the cell switch fabric. The VP/VC database contains the new VPI/VCI values for multicast cells, according to the multicast connection identifier in the internal routing tag attached to each cell.

The VP/VC database may also contain traffic-rate information about each connection, e.g., for traffic shaping the outgoing cell streams. Finally, the database may record measurement data about the egress traffic, such as egress cell counts or link utilizations for system management.

7.3.2 Signaling Cells Insertion

The signaling cells insertion block essentially performs the reverse function of the signaling cells filter in the IM. Recall that the signaling cells filter recognizes and sorts out signaling cells that require processing by the CAC (or IM-CAC) from the incoming cell stream. The CAC interprets the high-layer signaling messages carried within the signaling cells. Following the signaling protocol, the CAC may generate new signaling cells, which are sent to the output modules. The output module may receive signaling cells from the CAC (or OM-CAC) either directly or through the cell switch fabric. If directly, the signaling cells are mixed into the outgoing cell stream by the signaling cells insertion block.

7.3.3 Management Cells Insertion

Similarly, the management cells insertion block essentially performs the reverse function of the management cells filter in the IM. The management cells filter recognizes and sorts out management cells (e.g., ILMI and OAM cells) that require processing by the SM (or IM-SM) from the incoming cell stream. Not all management cells are diverted to the SM. For example, some OAM cells should be passed through transparently (e.g., if the switch is not an OAM flow endpoint), and some OAM cells (i.e., performance-monitoring cells) may be copied without extraction from the cell stream. For the cells routed to the SM, the SM processes these cells or the management information carried within them. Following management procedures, the SM may generate new management cells and send them to the output modules. The output module may receive management cells from the SM (or OM-SM) either directly or through the cell switch fabric. If directly, the management cells are mixed into the outgoing cell stream by the management cells insertion block.

7.3.4 Housekeeping and Processing

The housekeeping and processing functional block performs all ATM-layer processing before the cells are ready for physical transmission. First, using the VP/VC database, the new VPI/VCI values for multicast cells are determined and put into the cell headers. Outgoing cells should all have their proper new VPI/VCI values after this point.

An important task is removing and processing the internal tag attached to each cell in the input modules. The routing information in the tag is used for routing cells through the cell switch fabric. The housekeeping information in the tag is processed at the output module to monitor the internal performance of the switch. For instance, the cell sequence numbers will indicate whether any cells were lost or misinserted within the fabric. The timestamp will measure the delay experienced by the cells through the fabric. An error check may detect any bit errors introduced into the cells by the switch. The housekeeping information may be recorded in the VP/VC database for each connection, and unusual results may be reported to system management.

During housekeeping, it would be natural to make egress cell counts in support of accounting management (see Chapter 10). While monitoring outgoing cell streams for egress cell counts, it may be desirable to perform traffic shaping. Traffic shaping involves buffering the outgoing cells to smooth out the

ourstiness in a cell stream. Traffic shaping is an option for congestion avoid-
ance (see Chapter 4).

7.4 TRANSMISSION CONVERGENCE

The transmission-convergence block handles the media-independent functions
of the physical layer. As shown in Figure 7.3, transmission convergence consists of three components representing the steps of processing to prepare cells
for SONET transmission.

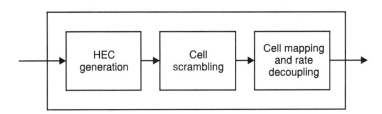

Figure 7.3 Transmission-convergence block.

The first two steps are HEC generation and cell scrambling. The HEC field
is generated using the first four bytes of the ATM cell header as described in
Section 6.4. The newly calculated HEC field is placed in the fifth byte of the cell
header. Cell scrambling is done on the cell information field, as mentioned in
Section 6.3.2. The sequence of these two steps can be interchanged because
they work on different parts of a cell.

The third step is cell mapping and rate decoupling to pack the ATM cells
onto the SONET payloads. The packing procedure preserves the sequential
order of cells and aligns the byte structure of cells with the byte structure of the
SONET payloads. To fill in the gaps between cells, unassigned ATM cells (i.e.,
cells with VPI = 0, VCI = 0) are generated and mixed with the outgoing (assigned) cells as needed to create a continuous cell stream to fill the SONET
payloads.

7.5 SONET FUNCTIONS

The SONET functional block is responsible for the transmission of SONET
frames over optical-fiber links. As shown in Figure 7.4, it consists of four
functions: SONET frame generation, SONET overhead generation, payload
scrambling, and electrical-to-optical signal conversion. The SONET frame for-

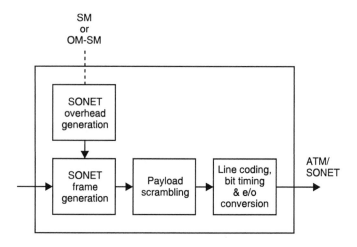

Figure 7.4   SONET functional block.

mat, including overhead bytes and payload scrambling, was described in Section 6.3.1.

As mentioned in Section 6.3.3, SONET OAM&P involves alarm surveillance, performance monitoring, and testing. These OAM&P functions are done in both the input modules and output modules with coordination by the system management. The output module will be responsible for its part in generating and passing alarm signals, data communication channel (DCC) messages, equipment monitoring, and testing.

7.6 OM-CAC

As mentioned earlier, the output module has a small role when the CAC is centralized. To alleviate the CAC from some processing, it may be desirable to distribute some CAC functions to the output module. For example, the OM-CAC could handle the SAAL functions to encapsulate outgoing high-layer signaling messages into signaling cells. The precise degree of distribution of CAC functions to the output module is a design issue. This issue will be investigated further in Chapter 9.

7.7 OM-SM

It was mentioned earlier that the output module naturally carries out some processing that might be considered part of system management, e.g., egress cell counts and SONET overhead generation. To alleviate the processing burden on the central SM, more system-management functions could be distributed to the output module. For example, the OM-SM, instead of the SM, could handle the generation of new OAM cells. The precise amount of distribution of SM functions to the OM-SM is a design issue. The distribution of system-management functions to the IM and OM will be revisited in Chapter 10.

7.8 CONCLUSIONS

Since the input module and output module handle the ingress/egress of traffic, the output module is a counterpart of the input module. There is some duality between the functions in the input module and output module. Many of the physical-layer (transmission convergence and SONET) and ATM-layer functions in the IM must be performed in reverse in the OM. Likewise, some portion of CAC and SM functions may be distributed to the output modules in the same manner as to the input modules.

However, the output module is certainly simpler than the input module. First, the UPC/NPC are not required in the output module. The VPI/VCI lookup is done for every cell in the IM, whereas VPI/VCI values are translated for only multicast cells in the OM. The IM must recognize and preprocess signaling cells and management cells to decide whether to route them to the CAC and SM; the OM simply inserts signaling and management cells into the outgoing cell stream. In general, the ATM-layer processing is more complicated for arriving cells at the IM than for departing cells at the OM.

References

[1]   ANSI, *American National Standard for Telecommunications—Frame Relay Bearer Service—Architectural Framework and Service Description*, T1.606, 1990.
[2]   ATM Forum, *B-ICI Specification Document (Version 1.0)*, ATM Forum/93-215R10, Aug. 1993.
[3]   Bellcore, *Broadband ISDN Switching System Generic Requirements*, TA-NWT-001110, Issue 2, Aug. 1993.
[4]   Bellcore, *Generic System Requirements in Support of Switched Multi-megabit Data Service*, TR-TSV-000772, Issue 2, May 1991.

Cell Switch Fabric

8

8.1 INTRODUCTION

Chapter 5 presented the main functional blocks of an ATM switching system. Chapters 6 and 7 covered the input modules and output modules, which handle the entry and departure of cells, respectively. This chapter examines the functions of the *cell switch fabric* (CSF) which, in a sense, is the central functional block in the ATM switching system. *ATM switch* is often meant to refer just to the switch fabric, and *switch architecture* typically to the design of the fabric.

In Chapter 5 we stated that the CSF is responsible for transferring cells between the other functional blocks in the switch. In particular, it routes user cells from the input modules to the appropriate output modules. This is the principal function associated with the switch fabric. In addition, because signaling and management cells are mixed in the same streams as user cells, the CSF can be used to pass signaling and management cells to the CAC or SM through special ports on the fabric.

The CSF is complicated by other requirements, such as:

- Multicasting;
- Fault tolerance;
- Loss and delay priorities.

When these requirements are considered, it becomes apparent that the CSF should have additional functions, e.g., concentration, duplication, cell scheduling, selective cell discarding, and congestion monitoring. We have defined the CSF as more than a simple fabric, which is usually thought to provide only routing and buffering functions. These basic functions are handled by a *routing and buffering functional block* within the CSF, as shown in Figure 8.1. Because the routing and buffering functional block is the main part of the CSF, its description occupies most of this chapter. The CSF also includes other functions, which will be described later in this chapter.

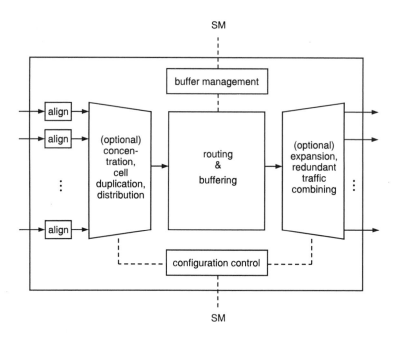

SM

Figure 8.1 Functional diagram of the CSF.

8.2 ROUTING AND BUFFERING

The routing and buffering functional block occupies the central portion of the
CSF in Figure 8.1. Its function is to route arriving cells from its inputs to the
appropriate outputs according to the internal routing tag attached to each cell
by the input modules. The routing is performed passively in the sense that the
routing tag identifies a path for each cell, and therefore no path computation
needs to be done by the CSF. Arriving cells may be aligned in time by means of
single-cell buffers at the inputs to the functional block. Because cells may be
addressed to the same output simultaneously, some buffering is necessary
within the functional block. Buffering approaches are discussed in more detail
later in the chapter.

  For the routing and buffering functional block, design principles are now
fairly well known. Several general surveys can be found [1–7]. These design
principles have been developed through a series of landmark switch designs.
One of the earliest prototype switches was Starlite, which used a Batcher-banyan network with a recirculating buffer [8]. Starlite demonstrated the applica-
bility of banyan networks to high-speed packet switching, but the
implementation of the recirculating buffer was complex. This buffer management complexity was avoided in another early design that used a banyan
network with internal buffering [9–11].

Another early switch prototype demonstrating the feasibility of ATM switching was the Prelude switch [12–15]. It is notable for using conventional time-slot interchange switching hardware. The idea of a central memory as a fabric was later refined in a design of a shared-buffer memory switch, which minimized the total amount of buffering [16,17].

A comparison of input buffering and output buffering established that output buffering could achieve optimal throughput while input buffering may result in less throughput due to so-called head-of-line blocking [18]. A landmark output buffered design was the Knockout switch [19]. At the cost of possible cell loss, this avoided the exponential growth in buffer space involved in output buffered switches such as the bus matrix switch [20].

Since then, research in switch designs has been widespread, and many first-generation commercial ATM switches have been developed based on ideas from the early research prototypes. It would be impractical, and not necessarily illuminating, to attempt an exhaustive survey of all switch designs. Instead we will describe four prototypical design approaches classified as:

- Shared memory;
- Shared medium;
- Fully interconnected;
- Space division.

Virtually all current switch designs are based on variations or combinations of these basic approaches. By contrasting the relative strengths and weaknesses of these different approaches, we will attempt to draw general design principles in Section 8.2.6.

8.2.1 Characteristics

For discussion, we will assume a routing and buffering functional block with N input ports and N output ports, with all port speeds equal to V cells per second. Generally, the number of inputs and outputs do not necessarily have to be the same; nor do the port speeds. A cell time is defined as the time required to receive or transmit an entire cell at the port speed, i.e., $1/V$ s. For the moment, an incoming cell is assumed to be destined for a single output port. Multicasting and broadcasting are considered in Section 8.4.

Some important parameters for consideration are:

- Throughput (total output traffic rate, which may be normalized by dividing it by the total input traffic rate);
- Utilization (the average input traffic rate divided by the maximum possible output traffic rate);
- Cell loss rate;

- Cell delays;
- Amount of buffering;
- Complexity of implementation.

For given input traffic, the routing and buffering functional block attempts to maximize throughput and minimize cell delays and cell loss. Of course, the total amount of buffering should be minimal and implementation should be simple. For the moment, we assume a single class of traffic; multiple priority classes of traffic are addressed later in Section 8.5.

8.2.2 Shared Memory Approach

A prototypical design of a shared memory fabric is shown in Figure 8.2. Incoming cells are converted from serial to parallel form. They are written sequentially into a dual port random access memory. Their cell headers with internal routing tags are delivered to a memory controller, which decides the order in which cells are read out of the memory. The outgoing cells are demultiplexed to the outputs, where they are converted from parallel to serial form.

Functionally, this is an output queuing approach, where the output buffers all physically belong to a common buffer pool. The output buffered approach is attractive because it can achieve a normalized throughput of one under a full load [18]. Sharing a common buffer pool has the advantage of minimizing the amount of buffers required to achieve a specified cell loss rate. If the rate of traffic to one output port is high, it can draw upon more buffer space until the common buffer pool is completely filled. Because the buffer space is completely shared, this approach requires the minimum possible

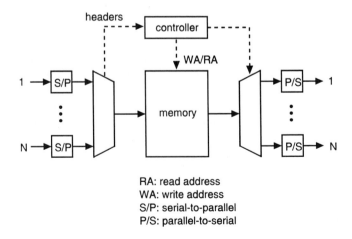

RA: read address
WA: write address
S/P: serial-to-parallel
P/S: parallel-to-serial

Figure 8.2 An example of shared memory approach.

amount of buffering and has the most flexibility to accommodate traffic dynamics, in the sense that the shared memory can absorb large bursts directed to any output. For these reasons, it is a popular approach; examples include Hitachi's shared buffer memory switch [16,17,21] and AT&T's GCNS-2000 switch.

Unfortunately, the approach has its disadvantages. As the cells must be written into and read out from the memory one at a time, the shared memory must operate at the total throughput rate. It must be capable of reading and writing a cell in every $1/NV$ s, that is, N times faster than the port speed. As the access time of random access memories is physically limited, this speed-up factor N limits the ability of this approach to scale up to large sizes and fast speeds. Either the size N or speed V can be large, but the memory access time imposes a limit on the product NV, which is the total throughput.

Moreover, the centralized memory controller must process the cell headers (and routing tags) at the same rate as the memory, i.e., one cell header in every $1/NV$ s. This might be difficult if, for instance, the controller must handle multiple priority classes and complicated cell scheduling. Multicasting and broadcasting in this approach will also increase the complexity of the controller, as discussed later in Section 8.4.

8.2.3 Shared Medium Approach

Instead of a shared memory, cells may be routed by means of a shared medium, e.g., ring, bus, or dual bus. An example of a fabric using a time-division multiplexed (TDM) bus is shown in Figure 8.3. Incoming cells are sequentially broadcast on the bus in a round-robin fashion. At each output, address filters examine the internal routing tag on each cell to determine if the cell is destined for that output. The address filter passes the appropriate cells through to the output buffers.

It is apparent that the bus must be capable of handling the total throughput. If the bus operates at a sufficiently high speed, at least NV cells/s, then there are no conflicts for bandwidth and all queuing occurs at the outputs. Naturally, if the bus speed is less than NV cells/s, some input queuing will probably be necessary.

The outputs are modular from each other, which has advantages in implementation and reliability. The address filters and output buffers are straightforward to implement. Also, the broadcast-and-select nature of this approach makes multicasting and broadcasting natural, unlike the shared memory approach. For these reasons, this approach is attractive for implementation; examples include IBM's PARIS [22,23], NEC's ATOM [24–27], IBM's plaNET [28], NET Adaptive's ATMX switch, Fore Systems' ForeRunner ASX-100, and Siemens' EWSM cell switch.

However, the address filters and output buffers must operate at the speed of the shared medium, which could be up to N times faster than the port speed.

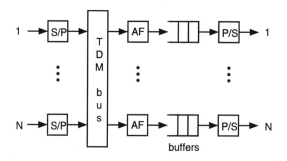

AF: address filter
S/P: serial-to-parallel
P/S: parallel-to-serial

Figure 8.3 An example of shared medium approach.

There is a physical limit to the speed of the bus, address filters, and output buffers; these limit the scalability of this approach to large sizes and high speeds. Either the size N or speed V can be large, but there is a physical limitation on the product NV.

As with the shared memory approach, this approach involves output queuing, which is capable of the optimal throughput. However, the output buffers are not shared, and hence this approach requires more total amount of buffers than the shared memory fabric for the same cell loss rate.

8.2.4 Fully Interconnected Approach

The fully interconnected output buffered approach is shown in Figure 8.4. Independent paths exist between all N^2 possible pairs of inputs and outputs. In this design, arriving cells are broadcast on separate buses to all outputs. Address filters at each output determine if the cells are destined for that output. Appropriate cells are passed through the address filters to the output queues.

This approach offers many attractive features. Naturally there is no conflict among the N^2 independent paths between inputs and outputs, and hence all queuing occurs at the outputs. As stated earlier, output queuing achieves the optimal normalized throughput. Like the shared medium approach, it is also broadcast-and-select in nature and, therefore, multicasting is natural. The address filters and output buffers are simple to implement. Unlike the shared medium approach, the address filters and buffers need to operate only at the port speed. All of the hardware operate at the same speed. There is no speed-up factor to limit scalability in this approach. For these reasons, this approach has been taken in Fujitsu's bus matrix switch [20], self-routing modules in Fujitsu's

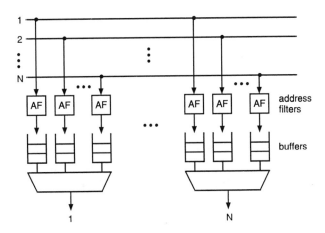

Figure 8.4 An example of fully connected approach.

FETEX-150 broadband switch [29], and GTE Government System's SPANet switch.

Unfortunately, the quadratic N^2 growth of buffers means that the size N must be limited for practical reasons. However, in principle, there is no severe limitation on V. The port speed V can be increased to the physical limits of the address filters and output buffers. Hence, this approach might realize a high total throughput NV cells per second by scaling up the port speed V.

The Knockout switch was an early prototype that suggested a trade-off to reduce the amount of buffers at the cost of higher cell loss [19]. Instead of N buffers at each output, it was proposed to use only a fixed number L buffers at each output (for a total of NL buffers which is linear in N), based on the observation that the simultaneous arrival of more than L cells to any output was improbable. It was argued that $L = 8$ is sufficient under uniform random traffic conditions to achieve a cell loss rate of 10^{-6} for large N.

8.2.5 Space Division Approach

A simple example of a space division fabric is a crossbar switch, which can physically connect any of the N inputs to any of the N outputs. Early work in *multistage interconnection networks* (MINs) began as a search for alternatives to the N^2 crosspoints in crossbar switches used for telephone switching [30]. Over the years MINs have been an active area of study for circuit switching [31,32], number sorting [33], multiprocessor interconnection [34–38], and more recently packet switching [39–42]. A historical perspective is given in [43].

Banyan networks are a common class of MINs. Figure 8.5 shows an example of an 8×8 banyan network constructed recursively from 2×2 switching elements. As shown in Figure 8.5(a), each 2×2 switching element routes an incoming cell according to a control bit. If the control bit is 0, the cell (on any input line) is routed to the upper output (address 0); otherwise, the cell is routed to the lower output (address 1). Thus, the output address of the incoming cell specifies its route.

Figure 8.5(b) shows a 4×4 banyan constructed by an interconnection of two stages of 2×2 switching elements. The first bit of the output address can be used to route the incoming cell through the first stage to either the upper or lower 2×2 switching element in the second stage (an example path is shown in bold). The second bit of the address will route the cell through the second stage to the appropriate output. The two-bit output address of the cell specifies its route through the two switching stages.

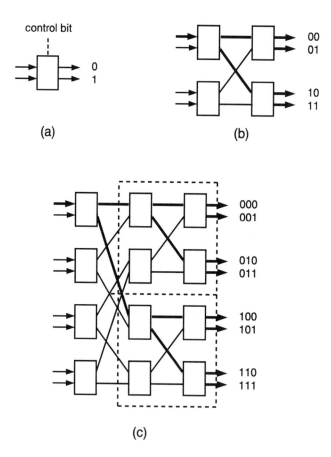

Figure 8.5 Examples of (a) 2×2 switching element, (b) 4×4 banyan, and (c) 8×8 banyan.

Figure 8.5(c) illustrates an 8×8 banyan constructed from 4×4 banyans. The first bit of the output address will route the cell through the first stage to either the upper or lower 4×4 network (dashed boxes). It is obvious that the last two bits of the output address will route the cell through the 4×4 network to the appropriate output. Continuing this recursion, it can be easily seen how to construct an $N \times N$ banyan network where the nth stage uses the nth bit of the output address to route the cell. If $N = 2^n$, the banyan will consist of $n = \log_2 N$ stages, each consisting of $N/2$ switching elements. When the output address specifies the route through the network, the MIN has the so-called self-routing property.

The banyan network has attracted a great deal of attention for a number of reasons: switching is performed by small, simple switching elements; cells are routed in parallel; all elements operate at the same speed; and larger fabrics can be constructed modularly and recursively. Implementation can be easily done in hardware. There is no special constraint on the size N or speed V except for physical limitations (more discussion in Section 8.2.7). Banyans or other MINs are used in Bellcore's Sunshine switch [44], Newbridge Networks' 36150 Main-Street switch, SynOptics' LattisCell switch, and Alcatel Data Networks' 1100 High Speed Switch.

More precisely, banyan networks are a broad class of MINs with exactly one path from any input to any output [45]. An n-level banyan has only neighboring stages connected by links such that each path through the network passes exactly n stages. Regular banyans consists of only one type of switching element. A subset of regular banyans is SW-banyans, which are constructed recursively from $L \times M$ switching elements. An n-level SW-banyan is constructed by the connection of several $(n - 1)$-level SW-banyans with an additional stage of switching elements.

Delta networks are a subclass of SW-banyan networks. They have the self-routing property, i.e., the output address also specifies the path between input and output. If the switching elements have the same number of inputs and outputs, it is a rectangular delta network. Delta networks can take different forms, depending on their method of construction, including omega, flip, cube, shuffle-exchange, and baseline networks [39,43,46]. A delta-b network of size $N \times N$ is constructed of $b \times b$ switching elements arranged in $\log_b N$ stages, each stage consisting of N/b switching elements. Figure 8.5(c) is an example of a delta-2 network with $\log_2 8 = 3$ stages.

Unfortunately, since banyans have less than the N^2 crosspoints of a crossbar switch, it can be easily seen that the routes of two cells addressed to different outputs might conflict before the last switching stage. In this situation, called internal blocking, only one of the two cells contending for a link can be passed to the next stage, while the other cell stays behind. Thus, the overall throughput is reduced.

A popular solution is to add a sort network, e.g., Batcher bitonic sort network [33], which rearranges cells with their addresses in increasing order before the banyan network [40]. A combined Batcher-banyan network is shown in Figure 8.6. The switching elements in the Batcher network sort the cells according to their addresses, with the larger address sorted to the output indicated by the arrow. It is internally nonblocking in the sense that a set of N cells addressed to N different outputs will not cause an internal conflict because they will be presented to the banyan network in sorted order.

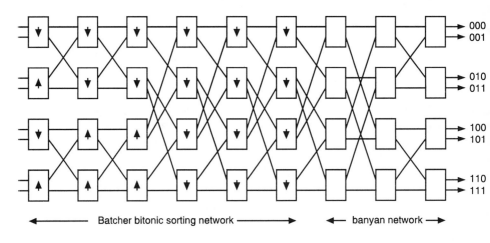

Figure 8.6   Example of 8 × 8 Batcher-banyan network.

However, output contention can still occur if two cells are addressed to the same output, and it must be resolved by buffering. One possibility is to position the buffers at the inputs of the Batcher network. If more than one cell is addressed to the same output, one cell is allowed to pass through the fabric by an arbitration algorithm (e.g. the method in [47]) while the other cells remain in the input buffers. However, this does not achieve full throughput due to the so-called head-of-line blocking, where a delayed cell prevents the other cells waiting behind it from going through the fabric. Head-of-line blocking might be alleviated by changing the first-in-first-out (FIFO) discipline in the input buffers, i.e., allowing a buffered cell to go through the fabric without waiting for the cells ahead of it to go first. The cost of this improvement is a substantial increase in the complexity involved for managing the first-in-random-out buffers.

Alternatively, buffers may be placed internally within the banyan switching elements [10,11,48]. If two cells arrive simultaneously to a switching element and attempt to go to the same outgoing link, one cell will be sent while the other is buffered within the switching element. This approach may be suitable to implement a backpressure control mechanism, if no cell loss is desired where queues in one stage of the banyan will hold up cells in the preceding stage by a feedback signal. Eventually, the backpressure may reach the first stage and create queues at the banyan network inputs. It can be seen that internal buffering does not achieve full throughput because head-of-line blocking may occur at each switching element.

A third alternative is a recirculating buffer external to the fabric, e.g. as in Starlite [8] and Sunshine [44]. After the Batcher sorter, output conflicts can be easily detected by comparing adjacent cell addresses. When multiple cells are addressed to the same output, a trap network selects one cell to go through the banyan network and recirculates the other cells back to the inputs of the Batcher network. However, a recirculating buffer involves complicated priority control to maintain cell sequential order (keeping count of the number of reattempts by each cell) and increases the size of the Batcher network to accommodate the recirculating cells.

As we will discuss in Section 8.2.6, output buffering is the most preferable approach. Unfortunately, banyans cannot realize output queuing straightforwardly because the banyan network delivers at most one cell per cell time to any output. To realize output queuing, there must be a way to deliver multiple cells per cell time to the same output. Some possible modifications include:

- Increasing the speed of internal links [10,11];
- Routing groups of links together as single links [2,49];
- Using multiple banyan planes in parallel [38,42,44,50];
- Using multiple banyan planes in tandem [51] or adding extra switching stages [52].

Details about the performances of these modifications are contained in the references.

MINs are certainly not restricted to banyan networks with a single path between any input-output pair. Classic examples of MINs with multiple paths between inputs and outputs are Benes and Clos networks, which are rearrangeably nonblocking and strictly nonblocking in the circuit-switching context, respectively [30–32]. Multipath MINs can also be constructed by adding switching stages to a banyan network; in fact, two cascaded banyans is equivalent to a Benes network. As another example, a distribution network could randomize the routes of cells before a banyan network [10,53]. Load distribution may be implemented by modification of the banyan network itself [54,55]. Alternatively, a multipath MIN can be constructed as a number of banyan planes in parallel [38,42,50]. Strictly nonblocking MINs constructed by extra staging and parallel planes are proposed in [56].

Multipath MINs have two potential advantages: the traffic distribution may be kept more uniform throughout the MIN to minimize internal conflicts, and the MIN is more fault tolerant. If cells can take independent paths with different delays, however, there must be a mechanism to preserve the sequential order of cells of the same virtual connection at the output. To minimize processing and ensure cell sequential order, it is probably more desirable to choose a path during connection set-up [53]. This path remains fixed for the duration of the connection and must be specified by a routing tag attached to each cell. This approach introduces a potential problem: paths must be selected during connection set-up with some care to prevent unnecessary blocking of subsequent calls. There has not been much work done on this problem.

8.2.6   General Principles

Thus far we have described four prototypical design approaches: shared memory, shared medium (TDM bus), fully interconnected, and space division (MINs). Needless to say, endless variations of these designs can be imagined, but it may be more useful to understand some general principles illustrated by a comparative discussion of these approaches. These principles will be applicable to understanding the trade-offs involved in any new design.

8.2.6.1   Internal Blocking

Recall that two cells addressed to different outputs can cause a conflict within a banyan network. In the example shown in Figure 8.7, the switching element in the second stage has a conflict because the two cells are attempting to go to the same link. This conflict is called internal blocking. A fabric is said to be internally blocking if a set of N cells addressed to N different outputs can cause conflicts within the fabric. Internal blocking can reduce the maximum possible throughput.

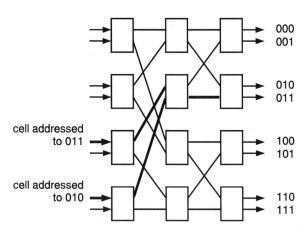

Figure 8.7   Example of internal blocking.

Internal blocking does not occur in some designs. By comparison, consider the example of a TDM bus in Figure 8.3. It is easy to see that the bus fabric is internally nonblocking if the bus operates at least N times faster than the port speed, i.e., at a speed of NV cells per second. At this bus speed, if N cells arrive for N different outputs, they will all successfully reach their outputs without conflicts. Likewise, the shared memory fabric in Figure 8.2 must read and write at a rate of NV cells per second to be internally nonblocking.

This illustrates a principle that can be generalized as follows: to prevent internal blocking, shared resources (e.g., bus, memory) must operate at some factor greater than the port speed (in these examples, by a factor of N). This speed-up factor will limit the total throughput and the ability to scale to larger sizes or faster speeds.

8.2.6.2 Buffering Approaches

Let us return again to the banyan network example. Suppose that two cells addressed to the same output have successfully reached the last switching stage simultaneously. Clearly only one of the two cells can be delivered to the output port at one time. This situation is called output contention, and it is unavoidable in all design approaches in the absence of buffering. The next principle is evident: buffering is necessary in all designs to resolve the output contention. The two main issues concerning buffers are their location and size (assuming no priorities for the moment).

Figure 8.8 shows four basic approaches to the placement of buffers (of course, combinations are possible). There have been several comparative studies of the different approaches [18,57,58], and numerous queuing analyses and simulations for dimensioning buffers can be readily found throughout the literature. Most studies assume uniform random traffic: in any time slot, a cell arrives at any input with probability ρ independent of all other inputs and is destined to any output with equal probability. There are various bursty traffic models that assume some correlation between consecutive cell arrivals.

Figure 8.8(a) shows buffers at the inputs of an internally nonblocking space division fabric, e.g., a Batcher-banyan network. It is well known that this approach suffers from head-of-the-line blocking. When two cells are destined for the same output simultaneously, one cell must wait in the input buffers. This cell prevents any cell behind it in the buffer from going through the fabric. Thus, some capacity in the fabric is wasted. Under assumptions of random uniform traffic, the maximum throughput is only $2 - \sqrt{2} = 0.586$ for large N [18].

Various methods have been proposed to reduce the head-of-line blocking at a cost in complexity. Increasing the internal speed of the space division fabric by a factor of 4 will achieve a normalized throughput greater than 99% [59–63]. A throughput of one can be achieved by changing the FIFO discipline

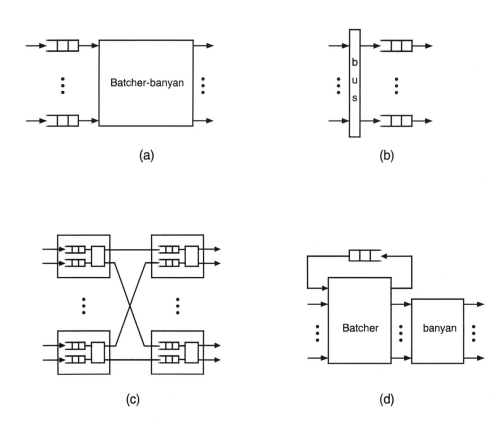

Figure 8.8 Examples of (a) input buffers, (b) output buffers, (c) internal buffers, and (d) a recirculating buffer.

of the input buffers to first-in-random-out, where cells may be extracted from the input buffers regardless of their positions [64].

In Figure 8.8(b), buffers are situated at the output ports of a shared bus fabric. It is generally agreed that the output queuing approach is optimal in terms of throughput and delays [18]. However, there must be a means to deliver multiple cells per cell time to any output. This implies either that the output buffers must be operating at some factor times the port speed (a speed-up factor of N for the TDM bus of Figure 8.3) or there must be multiple buffers at each output (e.g., N buffers at each output in Figure 8.4). In the former, the speed-up factor imposes a limit on the total throughput NV cells per second; the latter is limited by the exponential number of buffers.

Buffers are placed internally within a space division fabric in Figure 8.8(c). Each 2×2 switching element in the banyan network has buffers at its inputs. In he event of a conflict for the same outgoing link, one cell is forwarded to the ext stage while the other cell must be detained in the input buffers. Clearly ead-of-line blocking may occur within each switching element, which reduces he maximum throughput. Simulation results show that throughput is limited o around 0.45 for banyan networks with buffer sizes of one cell [65,66] and mproves only slightly for larger buffers [1,5]. The throughput becomes worse as he size of the network becomes larger. This was also observed under nonuni- orm traffic conditions [67].

Figure 8.8(d) shows a recirculating buffer that allows cells to re-enter the nternally nonblocking space division network. The network can deliver at nost one cell per cell time to any output. If more than one cell is addressed to he same output, the extra cells are routed through the recirculating buffer to he inputs of the network. This approach has the potential to achieve the ptimal throughput and delay performance of output buffering [57]. However, there are complications in its implementation. First, the size of the switching network must be larger than $N \times N$ to accommodate the recirculating cells. Second, there must be a control mechanism to ensure the correct sequential order of cells. Cells must keep track of the number of times they have recircu- lated. The switching network must give higher priority to the cells with the greater number of reattempts.

In general, output buffering is the preferred approach, but the routing fabric must be able to transfer multiple cells to the same output within one cell time. This involves either a speed-up factor or multiple buffers at each output.

8.2.6.3 Buffer Sharing

We have addressed one of the main issues concerning switch design—where to position the buffers—and concluded that output buffering is the preferred ap- proach. Another issue concerning the buffers is their number and size. First, let us consider the example of the shared memory fabric in Figure 8.2. A central buffer is most capable of taking advantage of statistical sharing. That is, if all of the traffic is routed to one output, the entire shared memory is available to buffer these cells. The remaining outputs will probably have little traffic, which leaves buffer space available. The central memory is thus capable of absorbing large traffic bursts to any output. It is known that this approach requires the least total amount of buffering. If traffic is random and uniform, for very large N, a buffer space of about $12N$ cells (or 12 cells per output) is required to achieve a cell loss rate of 10^{-9} under a load of 0.9 [16,17,57].

Next, we consider the example of the TDM bus fabric with N output buffers in Figure 8.3. Under the same traffic assumptions as before, the required buffer space is about $90N$ cells (or 90 cells per output) [57]. Here a large traffic burst to one output cannot be absorbed by the other output buffers. However, each output buffer does statistically multiplex the traffic from the N inputs.

That is, it takes advantage of the fact that it is unlikely that many incoming cells will be directed simultaneously to the same output.

We finally consider the fully interconnected fabric with N^2 output buffers in Figure 8.4. This approach takes advantage of neither statistical sharing between outputs nor statistical multiplexing at any output. There are no exact figures for buffer dimensions for any given cell-loss probability, but the buffer space is apparently exponential on the order of N^2 cells.

These examples illustrate the general principle that statistical sharing will minimize the total amount of buffers. It will also maximize the flexibility to handle traffic burstiness.

8.2.7 Construction of Large Fabrics

It might be assumed that ATM switches will eventually replace the large switching systems existing today in the public telephone network. To provide broadband services to the same number of customers as a typical central office, an ATM switch would require a throughput in the range of 1 Tbps or more [68,69]. If the argument for such large capacity switches is accepted, the next question is whether ATM switches can feasibly attain the desired throughput rates.

We have seen that all four basic design approaches are capable of realizing switch modules of limited throughput. The shared memory and shared medium approaches can achieve a throughput limited by the memory access time. Supposing a memory access time of 85 ns for example, switch modules can be as large as 32×32 with 155 Mbps ports (for a total throughput of approximately 5 Gbps). The size would have to be decreased proportionately for faster port speeds. Because the fully interconnected output buffered approach is not limited by a speed-up factor, its port speed may be as fast as 5 Gbps (assuming one cell every 85 ns). Unfortunately the size N must be constrained by practical limitations on the N^2 number of buffers.

Although the space division approach has no special constraints on throughput or size, physical factors do limit the maximum size in practice [70]. First, although Batcher-banyan networks of significant size can be implemented in single integrated circuits (e.g., 32×32 [69]), there are physical limits to the circuit density and number of input/output pins. Inevitably, a large number of circuit boards must be interconnected. Interconnection complexity and power dissipation become more difficult issues with increasing number of boards [68]. Second, the entire set of N cells must be synchronized at every stage. Third, reliability and repairability become more difficult with size. Finally, modifications to maximize the throughput of space division networks beyond 0.58 increases the implementation complexity.

It is clear that large ATM fabrics of 1 Tbps throughput or more cannot be realized simply by scaling up a fabric design in size and speed. Instead, large fabrics must be constructed by interconnection of switch modules of limited throughput. The small modules may be designed following any approach, and there are various ways to interconnect them.

The most straightforward and popular method of construction is multistage interconnection of small modules, e.g., configured in a three-stage Clos(N,n,m) network shown in Figure 8.9. The first stage consists of N/n switch modules each of size $n \times m$; the second stage is m modules of size $N/n \times N/n$; and the third stage is N/n modules of size $m \times n$. Examples of this construction approach are Fujitsu's multistage self-routing fabric in the FETEX-150 switching system [29,71], NEC's multistage ATOM switch [24,27], and Hitachi's hyper-distributed switching system constructed of shared buffer memory switch modules [21,72,73].

This configuration offers m possible paths between any pair of input and output ports. The choice of different paths is useful for balancing the traffic distribution. It is possible for each cell to take an independent, random path (and cell sequence is recovered at the outputs [74]), but more typically a least-congested path is chosen during connection set-up, which remains unchanged during the connection. However, it is possible to encounter internal congestion when a new connection request cannot be accepted.

In the circuit switching context, there is a well-known condition for strictly nonblocking Clos networks [30]. A network is strictly nonblocking if there always exists an available path between any free input-output pair, regardless of the other connections in the network. The meaning of nonblocking,

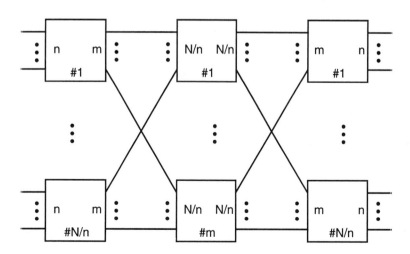

Figure 8.9 Clos(N,n,m) network.

and the nonblocking conditions for a Clos network, are much more complicated in the ATM context because more parameters are necessary to characterize ATM connections. A link is not either busy or idle; only part of the link bandwidth may be consumed by an ATM connection and the consumed bandwidth may be time-varying. Preliminary studies make the simplifying assumption that ATM connections can be described by a fixed-rate parameter (i.e., the connection is constant bit-rate). Then the problem is essentially similar to multirate circuit switching: a connection (of arbitrary bandwidth) is blocked if there is no path with sufficient available bandwidth. For multirate circuit switching, a general condition for a strictly nonblocking Clos network is given in [75]. Furthermore, a blocking probability is found under some probabilistic traffic assumptions.

The throughput of a Clos interconnection fabric can be increased by operating internal links at some factor greater than the port speeds. For example, in a Clos(1024,32,32) ATM fabric, it is suggested that the internal links should be four times faster to satisfy the nonblocking condition [73]. However, while this speed-up increases throughput, the buffers at the last switching stage should be carefully dimensioned because most of the queuing occurs at the outputs [76]. Channel grouping is another modification proposed to increase throughput [58].

It has been proposed to extend the output buffering principle to the Clos network [77]. In Figure 8.10, the first two switching stages constitute an interconnect network with no buffering. All buffering is located in the third stage, which consists of N/n output-buffered switching modules of size $m \times n$. This approach guarantees the optimal throughput and delay performance provided by output queuing. The important parameter m is chosen according to the so-called knockout principle: for sufficiently large m, the probability of more than m cells arriving simultaneously for the same last-stage module is very small [19]. For instance, if N is very large, $m = 40$ is sufficient to attain a cell-loss probability less than 10^{-9} for $n = 16$ and a load of 0.9 [77].

In contrast to the Clos approach of interconnecting small modules to construct a large fabric, we might begin with a large $N \times N$ fabric and seek an optimal partitioning of the fabric into smaller modules. A logical approach is shown in Figure 8.11 [70]. The entire set of N inputs is divided into K subsets. Each subset of inputs is handled by an $M \times N$ switch module where $M = N/K$. The parallel outputs from the K modules are multiplexed. As shown in Figure 8.12, it has been proposed to implement an $M \times N$ module as a combination of an $M \times M$ Batcher sorting network, $M \times N$ expansion network (a stack of M 1:K trees), and K parallel $M \times M$ banyan planes [70]. Each of these subnetworks is considerably simpler to implement than a large $N \times N$ Batcher-banyan network.

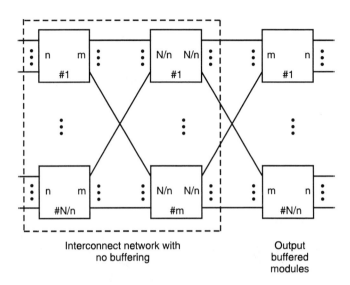

Interconnect network with
no buffering

Output
buffered
modules

Figure 8.10 *Growable* output buffered switch fabric.

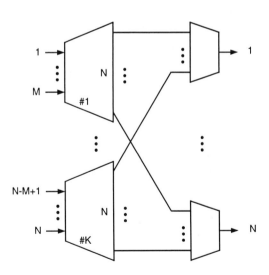

Figure 8.11 A partitioning of large $N \times N$ fabric into K modules with output multiplexing.

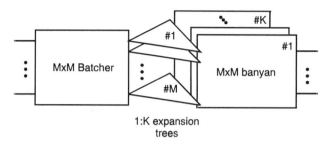

Figure 8.12   An implementation of *M* × *N* modules.

8.2.8 Fault Tolerance

Existing telephone switching systems are designed for a very high level of reliability; therefore reliability might be expected to be an important issue for ATM switching systems. As in any system, fault tolerance is achieved by adding redundancy to the crucial components. Of course, one of the most crucial components in the system is the routing and buffering fabric. Redundancy may be added in two ways: by duplicating copies of the fabric or by adding redundancy within the fabric. If redundancy exists, other considerations include: detection of faults and isolation and recovery.

It is straightforward to distribute the traffic among *K* parallel fabric planes (using the concentration and expansion functional blocks in Figure 8.1). There are three choices for the distribution of traffic: even division of all traffic into *K* disjoint subsets; division of all traffic into *K* partially overlapping subsets; or duplication of all traffic into *K* identical sets. The first approach provides the least redundancy because the fabric planes are all carrying different traffic. But each plane is burdened with only a small fraction $1/K$ of the total traffic. Thus, each fabric plane can be much smaller than $N \times N$ (and hence easily implemented [70]) or underutilized (for good throughput-delay performance [50,78]). The second approach is a compromise between the other two. The third approach provides the greatest redundancy because each fabric plane carries a separate copy of the entire traffic. In this case, it is clear that additional fabric planes will increase the fault tolerance but not improve the throughput-delay performance.

Even if the routing and buffering fabric is composed of parallel planes, it may still be desirable to add redundancy within each fabric plane. There has been a great deal of work on the design of fault-tolerant MINs [78–80]. In particular, banyans are susceptible to faults because a unique path exists between any pair of input and output. Multipath MINs are inherently more fault-tolerant than banyans. Techniques to add redundancy to banyans include: adding extra switching elements [81] or stages [52]; adding redundant links [82,83]; adding alternate links [84]; and increasing the number of input and output ports [79]. These modifications result in making multiple paths available between any input and output. The throughput may be increased as well as the fault tolerance. The cost is an increase in the complexity of implementation and route selection. Instead of space redundancy, it has been proposed to add *time redundancy*. Time redundancy allows cells to attempt multiple passes through the MIN [78].

With redundancy existing in the routing and buffering fabric, the next issue is fault detection. Basically, faults are detected by some testing mechanism to verify the proper operation of the MIN. Various mechanisms can be conceived [80]. One approach might consist of the periodic injection of test cells in a predetermined pattern and observations of the test cells at the outputs. If the outgoing cell pattern is different than expected, a fault may be inferred. Another approach might involve the addition of housekeeping information (e.g., sequence numbers, error detection codes, or timestamps) to each cell header to detect cell loss, cell misrouting, and cell delays.

After a fault is detected, the traffic should be redistributed around the fault. The fault can then be repaired without affecting the service. With parallel planes, the redistribution may be performed by the concentrator functional block in front of the routing fabric in Figure 8.1. Alternatively, the MIN itself may be designed to redistribute traffic internally around any faulty area.

8.3 CONCENTRATION AND EXPANSION

If the ATM switch is interfaced directly to customers, it is unlikely that most of the interfaces will be active even during the busy hour. It is therefore common practice to concentrate the traffic before the switch fabric. This could be performed either outside of the switch by a remote concentrator or within the switch. Figure 8.1 shows an optional concentration function within the CSF in front of the routing and buffering fabric (followed naturally by an optional expansion function).

The amount of concentration depends on the traffic characteristics, which are unknown at this time. A 10:1 concentration ratio is suggested in [68]; however, any ratio between 1:1 and 31:1 can be dynamically configured in a remote concentrator [85].

As we stated earlier, this concentration functional block may well serve additional purposes, such as distribution of traffic to multiple planes of the routing and buffering fabric to improve throughput, and duplication of traffic for fault tolerance. The distribution will be dynamically adjustable to route traffic around faults occurring in any fabric plane.

If the switch has interfaces to many subscribers, it may be necessary to expand the traffic after the routing and buffering fabric. This expansion functional block may also have the purpose of combining redundant traffic (duplicated for fault tolerance) from the fabric.

8.4 COPYING AND MULTICASTING

Thus far we have implicitly assumed that the routing and buffering fabric will transfer an incoming cell to a single output port. Of course, there will be services or applications (e.g., broadcast video) which will require the ATM switch to multicast an incoming cell to a number of selected outputs or broadcast it to all outputs. The design of multicasting capability may follow two approaches: each module (of any design) must be designed for multicasting if a large fabric is constructed as an interconnection of small switching modules, or a separate *copy network* can be added to a routing fabric.

Let us first consider multicasting in the four prototype designs in Section 8.2. Multicasting is inherently natural in two design approaches: the shared medium and fully interconnected output-buffered approaches. Both approaches consist of broadcasting incoming cells and selecting the appropriate cells with address filters at the output buffers. For multicasting, an address filter can recognize a set of multicast addresses as well as its output port address. As a result, multicasting is natural in these two broadcast-and-select approaches.

Multicasting is not natural to the shared memory approach but can be implemented with additional control circuitry. A multicast cell may be duplicated before the memory or read multiple times from the memory. The first approach obviously requires more memory because multiple copies of the same cell are maintained in the memory. In the second approach, a cell is read multiple times from the same memory location [16,17,21]. The control circuitry must keep the cell in memory until it has been read to all of the output ports in the multicast group.

Finally, multicasting in space division fabrics is simple to implement but has some consequences. For example, a crossbar switch (with input buffering) is naturally capable of broadcasting one incoming cell to multiple outputs. However, this would aggravate the head-of-line blocking at the input buffers. Approaches to alleviate the head-of-line blocking effect would increase the complexity of buffer control. As another example, a buffered banyan network can multicast if each switching element is capable of broadcasting. That is, in addition to routing two incoming cells to two different outputs, each 2×2 switching element can broadcast one incoming cell to both outputs while buffering the other cell. This has been called a broadcast banyan network [86].

As a consequence of the additional broadcasting capability, each switching element has four possible states, and each cell needs two bits of control information at each switching stage of the banyan. As a second consequence, a cell duplicated by a switching element would be identical and both copies would be self-routed by the banyan to the same output port. Two solutions are possible. First, multicast cells can carry a multicast address instead of output port address. The multicast address is carried unchanged and is used to look up routing information at each switching element [87]. Obviously, this requires some memory at each switching element. Second, each multicast cell can carry the entire set of output addresses. These are read at each switching element to decide the appropriate routing and duplication actions [86]. However, this approach is clearly awkward.

Because multicasting will increase the control complexity of space division fabrics, it may be desirable to separate the cell duplication and routing functions into a distinct copy network and routing network. The copy network makes duplicates of the multicast cells, and the routing network performs only point-to-point routing. If the copy network precedes the routing network, as usually proposed, it does not need to be concerned with the careful routing of the duplicated cells because it is the function of the routing network. The copy network must simply recognize multicast cells and make the indicated number of duplicates. The disadvantage is that the routing network must route all copies of the same cell. On the other hand, if the copy network follows the routing network, the copy network must duplicate cells and deliver them all to the correct outputs. This defeats the purpose of separating the duplication and routing functions.

A banyan was one of the earliest proposals for the copy network [88,89]. At each switching stage, a multicast cell is either routed randomly or duplicated. The action taken is decided following the principle that cell duplication should be done as late as possible within the copy network to minimize resource usage. Because all duplicates of the same cell will have identical addressing information, the copy network routes all cells randomly. The address information is changed to appropriate output addresses (according to the cells' multicast address) by translation tables after the copy network.

A modification has been proposed for adding concentration and processing before a broadcast banyan network [86]. It takes advantage of the observation that the broadcast banyan network is nonblocking (internal paths do not have common links) if the active inputs are concentrated (i.e., first M inputs are active while the others are inactive), there are N or fewer outputs, and the sets of outputs corresponding to inputs are disjoint and sequential. The multicast cells are concentrated and presented to the copy network each with two variables (min, max). The copy network then sends duplicates of the cells to the outputs numbered in the range (min, max). All duplicates are assigned a unique copy number. As before, address translation is done after the copy network (according to the cells' multicast address and copy number).

It was further observed that the nonblocking feature of broadcast banyans holds if the consecutiveness of inputs and outputs is regarded in cyclic (modulo N) fashion [90]. These conditions are ensured by a cyclic distribution network preceding the banyan network and a token-ring mechanism for reserving the outputs.

8.5 BUFFER MANAGEMENT

Thus far we have assumed a single type of traffic. In general, however, there will be a number of QOS classes of traffic in ATM (including a best-effort type of service being defined as *available bit rate* or ABR by the ATM Forum). The cell switch fabric must handle these classes of traffic differently according to their QOS requirements. Earlier we established that output buffering is the preferred approach. Hence, typically the CSF will have multiple buffers at each output port and one buffer for each QOS traffic class. The buffers may be physically separate or a physical buffer may be divided logically into separate buffers. Each buffer is typically FIFO to preserve the sequential order of cells within VPCs/VCCs, but the queuing discipline is not required to be FIFO.

Buffer management refers here to the discarding policy for the input of cells into the buffers and the scheduling policy for the output of cells from the buffers.

One can see that buffer management involves both dimensions of time (cell scheduling) and buffer space (cell discarding). The traffic classes are distinguished in the time and space dimensions by their cell-delay and cell-loss priorities.

Buffer management is a part of the general traffic control that is handled by the system-management (SM) functional block. Within the CSF, buffer management monitors the queues for signs for congestion, alerts the SM about congestion, and cooperates with the SM to control congestion.

8.5.1 Delay and Loss Priorities

Priorities are used to indicate the preferential treatment of one traffic class over another. In ATM, a two-level loss priority is indicated explicitly per cell by the CLP bit in the cell header. When it becomes necessary to discard cells due to buffer overflow, the queued cells with lower loss priority CLP = 1 should be discarded before CLP = 0 cells. The CLP bit may be set by the user to indicate that a CLP = 1 cell contains less important information, or it may be set (tagged) by the UPC function when the user source traffic exceeds the parameters in the established traffic contract.

A multiple-level delay priority can be associated implicitly with a VPC/VCC. There is no field for explicit delay priorities within the cell header. During the translation table look-up of the VPI/VCI values of incoming cells, a delay priority can be associated with the VPI/VCI number. This priority may be included in the internal routing tag attached to each cell. Cells of the same VPC/VCC must have the same delay priority to maintain sequential order, but they may have different cell-loss priorities.

8.5.2 Cell Scheduling

The cell-scheduling policy determines the order in which cells are transmitted out of the buffers. It is usually assumed that QOS classes will have different cell-delay requirements and higher delay priority should be given to the class with the strictest delay constraints. Static priorities are the simplest approach. A lower priority class will receive service only in the absence of higher priority class traffic. However, this simple approach is inflexible and allows for some unfairness. For example, a large burst of high-priority traffic might cause an excessively long queuing delay for low-priority traffic.

A more flexible approach is the well-known due-date (or deadline) scheduling. It is assumed that every cell has a target departure time (deadline) from the queue based on its QOS requirements. Those cells missing their deadlines are said to be late. If the deadlines are strict, late cells may be discarded; otherwise, late cells may still be transmitted later. The actions on late cells depends on the switch implementation and traffic requirements.

If late cells are discarded, the earliest-due-date policy, where service is given to the cell with the most imminent (but not past) deadline, is known to be optimal in minimizing the total number of discarded cells [91]. If late cells are still serviced, the earliest-due-date policy is known to be optimal in minimizing the maximum lateness of any cell and minimizing the range between the minimum and maximum lateness [92]. Due-date scheduling and other dynamic priority schemes have been widely studied in queuing theory.

A different scheduling approach consists of dividing time into cycles; the scheduling decisions are made only at the beginning of each cycle instead of before each cell. If there are n QOS classes, for example, time would be divided into cycles consisting of n subcycles [93,94]. The mth subcycle is available to transmit class m cells. At the beginning of each cycle, the contents of the buffers are examined and the lengths of the n subcycles in the next cycle are determined to satisfy the cell-delay requirements. For example, the subcycles might be chosen to transmit the minimum number of cells of each class that cannot be delayed until the next cycle to make their deadlines [93].

8.5.3   Cell Discarding

Cells of different cell-loss priorities may be mixed in the same buffer because cells of the same VPC/VCC must maintain sequential order. The cell-discarding policy determines how CLP = 0 and CLP = 1 cells will be admitted into the buffer when the buffer is full.

In the push-out scheme, an incoming CLP = 0 cell may be admitted to a full buffer only if space can be made available by discarding a CLP = 1 cell; CLP = 1 cells are not admitted [95]. In the partial-buffer sharing approach, both CLP = 0 and CLP = 1 cells may be admitted when the queue is below a given threshold. When the queue exceeds this threshold, only CLP = 0 cells may be admitted as long as there is buffer space available. Clearly, inefficiency could be an issue because a CLP = 1 cell may be blocked even though buffer space is available. The degree of inefficiency depends on the choice of the threshold. It has been observed that the push-out scheme is optimal, but the partial-buffer sharing scheme can be designed for a close performance and much simpler implementation [95].

Although not precisely the situation in ATM, a simple scenario for study can be made by assuming two traffic classes: one requires low delay (LD) while the other requires low loss (LL) [96,97]. Typical examples may be data and voice. In the LDOLL (low delay or low loss) queue, service priority is given to LD cells and space priority is given to LL cells [96]. If the buffer is full, arriving LL cells can push-out LD cells that have been waiting the longest. For a given threshold, LD cells are given service as long as the number of queued LL cells is less than the threshold; otherwise, service is given to LL cells. Variations of this buffer-management scheme have also been studied [97].

8.5.4 Congestion Indications

As mentioned earlier, buffer management is a part of traffic management, which is handled by the SM. Buffer management within the CSF will keep track of queue statistics and raise alarms to the SM if congestion is detected within the fabric. It must collect sufficient information to determine the state and nature of congestion in the routing and buffering fabric, e.g., whether congestion is increasing or receding and whether it is focused or widespread. To accomplish this, buffer management may use housekeeping or timing information (e.g., timestamps) in the internal routing tags attached to each cell.

Upon request from the SM, buffer management should be able to provide performance data, congestion information, records of discarded cells, and usage-measurement data for accounting management. Depending on the state and nature of congestion, the SM may instruct the buffer management to adjust the cell scheduling and discarding policies. The SM may decide to activate explicit forward congestion indication (EFCI), in which case the CSF will provide the capability to change the PT codes in cell headers to indicate congestion. The PT field changes are made at the buffers where the congestion occurs.

8.6 CONCLUSIONS

In addition to the routing and buffering fabric, the CSF consists of: (optional) concentration/duplication, (optional) expansion/combination, and buffer management. The routing and buffering fabric is, however, the central functional block in the CSF.

The design principles of the routing and buffering fabric are well known at least for fabrics with limited throughput. We have described four prototype designs: shared memory, shared medium, fully interconnected, and space division approaches. By a comparison of these approaches, some general design principles have been illustrated: shared resources imply a speed-up factor that will limit the total throughput, output buffering is the preferred approach, and statistical sharing will minimize the total amount of buffers.

Large fabrics (on the order of 1 Tbps total throughput) may be constructed by multistage interconnection of small switching modules of any design or by optimally partitioning the large fabric into manageable modules.

Although the design principles for the routing and buffering fabric are well established by now, the design is complicated by considerations for fault tolerance, multicasting, and priorities. Fault tolerance implies the necessity of redundant resources in the fabric. The straightforward approach of duplicating parallel planes may also improve throughput. Alternatively, various ways exist to add redundancy within a single fabric plane.

Multicasting depends on the fabric design because some design approaches inherently broadcast every cell. For space division fabrics, including large fabrics constructed by interconnection of small modules, there are two approaches to implement multicasting capabilities: add a cell-duplication (broadcast) capability to each switching element (or module); or separate the routing and duplication functions into a distinct routing network and copy network. The second approach is motivated by the increase in control complexity involved in the first approach. Most approaches for the copy network are based on the broadcast banyan network.

Finally, it will be necessary to manage multiple buffers at each output to satisfy the QOS requirements of the different traffic classes. Buffer management consists of cell scheduling and discarding policies, which determine the manner in which cells are input into and output from the buffers. The cell-scheduling policy attempts to satisfy the delay requirements as indicated by delay priorities. Scheduling decisions may be made on the basis of cells or cycles. The earliest-due-date policy is known to have optimal properties for per-cell scheduling. The cell-discarding policy attempts to satisfy the loss requirements as indicated by cell-loss priorities. The push-out approach is optimal, but the partial-buffer sharing approach may be designed for close performance and much simpler implementation.

References

[1]   Ahmadi, H., and W. Denzel, "A Survey of Modern High-Performance Switching Techniques," *IEEE J. on Selected Areas in Communications*, Vol. 7, Sept. 1989, pp. 1,091–1,103.

[2]   Pattavina, A., "Nonblocking Architectures for ATM Switching," *IEEE Communications Mag.*, Vol. 31, Feb. 1993, pp. 38–48.

[3]   Rathgeb, E., et al., "ATM Switches—Basic Architectures and Their Performance," *Int. J. of Digital and Analog Cabled Systems*, Vol. 2, 1989, pp. 227–236.

[4]   Takeuchi, T., et al., "Switch Architectures and Technologies for Asynchronous Transfer Mode," *IEICE Trans.*, Vol. E74, April 1991, pp. 752–760.

[5]   Tobagi, F., "Fast Packet Switch Architectures for Broadband Integrated Services Digital Networks," *Proc. of the IEEE*, Vol. 78, Jan. 1990, pp. 133–178.

[6]   Wulleman, R., and T. Van Landegem, "Comparison of ATM Switching Architectures," *Int. J. of Digital and Analog Cabled Systems*, Vol. 2, 1989, pp. 211–225.

[7]   Zegura, E., "Architectures for ATM Switching Systems," *IEEE Communications Mag.*, Vol. 31, Feb. 1993, pp. 28–37.

[8]   Huang, A., and S. Knauer, "Starlite: A Wideband Digital Switch," *GLOBECOM'84*, Atlanta, Dec. 1984, pp. 121–125.

[9]   Turner, J., and L. Wyatt, "A Packet Network Architecture for Integrated Services," *GLOBECOM'83*, San Diego, Nov. 1983, pp. 2.1.1–6.

[10] Turner, J., "Design of an Integrated Services Packet Network," *IEEE J. on Selected Areas in Communications*, Vol. SAC-4, Nov. 1986, pp. 1,373–1,380.

[11] Turner, J., "New Directions in Communications (Or Which Way to the Information Age?)," *IEEE Communications Mag.*, Vol. 24, Oct. 1986, pp. 8–15.

[12] Coudreuse, J., and M. Servel, "Prelude: An Asynchronous Time-Division Switched Network," *Int. Conf. on Communications '87*, Seattle, June 1987, pp. 769–773.

[13] Devault, M., et al., "The 'Prelude' ATD Experiment: Assessments and Future Prospects," *IEEE J. on Selected Areas in Communications*, Vol. 6, Dec. 1988, pp. 1,528–1,537.

[14] Gonet, P., "Fast Packet Approach to Integrated Broadband Networks," *Computer Communications*, Vol. 9, Dec. 1986, pp. 292–298.

[15] Gonet, P., et al., "Implementing Asynchronous Transfer Mode Concepts: Main Results of the Prelude Experiment," *GLOBECOM'87*, pp. 47.4.1–5.

[16] Endo, N., et al., "Shared Buffer Memory Switch for an ATM Exchange," *IEEE Trans. on Communications*, Vol. 41., Jan. 1993, pp. 237–245.

[17] Kuwahara, H., et al., "A Shared Buffer Memory Switch for an ATM Exchange," *Int. Conf. on Communications '89*, Boston, June 1989, pp. 118–122.

[18] Karol, M., et al., "Input Versus Output Queuing on a Space-Division Packet Switch," *IEEE Trans. on Communications*, Vol. COM-35, Dec. 1987, pp. 1,347–1,356.

[19] Yeh, Y., et al., "The Knockout Switch: A Simple, Modular Architecture for High-Performance Packet Switching," *IEEE J. on Selected Areas in Communications*, Vol. SAC-5, Oct. 1987, pp. 1,274–1,283.

[20] Nojima, et al., "Integrated Services Packet Network Using Bus Matrix Switch," *IEEE J. on Selected Areas in Communications*, Vol. SAC-5, Oct. 1987, pp. 1,284–1,292.

[21] Sakurai, Y., et al., "ATM Switching System for B-ISDN," *Hitachi Review*, Vol. 40, 1990, pp. 193–198.

[22] Cidon, I., et al., "Real-time Packet Switching: A Performance Analysis," *IEEE J. on Selected Areas in Communications*, Vol. 6, Dec. 1988, pp. 1,576–1,586.

[23] Gopal, I., et al., "Paris: An Approach to Integrated Private Networks," *Int. Conf. on Communications '87*, Seattle, June 1987, pp. 764–773.

[24] Itoh, A., et al., "Practical Implementation and Packaging Technologies for a Large-Scale ATM Switching System," *IEEE J. on Selected Areas in Communications*, Vol. 9, Oct. 1991, pp. 1,280–1,288.

[25] Suzuki, H., et al., "Output-Buffer Switch Architecture for Asynchronous Transfer Mode," *Int. Conf. on Communications '89*, Boston, June 1989, pp. 4.1.1–4.1.5.

[26] Suzuki, H. et al., "Output-Buffer Switch Architecture for Asynchronous Transfer Mode," *Int. J. of Digital and Analog Cabled Systems*, Vol. 2, 1989, pp. 269–276.

[27] Suzuki, K., et al., "An ATM Switching System—Development And Evaluation," *NEC Research & Development*, Vol. 32, April 1991, pp. 242–251.

[28] Gopal, I., et al., "ATM Support in a Transparent Network," *IEEE Network*, Vol. 4, Nov. 1992 pp. 62–68.

[29] Hajikano, K., et al., "ATM Switching Technologies," *Fujitsu Sci. Tech. J.*, Vol. 28, June 1992 pp. 132–140.

[30] Clos, C., "A Study of Non-Blocking Switching Networks," *Bell System Technical J.*, Vol. 32 March 1953, pp. 406–424.

[31] Benes, V., *Mathematical Theory of Connecting Networks and Telephone Traffic*, NY, Academic Press, 1965.

[32] Masson, G., et al., "A Sampler of Circuit Switching Networks," *IEEE Computer*, Vol. 12, June 1979, pp. 32–48.

[33] Batcher, K., "Sorting Networks and Their Application," *Spring Joint Computer Conf., AFIPS*, 1968, pp. 307–314.

[34] Bhuyan, L., and D. Agrawal, "Design and Performance of Generalized Interconnection Networks," *IEEE Trans. on Computers*, Vol. C-32, Dec. 1983, pp. 1,081–1,090.

[35] Chin, C-Y., and K. Hwang, "Packet Switching Networks for Multiprocessors and Data Flow Computers," *IEEE Trans. on Computers*, Vol. C-33, Nov. 1984, pp. 991–1,003.

[36] Dias, D., and J. Jump, "Packet Switching Interconnection Networks for Modular Systems," *IEEE Computer*, Vol. 14, Dec. 1981, pp. 43–54.

[37] Feng, T-Y., "A Survey of Interconnection Networks," *IEEE Computer Mag.*, Vol. 14, Dec. 1981, pp. 12–27.

[38] Kruskal, C., and M. Snir, "The Performance of Multistage Interconnection Networks for Multiprocessors," *IEEE Trans. on Computers*, Vol. C-32, Dec. 1983, pp. 1,091–1,098.

[39] Chen, X., "A Survey of Multistage Interconnection Networks in Fast Packet Switches," *Int. J. of Digital and Analog Communication Systems*, Vol. 4, 1991, pp. 33–59.

[40] Hui, J., "Switching Integrated Broadband Services by Sort-Banyan Networks," *Proc. of the IEEE*, Vol. 79, Feb. 1991, pp. 145–154.

[41] Lea, C-T., "Design and Performance Evaluation of Unbuffered Self-Routing Networks for Wide-Band Packet Switching," *IEEE Trans. on Communications*, Vol. 39, July 1991, pp. 1,075–1,087.

[42] Lea, C-T., "Multi-log$_2$N Networks and Their Applications in High-Speed Electronic and Photonic Switching Systems," *IEEE Trans. on Communications*, Vol. 38, Oct. 1990, pp. 1,740–1,749.

[43] McMillen, R., "A Survey of Interconnection Networks," *GLOBECOM'84*, Nov. 1984, pp. 105–113.

[44] Giacopelli, J., et al., "Sunshine: A High-Performance Self-Routing Broadband Packet Switch Architecture," *IEEE J. on Selected Areas in Communications*, Vol. 9, Oct. 1991, pp. 1,289–1,298.

[45] Goke, L. and G. Lipovski, "Banyan Networks for Partitioning Multiprocessor Systems," *First Annual Symp. on Computer Architecture*, Dec. 1973, pp. 21–28.

[46] Patel, J., "Performance of Processor-Memory Interconnections for Multiprocessors," *IEEE Trans. on Computers*, Vol. C-30, Oct. 1981, pp. 771–780.

[47] Hui, J., and E. Arthurs, "A Broadband Packet Switch for Integrated Transport," *IEEE J. on Selected Areas in Communications*, Vol. SAC-5, Oct. 1987, pp. 1,264–1,273.

[48] Dias, D., and J. Jump, "Analysis and Simulation of Buffered Delta Networks," *IEEE Trans. on Computers*, Vol. C-30, April. 1981, pp. 273–282.

[49] Pattavina, A., "Multichannel Bandwidth Allocation in a Broadband Packet Switch," *IEEE J. on Selected Areas in Communications*, Vol. 6, Dec. 1988, pp. 1,489–1,499.

[50] Corazza, G., and C. Raffaelli, "Performance Evaluation of Input-Buffered Replicated Banyan Networks," *IEEE Trans. on Communications*, Vol. 41, June 1993, pp. 841–845.

[51] Tobagi, F., et al., "Architecture, Performance, and Implementation of the Tandem Banyan Fast Packet Switch," *IEEE J. on Selected Areas in Communications*, Vol. 9, Oct. 1991, pp. 1,173–1,193.

[52] Urushidani, S., "Rerouting Network: A High-Performance Self-Routing Switch for B-ISDN," *IEEE J. on Selected Areas in Communications*, Vol. 9, Oct. 1991, pp. 1,194–1,204.

[53] Anido, G., and A. Seeto, "Multipath Interconnection: A Technique for Reducing Congestion within Fast Packet Switching Fabrics," *IEEE J. on Selected Areas in Communications*, Vol. SAC-6, Dec. 1988, pp. 1,480–1,488.

[54] Lea, C-T., "The Load-Sharing Banyan Network," *IEEE Trans. on Computers*, Vol. C-35, Dec. 1986, pp. 1,025–1,034.

[55] Lee, T-H., "Design and Analysis of a New Self-Routing Network," *IEEE Trans. on Communications*, Vol. 40, Jan. 1992, pp. 171–177.

[56] Shyy, D-J., and C-T. Lea, "Log$_2$(N,m,p) Strictly Nonblocking Networks," *IEEE Trans. on Communications*, Vol. 39, Oct. 1991, pp. 1,502–1,510.

[57] Hluchyj, M., and M. Karol, "Queuing in High-Performance Packet Switching," *IEEE J. on Selected Areas in Communications*, Vol. 6, Dec. 1988, pp. 1,587–1,597.

[58] Liew, S., and K. Lu, "A Three-Stage Architecture for Very Large Packet Switches," *Int. J. of Digital and Analog Cabled Systems*, Vol. 2, 1989, pp. 303–316.

[59] Chen, J., and T. Stern, "Throughput Analysis, Optimal Buffer Allocation, and Traffic Imbalance Study of a Generic Nonblocking Packet Switch," *IEEE J. on Selected Areas in Communications*, Vol. 9, April 1991, pp. 439–449.

[60] Genda, K., et al., "A High-Speed ATM Switch That Uses a Simple Retry Algorithm and Small Input Buffers," *IEICE Trans. on Communications*, Vol. E76-B, July 1993, pp. 726–730.

[61] Lee, M., and S-Q. Li, "Performance Trade-Offs in Input/Output Buffer Design for a Non-Blocking Space-Division Packet Switch," *Int. J. of Digital and Analog Communication Systems*, Vol. 4, 1991, pp. 21–31.

[62] Oie, Y., et al., "Performance Analysis of Nonblocking Packet Switches with Input and Output Buffers," *IEEE Trans. on Communications*, Vol. 40, Aug. 1992, pp. 1,294–1,297.

[63] Pattavina, A., and G. Bruzzi, "Analysis of Input and Output Queuing for Nonblocking ATM Switches," *IEEE/ACM Trans. on Networking*, Vol. 1, June 1993, pp. 314–327.

[64] Del Re, E., and R. Fantacci, "Performance Evaluation of Input and Output Queuing Techniques in ATM Switching Systems," *IEEE Trans. on Communications*, Vol. 41, Oct. 1993, pp. 1,565–1,575.

[65] Jenq, Y., "Performance Analysis of a Packet Switch Based on a Single-Buffered Banyan Network," *IEEE J. on Selected Areas in Communications*, Vol. SAC-1, Dec. 1983, pp. 1,014–1,021.

[66] Theimer, T., et al., "Performance Analysis of Buffered Banyan Networks," *IEEE Trans. on Communications*, Vol. 39, Feb. 1991, pp. 269–277.

[67] Kim, H., and A. Leon-Garcia, "Performance of Buffered Banyan Networks under Nonuniform Traffic Patterns," *IEEE Trans. on Communications*, Vol. 38, May 1990, pp. 648–658.

[68] Banwell, T., et al., "Physical Design Issues for Very Large Scale ATM Switching Systems," *IEEE J. on Selected Areas in Communications*, Vol. 9, Oct. 1991, pp. 1,227–1,238.

[69] Stephens, W., and K. Young, "Terabit-Per-Second Throughput Switches for Broadband Central Offices: An Overview," *IEEE LCS*, Nov. 1990, pp. 20–27.

[70] Lee, T., "A Modular Architecture for Very Large Packet Switches," *IEEE Trans. on Communications*, Vol. 38, July 1990, pp. 1,097–1,106.

[71] Murano, K., et al., "Technologies Towards Broadband ISDN," *IEEE Communications Mag.*, Vol. 28, April 1990, pp. 66–70.

[72] Kozaki, T., et al., "32 × 32 Shared Buffer Type ATM Switch VLSI's for B-ISDN's," *IEEE J. on Selected Areas in Communications*, Vol. 9, Oct. 1991, pp. 1,239–1,247.

[73] Sakurai, Y., et al., "Large-Scale ATM Multistage Switching Network with Shared Buffer Memory Switches," *IEEE Communications Mag.*, Vol. 29, Jan. 1991, pp. 90–96.

[74] Banniza, T., et al., "Design and Technology Aspects of VLSI's for ATM Switches," *IEEE J. on Selected Areas in Communications*, Vol. 9, Oct. 1991, pp. 1,255–1,264.

[75] Coppo, P., et al., "Optimal Cost/Performance Design of ATM Switches," *IEEE/ACM Trans. or Networking*, Vol. 1, Oct. 1993, pp. 566–575.

[76] Shobatake, Y., et al., "A One-Chip Scalable 8 × 8 ATM Switch LSI Employing Shared Buffer Architecture," *IEEE J. on Selected Areas in Communications*, Vol. 9, Oct. 1991, pp. 1,248–1,254.

[77] Eng, K., et al., "A Growable Packet (ATM) Switch Architecture: Design Principles and Applications," *IEEE Trans. on Communications*, Vol. 40, Feb. 1992, pp. 423–430.

[78] Kumar, V., and S. Wang, "Reliability Enhancement by Time and Space Redundancy in Multistage Interconnection Networks," *IEEE Trans. on Reliability*, Vol. 40, Oct. 1991, pp. 461–473.

[79] Adams, G., et al., "A Survey and Comparison of Fault-Tolerant Multistage Interconnection Networks," *IEEE Computer*, Vol. 20, 1987, pp. 14–27.

[80] Agrawal, D., "Testing and Fault-Tolerance of Multistage Interconnection Networks," *IEEE Computer*, Vol. 15, April 1982, pp. 41–53.

[81] Itoh, A., "A Fault-Tolerant Switching Network for BISDN," *IEEE J. on Selected Areas in Communications*, Vol. 9, Oct. 1991, pp. 1,218–1,226.

[82] Kumar, V., and S. Reddy, "Augmented Shuffle-Exchange Multistage Interconnection Networks," *IEEE Computer*, Vol. 20, June 1987, pp. 30–40.

[83] Yang, S-C., and J. Silvester, "A Reconfigurable ATM Switch Fabric for Fault Tolerance and Traffic Balancing," *IEEE J. on Selected Areas in Communications*, Vol. 9, Oct. 1991, pp. 1,205–1,217.

[84] Chen, W-S., et al., "FB-Banyans and FB-Delta Networks: Fault-Tolerant Networks for Broadband Packet Switching," *Int. J. of Digital and Analog Cabled Systems*, Vol. 2, 1989, pp. 327–341.

[85] Fischer, W., et al., "A Scalable ATM Switching System Architecture," *IEEE J. on Selected Areas in Communications*, Vol. 9, Oct. 1991, pp. 1,299–1,307.

[86] Lee, T., "Nonblocking Copy Networks for Multicast Packet Switching," *IEEE J. on Selected Areas in Communications*, Vol. 6, Dec. 1988, pp. 1,455–1,467.

[87] Knorr, R., and T. Wild, "Implementation of Multipoint Connections in an ATM Switching Network," *Int. J. of Digital and Analog Communication Systems*, Vol. 5, 1992, pp. 167–175.

[88] Bubenik, R., and J. Turner, "Performance of a Broadcast Packet Switch," *IEEE Trans. on Communications*, Vol. 37, Jan. 1989, pp. 60–69.

[89] Turner, J., "Design of a Broadcast Packet Switching Network," *IEEE Trans. on Communications*, Vol. 36, June 1988, pp. 734–743.

[90] Zhong, W., et al., "A Copy Network with Shared Buffers for Large-Scale Multicast ATM Switching," *IEEE/ACM Trans. on Networking*, Vol. 1, April 1993, pp. 157–165.

[91] Saito, H., "Optimal Queuing Discipline for Real-Time Traffic at ATM Switching Nodes," *IEEE Trans. on Communications*, Vol. 38, Dec. 1990, pp. 2,131–2,136.

[92] Chen, T., et al., "Dynamic Priority Protocols for Packet Voice," *IEEE J. on Selected Areas in Communications*, Vol. 7, June 1989, pp. 632–643.

[93] Hyman, J., et al., "Real-Time Scheduling with Quality of Service Constraints," *IEEE J. on Selected Areas in Communications*, Vol. 9, Sept. 1991, pp. 1,052–1,063.

[94] Takagi, Y., et al., "Priority Assignment Control of ATM Line Buffers with Multiple QOS Classes," *IEEE J. on Selected Areas in Communications*, Vol. 9, Sept. 1991, pp. 1,078–1,092.

[95] Kroner, H., et al., "Priority Management in ATM Switching Nodes," *IEEE J. on Selected Areas in Communications*, Vol. 9, April 1991, pp. 418–427.

[96] Awater, G., and F. Schoute, "Optimal Queuing Policies for Fast Packet Switching of Mixed Traffic," *IEEE J. on Selected Areas in Communications*, Vol. 9, April 1991, pp. 458–467.

[97] Ohnishi, H., et al., "Flow Control Schemes and Delay/Loss Tradeoff in ATM Networks," *IEEE J. on Selected Areas in Communications*, Vol. 6, Dec. 1988, pp. 1,609–1,616.

Connection Admission Control

9.1 INTRODUCTION

The previous chapters have described three of the major functional blocks in the ATM switch architecture model: input modules, output modules, and cell switching fabric. They collectively provide the necessary functions to route user cells through the switch. The present chapter covers the fourth functional block, *connection admission control* (CAC), named for the traffic-control function that it performs. Recall from Section 4.3 that CAC consists of the control functions for the establishment, supervision, and release of switched virtual connections (semi-permanent virtual connections are controlled by network management). As represented in the control plane, CAC is carried out through the exchange of signaling information between the user and network nodes (refer to Section 3.3). This chapter first describes the signaling protocols and then the decisions made by the network on the allocation of resources for connections.

A remark should be made about the difference between calls and connections in B-ISDN. B-ISDN calls and connections may be controlled separately. Connections may be point-to-point or multipoint, and symmetric or asymmetric; they are characterized by a specific QOS class and throughput. A call can consist of multiple connections, and any connection can be established, modified, or terminated during a call. However, initial (Release 1) B-ISDN signaling will be limited to single-connection calls, and the two terms will be used interchangeably in this chapter.

A functional diagram of the CAC is shown in Figure 9.1. The CAC has two main functions: interaction with a user (across the UNI) or another ATM switch (through the NNI or SS7 network) by means of signaling messages, and resource allocation to support the QOS of negotiated connections. For the moment, it is assumed that the CAC is centralized in the ATM switching system and receives signaling messages (carried in ATM cells) from the input modules. Alternatively, it is possible to receive signaling cells from the input modules through the cell switch fabric (CSF). We have also assumed interoffice signaling through direct links between ATM switches (through the NNI) rather than through the SS7 signaling network; otherwise, Figure 9.1 should show an interface to the SS7 network.

When the CAC receives signaling cells from the input modules, the high-layer signaling information is extracted by *signaling AAL* (SAAL) functions and interpreted by a negotiation functional block, which follows the high-layer signaling protocols (e.g., Q.2931 and BISUP). The SAAL functions also work in the reverse direction to encapsulate outgoing signaling messages into ATM cells sent to the output modules. Although metasignaling is considered part of the management plane, metasignaling is conveniently handled here using the same functional blocks. Signaling was introduced earlier in Section 3.3 and is covered in more detail in Section 9.2.

If a decision about the admission of a new connection is required, a request that follows a specified connection-admission policy is passed to a decision-making functional block. The admission policy will likely be deter-

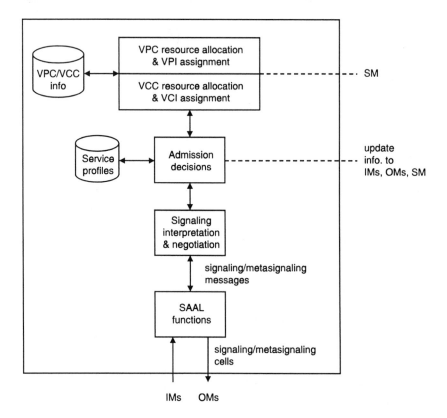

Figure 9.1 Functional diagram of the CAC.

mined by the network provider. As part of the admission-decision process, the needed resources will be sought through two functional blocks responsible for resource allocation at the levels of virtual paths and virtual channels. They maintain information about the current status of all virtual VPCs/VCCs and network resources. For a new VCC, available resources in an appropriate VP are sought and, if insufficient, reallocation of VP level resources is attempted. These functional blocks also respond to requests from the SM to allocate resources to semi-permanent virtual connections. Resource allocation is the topic of Section 9.3.

Status information about the VPCs/VCCs and network resources are conceptually kept in a database. Whenever a VPC/VCC is established or modified in any way, the database is updated. At the same time, update information is sent to the input modules and output modules concerning UPC/NPC parameters and VPI/VCI translations. The changes are also reported to the SM.

As noted in Chapters 5 and 6, the CAC is not necessarily centralized. Indeed it may be advantageous to distribute CAC functions to the input modules and output modules. This issue will be discussed further in Section 9.4.

9.2 SIGNALING

Switched VPCs/VCCs are controlled through the exchange of signaling messages. An ATM switch must support the access signaling protocol between itself and users (if the switch supports UNIs), and the interoffice signaling protocol with other switches. As mentioned in Section 3.3, the access signaling protocol across the UNI is the ITU-T standard Q.2931 (formerly Q.93B) [1,2]. SAAL is used to encapsulate Q.2931 messages into ATM cells. The ATM Forum has specified a version that contains a subset of Q.2931 for point-to-point connections and additional messages for point-to-multipoint connections [3]; a new version is being drafted in closer alignment with Q.2931.

The high-layer interoffice signaling protocol between ATM switches (across the public NNI) is the ITU-T standard BISUP (the ATM Forum is specifying a symmetric Q.2931 protocol across the private NNI). BISUP was derived from the ISDN user part of SS7 [4–8]. As shown in Figure 3.3, BISUP messages may be conveyed between ATM switching systems through the existing SS7 network, where the lower protocol layers will be MTP levels 1–3, or via direct ATM links, where the lower protocol layers will be SAAL and MTP-3 over ATM. Throughout this chapter, the latter case is assumed because it has more interesting implications on the ATM switch architecture.

As an introduction, the basic signaling procedure for a successful point-to-point connection is shown in Figure 9.2. It illustrates the three basic phases of the procedure: connection establishment, information transfer, and connection release. The connection establishment is initiated by a signaling message from a user to request a connection. The connection request is passed from node to node and finally to the called user. If the user accepts the connection, another signaling message is returned in the reverse direction to confirm the allocation of network resources and notify the calling user that the connection is active. Initial signaling capabilities do not allow signaling during the information transfer phase, but this capability will be included in future standards. When the information-transfer phase is complete, network resources for the connection are released by signaling. Of course, the complete signaling procedure is rather complicated, including time-outs and restarts to handle blocking and unusual conditions (e.g., faults, malfunctions).

9.2.1 Access Signaling

As mentioned earlier, the access signaling protocol between the user and network is the ITU-T standard Q.2931, which was derived from the ISDN access

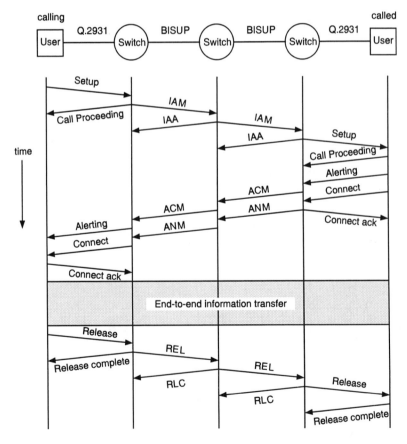

Figure 9.2 An example of the basic signaling procedure for a successful point-to-point connection.

signaling protocol Q.931. Release 1 signaling pertains to single connection, point-to-point calls between two parties [1,2]. The set of Q.2931 messages for connection control, including additional messages for point-to-multipoint connections from [3], are listed in Table 3.1. This set of messages is used to establish, monitor, and release connections. All messages have the format shown in Figure 3.4.

9.2.1.1 Point-to-Point Connections

Figure 9.3 shows the messages and states involved in access signaling for a successful outgoing point-to-point call ("outgoing" from the user's viewpoint). Before messages are exchanged, an assured mode SAAL connection must exist between the user and network (see Section 9.2.3). When no call actions exist, both user and network are in the *null* states. To begin an outgoing call, the user sends a *setup* message and enters the *call initiated* state. After checking that access to the requested service is authorized and available, the network acknowledges the request with a *call proceeding* message, which causes the user to enter the *outgoing call proceeding* state. When the network begins alerting the called user, the network enters the *call delivered* state and informs the calling user with an *alerting* message. The user enters the *call delivered* state. If the called user accepts, the network notifies the calling user with a *connect* message and enters the *active* state. The user acknowledges with a *connect acknowledge* and enters the *active* state.

During the active state, the network carries user cells between the two users. The connection is terminated with a *release* message from either user to request the network to release resources. When the network responds with *release complete*, the user returns to the *null* state. Alternatively, termination of the connection may be initiated by the network with a *release* message, upon which the user enters a *release indication* state. After internal clearing procedures, the user sends a *release complete* message and returns to the *null* state.

The connection establishment procedure may fail for various reasons. For instance, upon receipt of the *setup* message, the network may choose to reject the request by returning a *release* or *release complete* with any of these causes:

- #1 "unassigned (unallocated) number;"
- #3 "no route to destination;"
- #22 "number changed;"
- #28 "invalid number format (address incomplete);"
- #45 "no VPI/VCI available;"
- #49 "quality of service unavailable;"
- #51 "user cell rate unavailable;"
- #57 "bearer capability not authorized;"
- #63 "service or option not available, unspecified;"

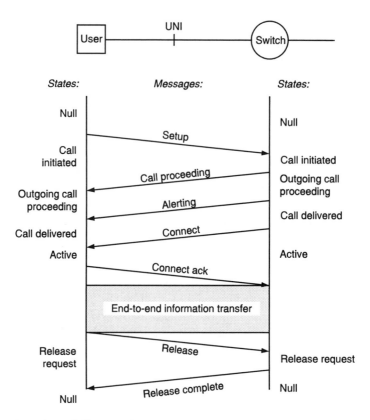

Figure 9.3 Outgoing call (from user).

- #65 "bearer service not implemented;"
- #73 "unsupported combination of traffic parameters."

A complete listing of causes can be found in the standards. In addition, the entire sequence of events in the connection-establishment procedure is governed by various timers that may terminate the call. For example, if the network takes too long to respond to the *setup* message, the user will retransmit the *setup* and eventually begin clearing procedures. In the *outgoing call proceeding* state, if the user does not receive an *alerting* or *connect* from the network after a certain time, it begins clearing procedures.

The messages and states for an incoming call ("incoming" to the user) are similarly shown in Figure 9.4. In this case, an unassured mode SAAL connection must exist between the user and network (see Section 9.2.3). The network notifies the user of an incoming call with a *setup* message, which causes the user to change from the *null* state to *call present*. The user checks the address and compatibility information in the *setup*. If compatible, the user may respond in any of three ways:

- Send a *call proceeding* message and enter the *incoming call proceeding* state;
- Send an *alerting* message and enter the *call received* state;
- Send a *connect* message and enter the *connect request* state.

In response to *call proceeding*, the network enters the *incoming call proceeding* state and waits for a subsequent *alerting* or *connect* message from the user. In response to *alerting*, the network enters the *call received* state, sends an *alerting* message to the calling user, and waits for a *connect* message from the called user.

The *connect* message indicates that the user accepts the call, and the user enters the *connect request* state. When the network confirms the connection with a *connect acknowledge*, the user enters the *active* state and is ready for end-to-end information transfer. The connection may be terminated by the

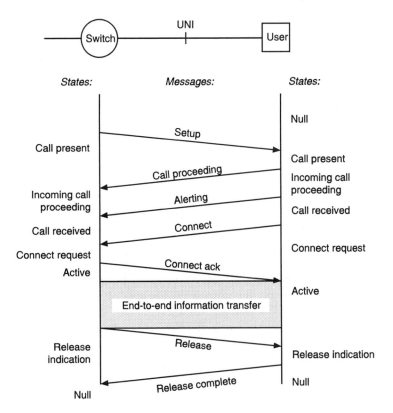

Figure 9.4 Incoming call (to user).

network with a *release* message to which the user responds with a *release complete*. The user may also initiate clearing with a *release* message, which is acknowledged with a *release complete*.

A fault or other unusual condition might happen to disrupt the continuity of a connection. The user or network can force a virtual connection to the *null* state with a *restart* message. The recipient of the *restart* message will take actions to clear its internal resources and returns a *restart acknowledge*. This procedure may be applied to a single virtual connection or all virtual connections controlled by a signaling virtual channel.

If there is confusion about the state of a connection, the user or network may send a *status enquiry* message. This message should prompt the return of a *status* message that reports the current call state. These messages do not affect the call state of the user or network.

9.2.1.2   Point-to-Multipoint Connections

Initial signaling procedures allow one user, called the root, to multicast to multiple users called leaves [3]. A point-to-multipoint connection is managed by additional signaling messages that allow the root to add or drop leaves to the connection.

The first leaf is set up by the root through the usual point-to-point connection-establishment procedure. The only difference is that the setup message from the root must contain the endpoint reference value of zero and the broad band bearer capability information element must indicate point-to-multipoint in the user plane connection configuration field (see [3]).

The root can request the addition of a new leaf by sending an add party message on the signaling virtual channel. The message has the same call reference value as specified in the initial set-up of the connection. It also contains the unique endpoint reference value assigned to the leaf. The QOS, bearer capability, and ATM user cell rate are the same for all leaves; thus, these are not indicated in the message. If the network can include the new leaf into the connection, it returns an add party acknowledge message. Otherwise, an add party reject message is returned with the appropriate cause number.

Similarly, the root can initiate the deletion of an existing leaf with a *drop party* message. After the network releases the leaf, a drop party acknowledge is returned to the root. A release message from the root will terminate the entire connection and all leaves. Alternatively, the network can initiate the deletion of a leaf with a drop party message or terminate the connection with release messages.

9.2.1.3   Metasignaling

Access signaling is normally exchanged across an UNI on a pre-established point-to-point signaling virtual channel indicated by VPI = 0, VCI = 5 in the headers of signaling cells. However, there may be multiple users or signaling endpoints sharing a single UNI that require their own signaling virtual channels. In that case, metasignaling is needed for the assignment and removal of individual signaling virtual channels [9]. Metasignaling messages are listed in Table 9.1.

Table 9.1
Metasignaling Messages

Message	Function
Assign Request	Sent by the user to request allocation of signaling resources
Assigned	Response from the network after successful allocation of signaling resources
Denied	Response from the network after unsuccessful allocation of signaling resources
Check Request	Sent by the network to verify the assignment of signaling resources
Check Response	Response by the user to a *Check Request*
Removed	Sent by user or network to indicate the removal of one or more signaling endpoints

Metasignaling between the user and network is carried on a pre-established metasignaling virtual channel indicated by VPI = 0, VCI = 1. A metasignaling VC between users, identified by VCI = 1 in any virtual path (other than VPI = 0), can be used to establish and manage signaling VCs within that virtual path.

In requesting a signaling VC, the metasignaling message identifies a service profile (if service profiles are implemented by the network provider). A service profile is a collection of information maintained by the network that characterizes a set of services to be provided to the user (e.g., subscription parameters, directory numbers, interface configuration). The service profile associates a level of service with the requested signaling VC.

Metasignaling messages are handled with the same CAC functional blocks as signaling messages. When a user requests a signaling VC, its service profile (according to the service profile identifier) is looked up to determine its level of service. A signaling VC is allocated resources and assigned a VCI value, which is passed to the user. The CAC updates its database to indicate that a signaling VC has been activated and allocated resources, and the CAC generates UPC parameters for the new signaling VC.

9.2.1.4 Message Formats

As described in Section 3.3, Q.2931 signaling messages have the general format shown in Figure 3.4. Every message contains these information elements:

- Protocol discriminator (1 byte);
- Call reference (4 bytes);
- Message type (2 bytes);
- Message length (2 bytes);
- Message-specific information elements (variable-length).

The 1-byte protocol-discriminator information element is used to distinguish user-network signaling messages from other types of messages. Normally, this field should be coded with the value of 9 to indicate B-ISDN access signaling.

The protocol discriminator is followed by the 4-byte call-reference information element. It consists of a 4-bit field of all zeros; 4 bits for the length (number of bytes) of the call-reference value, which should be coded with the value of 3; a one-bit flag; and a 23-bit call-reference value. The call-reference flag indicates whether the message is from the side originating the call reference (flag = 0) or to that side (flag = 1).

The call-reference value is assigned by the originating side at the beginning of the call. It is a unique value only within a particular signaling virtual channel. It remains fixed for the duration of the call. After the call, the call-reference value is released and can be used for a later call. The value of all zeros is reserved to indicate that the message pertains to all call references associated with the signaling virtual channel.

The 2-byte message-type information element identifies the function of the message. The first byte indicates the message type as listed in Table 9.2. The second byte contains fields for additional detailed actions, but for present purposes, is specified as coded to all zeros.

Table 9.2
First Byte of Message-Type Information Element in Q.2931 Messages

Code	Meaning
00000001	Alerting
00000010	Call Proceeding
00000011	Progress
00000101	Setup

Code	Meaning
00000111	Connect
00001101	Setup Acknowledge
00001111	Connect Acknowledge
01000110	Restart
01001101	Release
01001110	Restart Acknowledge
01011010	Release Complete
01101110	Notify
01110101	Status Enquiry
01111011	Information
01111101	Status
10000000	Add Party
10000001	Add Party Acknowledge
10000010	Add Party Reject
10000011	Drop Party
10000100	Drop Party Acknowledge

The 2-byte message-length information element identifies the number of bytes of the remaining message-specific variable-length information elements. There are many message-specific information elements that can be included, omitted, or repeated in a message (they may appear in any order but repeated information elements must occur consecutively). Some notable examples of information elements are listed in Table 9.3.

Table 9.3
Notable Examples of Message-Specific Information Elements in Q.2931 Messages

Information Element	Function
AAL parameters	To indicate the user requested AAL parameters for the connection (carried transparently end-to-end)

Table 9.3 (continued)

Information Element	Function
ATM traffic descriptor	To specify the traffic parameters for traffic control; peak cell rate is mandatory (including F5 OAM flow if OAM traffic descriptor is present)
Broadband bearer capability	To specify the ITU-T bearer service class, e.g., A, C, X
Broadband low-layer information	To allow compatibility checking by an addressed entity (carried transparently from calling user to addressed entity)
Broadband high-layer information	To allow compatibility checking by an addressed entity (carried transparently from calling user to addressed entity)
Cause	To explain the reason for certain messages to aid diagnostics
Call state	To describe the current state of a call/connection
Called-party number	To identify the called party
Called-party subaddress	To identify the subaddress of the called party
Calling-party number	To identify the originator of call
Calling-party subaddress	To identify the subaddress of the originator of call
Connection identifier	To identify local ATM connection resources on the interface, including virtual-path-connection identifier and virtual-channel identifier
End-to-end transit delay	To indicate the maximum acceptable one-way end-to-end transit delay between users
OAM traffic descriptor	To indicate the presence and handling of the end-to-end F5 OAM flow associated with the user connection (if present, ATM traffic descriptor is peak cell rate for user cells + F5 OAM flow)
QOS parameter	To specify a particular QOS class (in addition to end-to-end transit delay)
Transit network selection	To identify a requested transit carrier network

For instance, a *setup* message must contain the ATM traffic descriptor, broadband bearer capability, connection identifier, and QOS parameter; optionally, it might include several additional information elements such as the calling-party number, called-party number, AAL parameters, end-to-end transit delay, OAM traffic descriptor, and transit network selection. A *connect* message might optionally contain AAL parameters, connection identifier, and end-to-end transit delay. A *release* message must contain a cause information element. The exact contents of messages involve a great amount of details, which are documented in [2,3].

9.2.2 Interoffice Signaling

The high-layer signaling protocol between ATM switching systems (across the public NNI) is the ITU-T standard BISUP, which was derived from the ISDN user part of signaling system number 7 [4–8,10,11] (for the private NNI, a symmetric Q.2931 protocol is being specified by the ATM Forum). The initial specifications referred to as BISUP Capability Set 1 (CS1) are designed for the control of simple point-to-point single-connection calls with no in-call bandwidth modification. BISUP messages for call control are listed in Table 3.2 and the BISUP message format is shown in Figure 3.5.

9.2.2.1 BISUP

Interoffice signaling proceeds from the originating switch (interfacing with the calling user) through intermediate switches to a destination switch (interfacing with the called user). An example of the procedure for a successful connection is shown in Figure 9.5.

When a switch receives a *setup* message from a user, it has an outgoing call to propagate to the destination switch, where the called user is located. The originating switch must select a route based on information in the *setup* message (e.g., called-party number, broadband bearer capability, ATM traffic descriptor, and transit network selection), the user's subscribed service, and state of network resources. Routing information is assumed to be available at the switch or accessible at a remote database. Within a carrier network, the algorithm for route selection will most likely be proprietary (see Section 9.3.2).

After the next switch is selected, appropriate VPCI/VCI values and bandwidth are assigned if available. The originating switch sends an *initial address message* (IAM) containing all of the information required to route the call to the destination switch and called user, i.e., called-party number, broadband bearer capability, ATM traffic descriptor, calling party's category (usually "ordinary calling subscriber"), and other parameters.

When the IAM is received at the next switch, an *IAM acknowledgment* (IAA) is returned in confirmation. This intermediate switch makes a routing

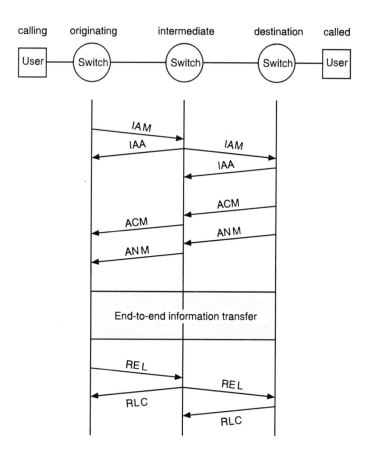

Figure 9.5 BISUP messages for a successful point-to-point call.

selection and follows the same procedure to send an IAM to the next switch. When the IAM finally reaches the destination switch, it returns an IAA as usual. After determining the called user, it checks whether the user is allowed to receive the call. If the call is allowed, the switch sends a *setup* message and waits for a response from the user.

The user may respond first with a *call proceeding* message to indicate recognition of the call request. This may be followed by an *alerting* message, which indicates that the user is being alerted. When the switch has determined that the complete called-party number has been received and the called user is being alerted, it sends an *address complete* message (ACM) backward through the network. An ACM might also be sent if there has been no user response after a certain time since the *setup* message; the switch sends an ACM backward to indicate no action and sends another *setup* message to the user.

The user must eventually respond with a *connect* message in order to accept the call. When the user responds with a *connect*, the switch returns an *answer* message (ANM) backward to notify all nodes and the calling user that the connection is active and charging can begin.

At any point in the setup procedure, a switch can block the call with an *IAM reject* (IAR) message in response to an IAM. The IAR contains a cause number to explain the reason for blocking, e.g.:

- #47 "resource unavailable—unspecified;"
- #45 "no VPCI/VCI available;"
- #51 "user cell rate not available."

If the call is blocked, the switch receiving the IAR might attempt an alternate route. If all attempts fail, the switch will return a *release* message (REL) backward to the originating switch, which in turn sends a *release* to the calling user.

The procedure for clearing a call is similar regardless of which user initiates it. A REL initiates release of the VPI/VCI values and assigned bandwidth so that they may be used again for a future connection. When these are released, a *release complete* (RLC) is returned in response to the REL.

In addition to the messages in Table 3.2 for call control, there are a number of BISUP messages useful for maintenance control. For example, a *blocking* (BLO) message initiated by a VPC endpoint can make a specified VP unavailable for user cells; it is confirmed with a *blocking acknowledgment* (BLA) from the other VP endpoint. The VP remains available to carry test cells for verifying the consistency of the VPC. After testing, the VP can be made available again for user cells by *unblocking* (UBL) and *unblocking acknowledgment* (UBA) messages. For other messages and more details, the interested reader is referred to the standards and references.

9.2.2.2   *Message Formats*

As described in Section 3.3, BISUP messages have the general format shown in Figure 3.5. Every message contains these fields:

- Routing label (4 or 7 bytes);
- Message-type code (1 byte);
- Message length (1 or 2 bytes);
- Message-compatibility information (1 byte);
- Message content (variable length).

The routing labels are unchanged from ISUP messages. The standard international routing label is 4 bytes, and the U.S. national routing label is 7 bytes. It contains codes for the origination and destination points. All BISUP messages in a virtual connection use the same routing label.

The message-type code defines the function and format of the message. These codes are given for the BISUP messages listed in Table 9.4.

Table 9.4
Message-Type Codes for BISUP Messages for Call Control

Code	Message Type
00000001	Initial Address (IAM)
00000010	Subsequent Address (SAM)
00000110	Address Complete (ACM)
00001001	Answer (ANM)
00001010	IAM Acknowledgment (IAA)
00001011	IAM Reject (IAR)
00001100	Release (REL)
00001101	Suspend (SUS)
00001110	Resume (RES)
00010000	Release Complete (RLC)
00101100	Call Progress (CPG)

The message length is the number of bytes of the message content (excluding the routing label, message-type code, message length, and message-compatibility information).

The message-compatibility information defines the switch behavior in the event that the message is not understood. This is a possibility because the signaling protocol is expected to undergo a number of revisions. New protocol versions should be transparent to existing equipment. Hence, all messages contain compatibility handling directives (as seen later, each parameter within a message also has compatibility information). Examples of actions are pass message; discard message; release call; or send notification.

The message content consists of a variable number of parameters that are specific to each type of message. Every parameter consists of these parts:

- *Parameter name* (1 byte);
- *Length indicator* (1 or 2 bytes): the number of bytes of parameter content;

- *Parameter-compatibility information* (1 or 2 bytes): to define the switch behavior if the parameter is not understood;
- *Parameter content* (variable length): parameter-specific subfields.

Some notable examples of parameters are listed in Table 9.5. In most cases, the BISUP message carries the same parameters as the corresponding access signaling message. For example, the ATM traffic descriptor, broadband bearer capability, called-party number, OAM traffic descriptor, and transit network selection, and other information elements contained in the *setup* message are mapped directly into corresponding parameters in the IAM message (the end-to-end transit delay information field is mapped into a field in the propagation delay counter parameter). Details about the BISUP parameters can be found in [7,11,12].

Table 9.5
Notable Examples of Message-Specific Parameters in BISUP Messages

Parameter	Function
AAL parameters	To indicate the user-requested AAL parameters for the connection (carried transparently end-to-end)
ATM traffic descriptor	To specify the traffic parameters for traffic control; peak cell rate is mandatory (including F5 OAM flow if OAM traffic descriptor is present)
Broadband bearer capability	To specify the ITU-T bearer service class, e.g., A, C, X
Broadband low-layer information	To allow compatibility checking by an addressed entity (carried transparently from calling user to addressed entity)
Broadband high-layer information	To allow compatibility checking by an addressed entity (carried transparently from calling user to addressed entity)
Cause	To explain the reason for certain messages to aid diagnostics
Called-party number	To identify the called party
Called-party subaddress	To identify the subaddress of the called party
Calling-party number	To identify the originator of call
Calling-party subaddress	To identify the subaddress of the originator of call
Connection-element identifier	To identify local ATM connection resources on the interface, including virtual-path-connection identifier and virtual-channel identifier

Table 9.5 (continued)

Parameter	Function
OAM traffic descriptor	To indicate the presence and handling of the end-to-end F5 OAM flow associated with the user connection (if present, ATM traffic descriptor is peak cell rate for user cells + F5 OAM flow)
Propagation delay counter	To indicate the propagation delay of a call in ms accumulated during call set-up
QOS information	To specify a particular QOS class
Transit network selection	To identify a requested transit carrier network

9.2.3 Signaling AAL

The CAC receives and sends Q.2931 and BISUP signaling messages encapsulated in ATM cells. In order to interpret the high-layer signaling messages, the CAC performs the SAAL functions, which reside between the high-layer signaling protocols and the ATM layer. As shown in Figure 9.6, SAAL consists of a common part and a service-specific convergence sublayer (SSCS) [13]. The SAAL common part is the AAL5 common part (refer to Appendix C). The SSCS is further divided into *service-specific coordination functions* (SSCF) and a *service-specific connection-oriented protocol* (SSCOP). Strictly speaking, SSCF and SSCOP are not protocol sublayers (in the OSI sense) but a separation of functions.

9.2.3.1 SSCF

There are two versions of SSCF for the UNI [14] and the NNI [15]. In general, the SSCF was designed to allow the exchange of messages between high-layer signaling entities by using the services of the lower SSCOP. It provides for the establishment and release of two types of connections to the signaling entities: *assured* and *unacknowledged* (unassured). For assured connections, variable-length signaling messages (up to 4,096 bytes) are carried with protection from loss, misinsertion, corruption, and disordering. For unacknowledged connections, signaling messages are not protected from possible loss, misinsertion, or disordering.

These connections are managed by specified procedures for invoking the services of SSCOP. It might be noticed from Figure 9.6 that there is no communication between peer SSCF entities, i.e., SSCF does not add or remove AAL

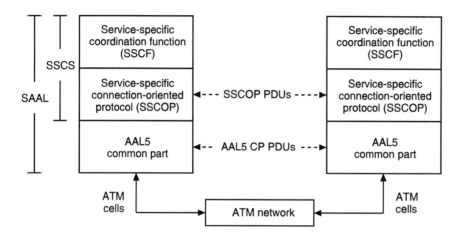

Figure 9.6 SAAL sublayers.

information to the signaling messages. The only actions of SSCF are passing data between the higher layer signaling entity (Q.2931 or BISUP) and SSCOP, and invoking the services of SSCOP. Thus, SSCF is merely a coordination function that maps SSCOP services to the needs of the higher layer signaling entities. To invoke SSCOP services, it follows procedures and state-transition diagrams whose details are specified in [14,15].

9.2.3.2 SSCOP

SSCOP uses the unguaranteed delivery service of the SAAL common part to provide a reliable transport service of variable-length data units up to 65,527 bytes between its users (i.e., SSCF entities) [16]. SSCOP relies on error detection in AAL5 and adds loss-recovery and error-control functions above the AAL5 common part. Specific functions are:

- Preserves sequence of data units received from SSCF;
- Loss detection and recovery by retransmission;
- Connection control (establishment and release);
- Flow control;
- Assured and unassured transport of data units.

These functions are performed by means of messages (SSCOP protocol data units or PDUs) between peer SSCOP entities. The set of SSCOP messages are shown in Table 9.6. These messages have different formats, but all contain a four-bit PDU type field, which identifies the message function according to the codes in Table 9.6. As an example, the format of a *sequenced data* (SD) message used for error-free sequential data transfer is shown in Figure 9.7 (transmitted from left to right). It consists of these fields:

- *Information field* (variable length up to 65,527 bytes);
- *PAD* (0–3 bytes): padding to make the SD message an integer multiple of four bytes;
- *PL* (2 bits): length of PAD in bytes;
- *RES* (2 bits): reserved;
- *PDU* type (4 bits): message function (PDU type = 1000 denotes SD message);
- *SN* (3 bytes): sequence number.

Table 9.6
SSCOP Protocol Data Units

PDU Type	Code	Function
Begin (BGN)	0001	Request a new connection establishment or re-establish an existing connection
Begin acknowledge (BGAK)	0010	Acknowledge acceptance of a connection request
Begin reject (BGREJ)	0111	Reject a connection request
End	0011	Release a connection
End acknowledge (ENDAK)	0100	Confirm the release of a connection
Resynchronization command (RS)	0101	Resynchronize the buffers and state variables in the forward direction of a connection
Resynchronization acknowledge (RSAK)	0110	Acknowledge the resynchronization
Sequenced data (SD)	1000	Transfer sequentially numbered data units from SSCF
Sequenced data with poll (SDP)	1001	Transfer sequentially numbered data units from SSCF and request status information
Status request (POLL)	1010	Request for status information
Solicited status response (STAT)	1011	Returns status information in response to POLL or SDP messages
Unsolicited status response (USTAT)	1100	Respond to detection of missing SD or SDP PDU based on sequence numbers

PDU Type	Code	Function
Unnumbered data (UD)	1101	Unassured transfer of data units from SSCF without sequence numbers
Management data (MD)	1110	Unassured transfer of management data between SSCOP entities

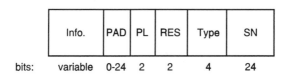

bits: variable   0-24   2   2   4   24

Figure 9.7 Format of SSCOP SD message.

Connection establishment is initiated by a *begin* message, and acknowledged with a *begin acknowledge* (BGAK) or rejected by a *begin reject* (BGREJ). Connection release is done by an *end* message confirmed by an *end acknowledge* (ENDAK).

Data not requiring error control may be sent within *unnumbered data* (UD) messages that do not have sequence numbers. In the error-controlled data transfer, SD messages (carrying SSCF data) with sequence numbers are transmitted. These are not acknowledged individually, but a group of them may be acknowledged with a *solicited status response* (STAT) message in response to a *status request* (POLL) or *sequenced data with poll* (SDP) message. Lost and corrupted data may be detected by the transmitter by this means. A missing SD message may be detected by the receiver based on sequence numbers, in which case the receiver will send an *unsolicited status response* (USTAT) to inform the transmitter. Specific details can be found in [16].

9.3 RESOURCE ALLOCATION

Thus far we have discussed signaling, the means by which the CAC communicates with users and other switches to coordinate the actions taken on connections. The other task of the CAC functional block is making decisions about the acceptance or rejection of new connection requests. It will follow a connection-admission policy that will probably be proprietary to the network provider. In B-ISDN, the connection-admission decision making is complicated by the existence of connections with widely different characteristics and QOS requirements. It is unclear how to decide acceptance or rejection of connections among different services on a fair and equitable basis. For instance, acceptance of a high-bandwidth connection could result in the blocking of a number of low connections. For fairness, it has been proposed to divide the bandwidth resources into separate *bandwidth pools* for each type of service, and a new connection cannot use bandwidth reserved for other types of services [17].

In order to make decisions, the CAC must have information about the new connection (from the signaling information and subscriber's service parameters), available resources, and existing traffic. The admission decision depends on a resource-allocation algorithm that determines whether and where sufficient network resources are available. If sufficient resources cannot be found, the connection request is denied immediately. If resources are available, the admission decision can proceed; acceptance may not be immediate if the decision must take additional factors into consideration, e.g., priorities or fairness.

The main issue in resource allocation is how resources are judged to be sufficient or insufficient for the requested connection. Although a considerable number of studies have been done, there has been little validation of theories with real experiences. Validation will become possible as ATM networks are deployed more widely. This section discusses three factors considered in resource allocation: virtual paths, route selection, and QOS estimation.

9.3.1 Virtual Paths

Recall from Sections 2.5.2 and 4.3.4 that ATM connections exist at both levels of virtual paths and virtual channels. Figure 9.8 shows an example of virtual-path connections. Nodes A, C, and D are endpoints of three virtual-path connections designated as VPC1, VPC2, and VPC3 (through node B). As a VPC connecting point, node B is a VP switch or VP crossconnect; it routes cells according to their VPI values only. A number of VCCs may exist within each VPC, and multiple VPCs may exist on a physical link. It has been noted that statistical multiplexing at the VP and VC levels may be independent of each other [18]. That is, VCCs may be statistically multiplexed or segregated (allocated peak rates) within a VPC, and VPCs may be statistically multiplexed or segregated on a physical link.

The use of VPs have been advocated to simplify CAC [18–24]. For example, suppose a new VCC is requested in VPC1. Nodes A and D determine whether sufficient bandwidth is available in VPC1, and, if so, establish the new VCC; if insufficient, the bandwidth allocated to VPC1 is increased (if possible) or else the new VCC is denied. No call processing is required at node B because it is not concerned with connections at the VC level. The addition of a new VCC does not require routing changes or bandwidth allocation decisions at node B. Once VPC1 has been established at node B, it need not be involved in subsequent set-ups of VCCs within VPC1. This reduces the amount of processing involved in VCC establishment as well as the implementation complexity of VPC connecting points (i.e., VP switches and crossconnects).

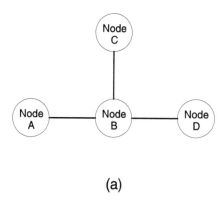

(a)

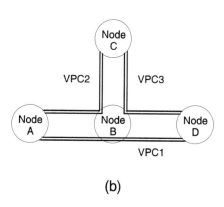

(b)

Figure 9.8 (a) Physical interconnection of four nodes, and (b) virtual path connections between the nodes.

Virtual paths also offer advantages for managing existing connections. For instance, a group of VCCs can be policed more simply together as a VPC, requiring one UPC/NPC mechanism instead of many. In addition, the paths of multiple VCCs may be changed simultaneously by simple routing changes at the VP level. For example, suppose that VPC1 has a back-up virtual path VPC4 along a different route between the same two endpoints, nodes A and D. In normal operation, VPC4 is inactive and has no reserved bandwidth. If VPC1 fails, however, the sources are given a new VPI value corresponding to VPC4, and all the traffic in VPC1 is immediately routed along the back-up VPC4. The VCCs do not have to be rerouted individually.

Different strategies have been suggested for allocating bandwidth to VPCs on a physical link and to VCCs within a VPC. A simplistic approach based on peak-rate allocation (without statistical multiplexing) is proposed in [21,23]. When a new VCC is requested, its peak cell rate is compared with the available (allocated but unused) bandwidth of an appropriate VPC along the desired route. If the available bandwidth is sufficient, the new VCC is accepted and its peak rate is allocated. If insufficient, the bandwidth of the VP is increased by constant increments if possible, until it is sufficient to accept the call; if impossible—if not enough link bandwidth is available—the VCC is denied. An analysis is provided under the assumption of Poisson arrivals for VCC requests and exponential holding times. The allocated bandwidth of VPCs are calculated such that the blocking probability for VCCs is bounded.

Statistical multiplexing of virtual paths is considered in [19]. A reserved-mode connection is proposed, where a VPC is guaranteed a minimum bandwidth W_1 that can be increased to a predetermined amount $W_1 + W_2$ when needed, if sufficient bandwidth is available. The bandwidth is reduced from $W_1 + W_2$ back down to W_1 when the extra bandwidth is not used. This scheme allows the physical-link bandwidth to be statistically shared among VPCs as needed, while also maintaining a minimum guaranteed bandwidth per VPC.

Two variations of a similar scheme for statistically multiplexing VPCs are studied in [25]. In the first variation, VPCs have no reserved bandwidth when idle, and the bandwidth jumps to a predetermined amount W (same for all VPCs) when the VPC is active, if sufficient link bandwidth is available. In the second variation, VPCs may have different values of W depending on the type of service.

A comparison of two bandwidth-allocation schemes is made in [26]. In the first scheme, no link bandwidth is reserved for any VPCs; all traffic is statistically multiplexed without regard to the data's VPC. In the second scheme, an amount of link bandwidth is reserved for each VPC and the amount is adjusted at periodic time intervals according to usage measurements. Under given traffic assumptions, the two schemes are evaluated in terms of required bandwidth and control costs. It is concluded that the strategy of reserving bandwidth to VPCs can provide significant advantages if the cost of bandwidth is relatively less than control costs.

An elaborate bandwidth-allocation scheme is proposed for statistically multiplexing VCCs within a VPC in [27,28]. First, each VCC flow is monitored—each flow's first two statistical moments (average and variance) are estimated from cell counts. Assuming that VCCs are independent, the sum of the moments of all VCCs is used to estimate the moments of the total traffic flow. Next, by matching the moments, the total traffic flow is modeled by a renewal process with hyperexponentially distributed interarrivals. The bandwidth of the VPC is estimated from a queuing model with this hyperexponentially distributed arrival process and deterministic (constant) service times, such that the estimated cell-loss probability is less than a given bound.

9.3.2 Route Selection

A resource-allocation algorithm seeks a route with sufficient resources at each node. A choice among multiple paths may be necessary, and routing (or path computation) generally attempts to select routes to maximize the long-term network throughput by uniformly distributing traffic to utilize the network efficiently while minimizing end-to-end delays. Although an extensive amount of work has been done on routing in conventional packet-switched networks (e.g., see [29,30]), there has not been much research on routing specific to ATM networks.

Some early progress on routing has been made by the ATM Forum for the private NNI. For the private NNI, agreement has been reached on multilevel hierarchical link-state routing, although the details are still under development. Within each level, routing is done between *peer groups*, which are collections of switches or individual switches (at the lowest level). The higher level routing will work correctly even if a lower level peer group is using different routing internally, as long as it exhibits the correct external behavior.

In link-state routing, each node typically monitors the state of its links (in terms of certain defined parameters) and, when the parameters change significantly, broadcasts the new link-state information to all other nodes. Each node keeps a view of the entire network state based on the link-state messages received from the other nodes. It calculates the shortest (or optimal according to some criteria) path using the well known Dijkstra's algorithm or a variation. An example of link-state routing is *open shortest path first* (OSPF), an interior gateway protocol developed for the Internet.

It is most likely that network providers will have a large amount of freedom to implement their own route-selection algorithms within constraints for internetworking. While it would be desirable to comparatively evaluate routing algorithms, it is probably premature at this time without more experience with actual networks. For the interested reader, several overviews of routing algorithms for packet-switched networks are widely available.

9.3.3 QOS Estimation

Assuming that a prospective route (or set of routes) is selected, each switch along the route must determine whether it has sufficient resources (bandwidth, buffers, processors) to support the throughput and QOS of the new connection. Each switch estimates the required resources and the effect of allocating these resources on the QOS of existing connections. However, before the effect of a new connection can be estimated, the behavior of the source traffic must be well understood. Unfortunately, traffic modeling is the single most difficult and uncertain problem in ATM [31,32]. There is a need for actual traffic measurements to validate traffic models. Also, some types of sources—such as data and video—have widely variable characteristics depending on the application.

Of course, CBR sources can be characterized simply by their constant bit-rate. VBR sources, described by at least the peak cell rate and perhaps the sustainable cell rate and burst tolerance, are more problematic because these parameters may not fully characterize a VBR source. At this time, it is not certain which set of traffic parameters are necessary and sufficient for VBR sources.

VBR speech has fairly consistent characteristics and has been studied extensively for the telephone network. It is considered to be well modeled by an on/off model with exponentially distributed bursts (talkspurts) and idle periods (silences), or by variations of this model with more complicated probability distribution functions for the silences [32].

Data traffic has been traditionally modeled in computer networks by a Poisson process (i.e., independent exponentially distributed times between data messages) or compound Poisson (batches separated by exponential times). However, the Poisson model has been increasingly challenged, particularly for B-ISDN. The packet train, a variation of the on/off model, is an example of an alternate model [33]. A string of packets (train) separated by small intercar intervals is generated when the source is active, and trains are separated by relatively longer intertrain intervals when the source is idle. Also, there is evidence from LAN measurements that data may exhibit a so-called self-similar characteristic; i.e., the burstiness of the data traffic is the same regardless of timescale and traffic aggregation by multiplexing [34].

VBR video is especially difficult to model because the characteristics depend on several factors such as the video content, activity (motion), coding algorithm, and application. Many traffic models have been proposed but are useful as approximations at best. Low-motion videoconference traffic has been modeled both as a continuous-state first-order autoregressive process and a discrete-state, continuous-time Markov process [35]. Based on testbed network measurements, VBR video sources have been characterized by an on/off model where the bursts begin periodically (at the beginning of each frame) and burst lengths are uniformly distributed depending on the instantaneous activity in the video [36]. Other models and variations can be found throughout the literature, e.g., see [31,32].

A number of general VBR traffic models, not particular to any service, have been used in performance analyses. The most common might be the on/off model, where bursts at peak rate alternate with periods of inactivity [17,22,31,32,37–46]. This model is convenient because a queuing analysis of statistically multiplexed on/off sources is tractable, e.g., by the fluid-flow analysis presented in [47]. Another popular traffic model is the Markov-modulated Poisson process, where the rate of the Poisson process varies according to the state of a continuous-time Markov chain [31,32,48].

The importance of certain traffic parameters was studied in [43]. The ratio of the peak rate per connection to the link rate was observed to have a major effect on the maximum link utilization. It is claimed that high-link utilization and significant statistical multiplexing gain is possible when R is less than 0.1. When R is small, it is claimed that minimal source characteristics need to be known for call admission because of the high degree of statistical multiplexing. When R is large, it is more important to know complete source characteristics. Another important parameter is the *traffic density* of a call—the fraction of time that the source is active. It was observed to be more significant when R is large. A higher link utilization can be realized when the traffic density is large.

Assuming the source traffic can be modeled (albeit approximately), the effect of accepting a new connection must be evaluated. Typically, a queuing analysis is performed to calculate cell-loss probabilities. It would be difficult to present a comprehensive survey of the many mathematical treatments that have appeared (the interested reader can readily find them, e.g., see the surveys [22,46]). Also, there is little point in mathematical expositions without more validation of these approaches with real experiences. Instead, a few examples are offered below to highlight some differences among approaches.

Connections are classified into distinct classes in the class-related rule proposed in [38]. Sources are described by their peak rate, average rate, and average burst length. Sources with similar characteristics are classified into the same traffic class. Through simulations for each traffic class, plots of required bandwidth and cell-loss probabilities are derived for statistical multiplexing a number of sources. The plots are used to calculate the bandwidth required for the new connection. The result is added to the bandwidth allocated to the existing connections to determine the total bandwidth. A second calculation is made for the total mean bandwidth, assuming that the new connection belongs to the traffic class requiring the most bandwidth. The class-related rule accepts the new connection if the minimum of the two calculations is less than the link rate.

Instead of grouping connections according to the source characteristics, connections are classified as either deterministic (with a hard delay bound) or statistical (with probabilistic delay bound) in [49]. It is also assumed that cells are assigned deadlines (the desired time of departure) at each switch, and cells with earlier deadlines are given higher service priority. Three tests are suggested to determine whether there is sufficient bandwidth, processing, and buffer space at each node. These tests are called the deterministic test, statistical test, and delay bound test. A new connection is accepted only if the tests are passed at each node along the route. For deterministic connections, the *deterministic test* ensures that sufficient processing capability exists at each node. The test simply determines whether the total peak rates of all deterministic connections exceeds the link rate. The *statistical test* estimates the probability of cells missing their deadlines. This is compared with the allowed probabilistic bound for each statistical connection. The *delay-bound test* determines the minimum delay bound for the new connection so that a feasible schedule exists to meet all deadline constraints.

It is proposed to use the *virtual peak rate* and *virtual mean rate* of sources to calculate worst-case results in [50,51]. The virtual peak rate is calculated from the maximum number of cells measured over any short period of duration T_p. The virtual mean rate is the average rate measured over a longer period T_m. These definitions are proposed because they can be monitored by a simple sliding window UPC. Given the virtual peak and mean rates of sources, an upper bound on the time congestion (the average fraction of time that a buffer is full) is given.

In [52], a new connection is characterized by the average and maximum number of cells within a fixed interval. A method is given for calculating an upper bound on the cell-loss probability. If the probability distribution of the number of cells within a fixed interval is also known, a bound on cell-loss probability is calculated in [53].

The notion is suggested in [37] that a connection can be characterized by an *equivalent bandwidth*. The connection request includes the peak cell rate, the fraction of time the source is active, and the average duration of an active period. From these parameters, the amount of bandwidth required for the QOS of the connection, called the equivalent bandwidth, is calculated by an analytical method described in [37,40]. The new connection is accepted only if the equivalent bandwidth is available on all links along the selected route.

Two components of the buffer-overflow probability, called *cell-scale* and *burst-scale* congestion, have been identified in [44]. Cell-scale congestion is caused by the coincidentally simultaneous arrivals of cells when the total source rate is not greater than the link rate. Burst-scale congestion occurs when the total source rate temporarily exceeds the link rate. It is suggested that the connection-admission policy keeps congestion to either the cell scale (by restricting the total source rate to less than the link rate) or the burst scale (the necessary buffer size then depends on the burstiness of the sources).

9.4 DISTRIBUTION OF CAC

Up to this point, we have discussed the functions of a centralized CAC. It might be noticed from Figure 9.1, however, that the CAC must perform a tremendous amount of processing. It receives signaling cells from the input modules, performs SAAL functions for each signaling cell, and interprets high-layer signaling messages. It then makes decisions about resources and updates all tables. The amount of processing increases with the volume of signaling traffic, which may be proportional to the size of the switch. For large switches, the centralized CAC may become a processing bottleneck.

To overcome this bottleneck, it may be desirable to distribute some of the CAC functions to the input modules and output modules. The portion of CAC functions in the input and output modules are referred to as IM-CACs and OM-CACs, respectively. The precise amount of distribution is dependent on implementation. A trade-off is involved between performance and consistency. As more CAC functions are distributed, the switch is more scalable to larger sizes because the centralized processing bottleneck is alleviated. However, there must be more coordination to ensure that the distributed CAC functions behave consistently, as they affect the common resources of the switch.

As an example, SAAL functions may be distributed to the IM-CAC. The IM recognizes the signaling cells that require processing, extracts them from the cell stream, and passes them to the IM-CAC; the other signaling cells are allowed to pass through the IM to the cell switch fabric like user cells. In this scenario, the IM-CAC carries out the SAAL functions for every signaling cell and extracts the high-layer signaling messages to be interpreted by the centralized CAC function. Relieved of the SAAL processing, the centralized CAC handles only the high-layer signaling protocols and resource-allocation decision making. Likewise, SAAL functions may be distributed to the OM-CAC to encapsulate high-layer signaling messages into outgoing cells.

In an extreme scenario, the CAC functions could be completely distributed. Each IM-CAC could handle all signaling functions and resource allocation for the connections going through that IM. Each IM would then maintain its own information about the switch resources and existing connections. There must be communication between all of the IMs to keep the separate databases consistent and current. Thus, performance becomes more scalable at the cost of possible inconsistency, greater intermodule communications, and more databases.

9.5 CONCLUSIONS

The CAC has two main functions: interaction with users and other switches through signaling, and resource-allocation decisions for requested connections. The signaling information is carried in ATM cells and must be extracted by SAAL functions. The CAC handles the SAAL functions and the higher layer signaling protocols (Q.2931 and BISUP).

With the information about the new connection, the CAC uses its information about network resources and existing traffic to decide on a connection request according to a connection-admission policy. This policy depends on a resource-allocation algorithm, which determines whether and where sufficient switch resources are available. This allocation algorithm will probably be proprietary to the network provider. Several examples of possible approaches have been highlighted, but it is premature to meaningfully evaluate them without more experience with actual networks.

The signaling and resource allocation done by the CAC implies a considerable amount of centralized processing, which may become a bottleneck in large switches. It may be desirable to distribute the CAC functions to the input modules and output modules. The precise amount of distribution depends on a trade-off between performance and consistency. We have suggested an example where the IM-CACs and OM-CACs relieve the centralized CAC of the burden of SAAL processing for each signaling cell. The centralized CAC still handles the high-layer signaling protocols and resource allocation for all connections. Naturally, the CAC may be distributed further. The performance trade-off remains for future study.

References

[1]   Bellcore, *B-ISDN Access Signaling Generic Requirements*, TA-NWT-001111, Issue 1, Aug. 1993.
[2]   ITU-T Draft Rec. Q.2931, *B-ISDN Access Signaling System DSS2 (Digital Subscriber Signaling System No. 2)*, Geneva, Dec. 1993.
[3]   ATM Forum, *ATM User-Network Interface Specification Version 3.0*, Sept. 10, 1993.
[4]   Bellcore, *Broadband Switching System SS7 Requirements Using the Broadband Integrated Services Digital Network User Part (BISUP)*, GR-1417-CORE, Issue 1, Feb. 1994.
[5]   ITU-T Draft Rec. Q.2761, *BISUP—Functional Description*, Geneva, Dec. 1993.
[6]   ITU-T Draft Rec. Q.2762, *BISUP—General Functions of Messages and Signals*, Geneva, Dec. 1993.
[7]   ITU-T Draft Rec. Q.2763, *BISUP—Formats and Codes*, Geneva, Dec. 1993.
[8]   ITU-T Draft Rec. Q.2764, *BISUP—Basic Call Procedures*, Geneva, May 1993.
[9]   ITU-T Draft Rec. Q.1420, *B-ISDN Meta-Signaling Protocol*, Geneva, May 1993.
[10] Bellcore, "General Functions of BISUP Messages and Signals," Chapter BT1.113.2 in *Bell Communications Research Specification of Signaling System Number 7*, TR-NWT-000246, Issue 2, Rev. 3, Dec. 1993.
[11] Bellcore, "B-ISDN User Part (BISUP) Formats and Codes," Chapter BT1.113.3 in *Bell Communications Research Specification of Signaling System Number 7*, TR-NWT-000246, Issue 2, Rev. 3, Dec. 1993.
[12] ITU-T Draft Rec. Q.2650, *Interworking Between Signaling System No. 7 Broadband ISDN User Part (BISUP) and Digital Subscriber Signaling System No. 2 (DSS2)*, Paris, March 1994.
[13] ITU-T Draft Rec. Q.2100, *B-ISDN Signaling ATM Adaptation Layer Overview Description*, Geneva, Nov. 29–Dec. 17, 1993.
[14] ITU-T Draft Rec. Q.2130, *B-ISDN Signaling ATM Adaptation Layer—Service Specific Coordination Function for Support of Signaling at the User-to-Network Interface (SSCF at UNI)*, Geneva, Nov. 29–Dec. 17, 1993.
[15] ITU-T Draft Rec. Q.2140, *B-ISDN Signaling ATM Adaptation Layer—Service Specific Coordination Function for Support of Signaling at the Network-Node Interface (SSCF at NNI)*, Geneva, Nov. 29-Dec. 17, 1993.
[16] ITU-T Draft Rec. Q.2110, *B-ISDN ATM Adaptation Layer—Service Specific Connection Oriented Protocol (SSCOP)*, Geneva, Nov. 29–Dec. 17, 1993.
[17] Cooper, C., and K. Park, "Toward a Broadband Congestion Control Strategy," *IEEE Network Mag.*, Vol. 14, May 1990, pp. 18–23.
[18] Hughes, D., and K. Wajda, "Comparison of Virtual Path Bandwidth Assignment and Routing Methods," *Annals Telecommunications*, Vol. 49, 1994, pp. 80–89.
[19] Aoyama, T., et al., "Introduction Strategy and Technologies for ATM VP-Based Broadband Networks," *IEEE J. on Selected Areas in Commun.*, Vol. 10, Dec. 1992, pp. 1,434–1,447.
[20] Burgin, J., and D. Dorman, "Broadband ISDN Resource Management: The Role of Virtual Paths," *IEEE Communications Mag.*, Sept. 1991, pp. 44–48.
[21] Ohta, S., and K-I. Sato, "Dynamic Bandwidth Control of the Virtual Path in an Asynchronous Transfer Mode Network," *IEEE Trans. on Communications*, Vol. 40, July 1992, pp. 1,239–1,247.

22] Saito, H., et al., "Traffic Control Technologies in ATM Networks," *IEICE Trans.*, Vol. E74, April 1991, pp. 761–771.

23] Sato, K., et al., "Broadband ATM Network Architecture Based on Virtual Paths," *IEEE Trans. on Communications*, Vol. 38, pp. 1212-1222, Aug. 1990.

24] Sato, K., et al., "The Role of Virtual Path Crossconnection," *IEEE LTS*, Aug. 1991, pp. 44–54.

25] Kawamura, R., et al., "Fast VP-Bandwidth Management with Distributed Control in ATM Networks," *IEICE Trans. Communications,* Vol. E77-B, Jan. 1994, pp. 5–14.

26] Burgin, J., "Broadband ISDN Resource Management," *Computer Networks and ISDN Systems*, Vol. 20, 1990, pp. 323–331.

27] Sato, Y., and K-I. Sato, "Virtual Path and Link Capacity Design for ATM Networks," *IEEE J. on Selected Areas in Communications*, Vol. 9, Jan. 1991, pp. 104–111.

28] Yamanaka, N., et al., "Usage Parameter Control and Bandwidth Allocation Methods Considering Cell Delay Variation in ATM Networks," *IEICE Trans. on Communications*, Vol. E76-B, March 1993, pp. 270–279.

29] Bell, P., and K. Jabbour, "Review of Point-to-Point Network Routing Algorithms," *IEEE Communications Mag.*, Vol. 24, Jan. 1986, pp. 34–38.

30] Bertsekas, D., and R. Gallager, *Data Networks*, Englewood Cliffs, NJ: Prentice-Hall, 1987.

31] Bae, J., and T. Suda, "Survey of Traffic Control Schemes and Protocols in ATM Networks," *Proc. of the IEEE*, Vol. 79, Feb. 1991, pp. 170–189.

32] Stamoulis, G., et al., "Traffic Source Models for ATM Networks: A Survey," *Computer Communications*, Vol. 17, June 1994, pp. 428–438.

33] Jain, R., and S. Routhier, "Packet Trains—Measurements and a New Model for Computer Network Traffic," *IEEE J. on Selected Areas in Communications*, Vol. SAC-4, Sept. 1986, pp. 986–995.

34] Leland, W., et al., "On the Self-Similar Nature of Ethernet Traffic," *IEEE/ACM Trans. on Networking*, Vol. 2, Feb. 1994, pp. 1–15.

35] Maglaris, B., et al., "Performance Models of Statistical Multiplexing in Packet Video Communications," *IEEE Trans. on Communications*, Vol. 36, July 1988, pp. 834–844.

36] Hyman, J., et al., "Real-Time Scheduling with Quality Of Service Constraints," *IEEE J. on Selected Areas in Communications*, Vol. 9, Sept. 1991, pp. 1,052–1,063.

37] Cidon, I., et al., "Bandwidth Management and Congestion Control in PlaNET," *IEEE Communications Mag.*, Oct. 1991, pp. 54–64.

38] Gallassi, G., "Resource Management and Dimensioning in ATM Networks," *IEEE Network Mag.*, Vol. 4, May 1990, pp. 8–17.

39] Gilbert, H., et al., "Developing a Cohesive Traffic Management Strategy for ATM Networks," *IEEE Communications Mag.*, Oct. 1991, pp. 36–45.

40] Guerin, R., et al., "Equivalent Capacity and its Application to Bandwidth Allocation in High-Speed Networks," *IEEE J. on Sel. Areas in Communications*, Vol. 9, pp. 968–981, Sept. 1991.

41] Habib, I., and T. Saadawi, "Controlling Flow and Avoiding Congestion in Broadband Networks," *IEEE Communications Mag.*, Oct. 1991, pp. 46–53.

42] Hong, D., and T. Suda, "Congestion Control and Prevention in ATM Networks," *IEEE Network Mag.*, July 1991, pp. 10–16.

43] Ohnishi, H., et al., "Flow Control Schemes and Delay/Loss Tradeoff in ATM Networks," *IEEE J. on Selected Areas in Communications*, Vol. 6, Dec. 1988, pp. 1,609–1,616.

44] Roberts, J., "Variable Bit-Rate Traffic Control in B-ISDN," *IEEE Communications Mag.*, Sept. 1991, pp. 50–56.

45] Turner, J., "Managing Bandwidth in ATM Networks with Bursty Traffic," *IEEE Network*, Vol. 6, Sept. 1992, pp. 50–58.

46] Vakil, F., and H. Saito, "On Congestion Control in ATM Networks," *IEEE LTS*, Aug. 1991, pp. 55–65.

47] Anick, D., et al., "Stochastic Theory of a Data-Handling System with Multiple Sources," *Bell System Technical J.*, Vol. 61, Oct. 1982, pp. 187–194.

[48] Heffes, D., and D. Lucantoni, "A Markov Modulated Characterization of Packetized Voice and Data Traffic and Related Statistical Multiplexer Performance," *IEEE J. on Selected Areas in Communications*, Vol. SAC-4, Sept. 1986, pp. 856–868.

[49] Ferrari, D., and D. Verma, "A Scheme for Real-Time Channel Establishment in Wide-Area Networks," *IEEE J. on Selected Areas in Communications,* Vol. 8, April 1990, pp. 368–379.

[50] Rasmussen, C., et al., "Source-Independent Call Acceptance Procedures in ATM Networks," *IEEE J. on Selected Areas in Communications*, Vol. 9, April 1991, pp. 351–358.

[51] Rasmussen, C., and J. Sorensen, "A Simple Call Acceptance Procedure in an ATM Network," *Computer Networks and ISDN Systems*, Vol. 20, 1990, pp. 197–202.

[52] Saito, H., "Call Admission Control in an ATM Network Using Upper Bound of Cell Loss Probability," *IEEE Trans. on Communications,* Vol. 40, Sept. 1992, pp. 1,512–1,521.

[53] Saito, H., and K. Shiomoto, "Dynamic Call Admission Control in ATM Networks," *IEEE J. on Selected Areas in Communications*, Vol. 9, Sept. 1991, pp. 982–989.

System Management 10

10.1 INTRODUCTION

The previous chapters described four of the five major functional blocks in the ATM-switch architecture model. They involved well-defined functions implied by the user plane and control plane of the B-ISDN protocol reference model. By contrast, this chapter enters a broader, less certain territory related to the management plane, where the ATM standards are not nearly as well developed. It covers the final functional block referred to as *system management* (SM) for the lack of a better term. It is intended to emphasize the system aspect of the switch but is not used in the identical sense as OSI system management, which refers to specific management functions in the application layer. Generally, the SM is responsible for the correct and efficient internal operation of the switching system, and supports networkwide operations and management.

The SM is obviously an important functional block, but it is also the most difficult in several ways. First, management covers an extremely wide spectrum of activities. Historically, management and operations have been enormously labor-intensive and complex in the public switched network. Within the ATM switch, the SM involves the cooperation of all other functional blocks. Indeed, SM functions might be viewed as resident in all of the functional blocks, depending on precisely how the functional partitioning is chosen.

Second, the level of management functions implemented in the switch can vary between minimal to complex. Network operations is largely determined by the network provider and is specified in the standards only to the degree of ensuring interoperability between different networks. It is not necessary to implement sophisticated operations and management to begin to offer basic ATM bearer services. Hence, management and control issues are being studied in the industry much later than other network aspects.

Third, the area of network operations and management is closer to an art than a science. For example, consider the inconsistent use of the terms *network management* and *operations*. In traditional telephony, operations is a broad term that includes the general functions of provisioning, administration, and maintenance [1]. It covers all aspects of installing facilities, bringing them into service, and maintaining their proper and efficient operation. In this case network management refers to a subset of operations responsible for sustaining grade of service and network efficiency in the face of traffic congestion and equipment failures [1,2,39]. It generally involves real-time surveillance, congestion detection, and expansive or restrictive traffic controls.

On the other hand, network management is used more broadly in the context of data networks to mean everything related to planning, implementation, operation, and maintenance [4,5]. It is often categorized into five separate functions: configuration management, fault management, performance management, security management, and accounting management. Operations is not a commonly used term.

Recognizing these difficulties, a functional overview of the SM is shown in Figure 10.1. It is not unique; different partitions of the SM functions are feasible. The diagram is based on the presumption that the SM must perform a few basic tasks:

- Carry out specific management responsibilities;
- Collect and administer management information;
- Communicate with users and network managers;
- Supervise and coordinate all management activities.

These are represented by separate functional blocks in the SM.

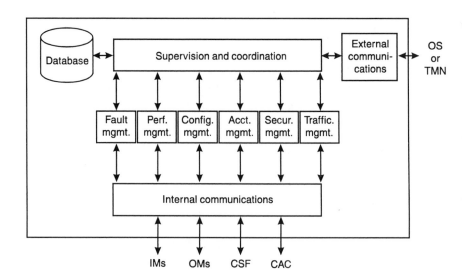

Figure 10.1 Functional diagram of the SM.

The specific management responsibilities, shown as six functional blocks, are consistent with the OSI management functional areas:

- Fault management;
- Performance management;
- Configuration management;
- Accounting management;
- Security management;
- Traffic management.

Traffic management is important to include because of the random and asynchronous nature of ATM. These six functions are categorized together as *operations and maintenance* in Section 10.2. To carry these out, the SM depends on cooperation from the other functional blocks in the switch: input modules, output modules, cell switch fabric, and connection admission control. There is a great deal of intraswitch communications between the SM and the other functional blocks.

Most management activities involve alarms, measurements, statistics, or other types of information. The SM collects such management information in order to make control decisions. This information is also necessary to record and exchange with users and network managers for purposes of control, planning, and provisioning. The administration of management information is the subject of Section 10.3.

The communication of management information to network managers or users will follow protocols, such as the *simple network management protocol* (SNMP) or *common management information protocol* (CMIP). Communications with parties outside of the switch is the topic of Section 10.4.

Section 10.5 discusses the necessity of supervising and coordinating all management activities. For example, a fault might be detected by both fault monitoring and performance monitoring; it would be desirable to correlate data from fault management and performance management.

In Section 10.6, it will be observed that SM functions may be distributed to the input modules and output modules. Indeed, it might be argued that SM functions are inherent in all functional blocks, depending on how the functional partitioning is chosen to be drawn.

10.2 OPERATIONS AND MAINTENANCE

A few specific management responsibilities can be identified within system management. In Chapter 3, the management plane in the B-ISDN protocol reference model was seen to include: fault management, performance management, configuration management, accounting management, and security management (consistent with OSI management functional areas). Traffic management can be included as well because of its importance in ATM (see Chapter 4). These management functions operate more or less independently according to defined procedures. Of these functions, fault management and performance management have been addressed the most in the current standards for the physical and ATM layers.

As described in Chapter 6, the SONET-based physical layer uses overhead fields in the SONET frame for the F1-F3 OAM flows [6]. The F1-F3 flows correspond to the SONET section, line, and path levels. The SONET overhead is processed in the input modules, where the incoming SONET signals are terminated, but overhead information is reported to the SM. The SM collects overhead information from all input modules, decides on the appropriate actions, and sends instructions to the output modules, where the outgoing SONET signals are generated.

In the ATM layer, recall from Chapter 3 that OAM information is carried in F4 and F5 OAM flows [6]. Switches acting as endpoints can generate, insert, process, and terminate OAM cells. Switches acting as connecting points can monitor passing OAM cells and insert new cells but cannot terminate them. The input modules will recognize OAM cells and, if appropriate, route them to the SM for processing. After processing, the SM will decide on the appropriate control actions and may generate new OAM cells to the output modules for transmission.

10.2.1   Fault Management

Fault management is responsible for detection, isolation, and recovery from troubles such as failures. It depends on alarm surveillance, the continuous monitoring and reporting of troubles. Another part of fault management is mechanisms for fault localization and testing. Fault management is performed in both physical layer and ATM layer.

10.2.1.1   Physical Layer

As described in Chapter 6, the input modules terminate incoming SONET signals and process the SONET overhead [7–9]. These types of faults may be detected:

- Loss of signal (LOS);
- Loss of frame (LOF);
- Loss of pointer (LOP);
- Troubles on the APS channel;
- Loss of synchronization;
- STS or VT signal label mismatch.

The IMs also look for incoming messages in the form of:

- AIS, RDI, and RFI signals;
- Embedded operations channels.

In addition to SONET signal processing, the IMs detect internal equipment failures and loss of cell delineation.

All physical layer fault information is reported to the SM, which then determines the appropriate actions, if any are required beyond the automatic actions of the IMs (e.g., protection switching). Actions may consist of instructing the output modules to generate the appropriate overhead in the outgoing SONET signals:

- Downstream line or path AIS;
- Upstream line RDI or path RFI;
- Embedded operations channels.

Other actions of the SM could include isolation of faults using the testing, diagnostics, and loopback functions mentioned in Section 6.3.3.3.

10.2.1.2 ATM Layer

From Chapter 3, recall that the ATM layer uses F4 and F5 OAM fault management cells for alarm surveillance, continuity checks, and loopback testing [6,10]. The input modules will recognize OAM fault-management cells and, if appropriate, extract or copy them for processing by the SM. The OAM cells are routed to the SM for processing. The SM determines the appropriate actions according to the ATM layer fault-management procedures. The SM may generate outgoing OAM cells and send them to the output modules.

If the SM detects an uncorrected physical layer failure, it generates AIS cells to notify downstream nodes of the failure. In response to incoming AIS cells, the SM will generate AIS cells in the same direction if the switch is a connecting point or generate RDI cells in the reverse direction if it is an endpoint. In response to incoming RDI cells, the SM will generate RDI cells in the same direction if the SM is a connecting point or terminate them if it is an endpoint.

In the continuity-check procedure, the SM may be informed by the input modules about idle virtual connections with no continuity check cells, in which case the SM will generate RDI cells upstream. On the output side, the SM will generate continuity check cells to the output modules as required for idle virtual connections.

The SM may respond to incoming loopback cells or generate a loopback cell upon request from network management. Incoming loopback cells are either passed along (if the switch is a connecting point), looped back (if the switch is the loopback point), or terminated (if the switch is the originator).

10.2.2 Performance Management

Performance management concerns the evaluation of how well the system is carrying out its designed functions by means of continuous performance monitoring and reporting. Within the ATM switching system, performance monitoring covers:

- Physical layer transmission;
- VPCs/VCCs in the ATM layer;
- ATM and AAL protocol processing.

10.2.2.1 Physical Layer

As in fault management, SONET uses overhead bytes for in-service monitoring of transmission quality. Performance parameters include:

- Errored seconds;
- Severely errored seconds;
- Coding violations (BIP errors);
- Pointer justifications;
- Unavailable seconds.

The complete list of parameters monitored at each level can be found in Section 6.3.3 and [7]. These parameters are measured over specific time intervals and recorded in the input modules.

The accumulated performance data can be read by the SM upon query. The IMs also contain thresholds for certain parameters and automatically report threshold crossings to the SM when they occur. The SM determines if and what actions are appropriate, e.g., reconfiguration or repair.

10.2.2.2 ATM Layer

In Chapter 3, it was noted that OAM performance-management cells are used in the ATM layer for performance monitoring and reporting [6,10]. In the forward monitoring procedure, OAM cells are transmitted between blocks of user cells. The OAM cells contain the preceding block size (in number of user cells), an error-detection code computed over the information fields of the block, and an optional timestamp. At the destination endpoint, the switch can infer the number of lost/misinserted cells and detect bit errors. From the timestamp field, the switch can observe the relative distribution of cell delays. The results are reported backward in the reverse OAM flow.

As with OAM fault-management cells, the input modules will recognize OAM performance-management cells. Forward monitoring cells will be allowed to pass through if the switch is a connecting point; the IM may monitor (copy and process nonintrusively) them as an option. If the switch is an endpoint, the IM must count the number of user cells in the block preceding the OAM cell and calculate the BIP-16 code over the cell block. The OAM cell will be processed and terminated. The IM will report the results to the SM. The SM may keep counts of: errored blocks, errored cells, lost cells, misinserted cells, total transmitted cells, and total received cells. The SM will generate a backward reporting cell with the results and send it to the output module to be sent in the reverse OAM flow.

Incoming backward reporting cells will be passed through by the IM if the switch is a connecting point. If the switch is an endpoint, the IM will record the results contained in the cell and terminate it. All information is reported to the SM.

It is important to note that OAM performance-management cells require special handling at the input modules for two reasons. First, they must maintain their relative positions within the user cell stream (so that the cell block sizes remain fixed). Hence, the OAM cells cannot be extracted from the user cell stream at the IMs, processed by the SM, and then re-inserted later at the output modules unless they can be guaranteed to resume their original positions in the user cell stream. OAM performance-management cells must be monitored within the input modules without extracting them from the user cell stream. Second, the OAM performance-monitoring procedure requires a cell count and error check to be calculated over the user cell block. This must be done within the input module. The OAM performance-management cell should be processed in the input module, rather than the SM, because the SM does not see the user cells.

10.2.2.3 ATM and AAL Protocol Monitoring

Protocol monitoring checks that the ATM cell headers and AAL information are processed correctly (AAL processing within the switch will be required for signaling cells and ILMI cells, for example). For cell-header processing, possible anomalies might be:

- Cells discarded due to HEC violations;
- Out of cell delineation anomalies (when seven consecutive cells are discarded due to HEC violations);
- Cells discarded due to ATM-layer error (e.g., unassigned VPI/VCI, reserved PT).

Because cell header processing is performed in the IMs, these anomalies can be detected there. The IMs may report counts of these events or an alert of threshold crossing to the SM. Supplementary information may well be included, e.g., time of occurrence, reason for discarding, VPI/VCI, or type of cell (user or OAM).

For user data cells, no AAL processing is involved because the information fields are carried transparently through the switch. However, the switch must perform some AAL processing for signaling cells and ILMI cells [11]. Protocol monitoring checks that the AAL processing is done correctly. There are various fields in the AAL PDUs useful for detecting errors, misassembly, length violation, or other errors at the destination. The AAL fields and possible errors depend on the particular AAL type. For details, the reader should consult Appendixes A to C and [12,13].

In particular, it may be important for the switch to monitor SAAL processing, consisting of the common part of AAL5 and SSCOP (see Chapter 9). Since SSCF does not involve additional protocol information, it is not monitored. For SSCOP, these anomalies might be detected:

- Loss of SSCOP connection;
- Inability to establish SSCOP connection;
- Re-establishment or resynchronization of SSCOP connection;
- PDU retransmission;
- Errored PDU received.

These are monitored wherever the SAAL is processed, whether it is in the input modules or the CAC. As usual, anomalies are recorded and reported to the SM.

Protocol monitoring is also done on the high-layer signaling protocols above SAAL, i.e., BISUP and Q.2931. Examples of protocol abnormalities could be unrecoverable call termination, status errors, errored messages, or restarts. In general, abnormalities can be categorized into: resource unavailability, user and network errors, timer expirations, and restarts. There are many possibilities in each category; the interested reader is referred to [10].

10.2.3 Configuration Management

Generally configuration management is concerned with bringing components of the switching system into and out of service. Configuration refers to the relationships among the various components of the system, which can be specified through a set of attributes. These components may be physical or logical (e.g., timers or counters). Configuration management can initialize components into service and shut down components. During service, the configuration can be monitored and changes can be made by altering attribute values. Configuration management in ATM has not been addressed in the standards yet, but some preliminary specifications can be found in [10].

It may be assumed that the configuration information is maintained within the SM database. The information consists of all managed resources and their attributes. Configuration management is responsible for these functions:

- Report configuration status or changes to network management;
- Make configuration modifications requested by network management;
- Respond to database queries from network management;
- Backup configuration information;
- Allow software to be downloaded.

More specifically, two examples of managed resources are switch interfaces and VP/VC links. For each switch interface, attributes could include [10]:

- Unique interface identifier;
- Maximum bandwidth for ATM connections;
- Maximum number of VPCs/VCCs allowed;
- Number of allocated VPI/VCI bits;
- ILMI channel identifier (for UNI only);
- Valid calling party addresses (for UNI only);
- Default calling party address (for UNI only);
- Downstream carrier network (for NNI only).

For VP/VC links, attributes could include:

- Unique link identifier;
- VPI/VCI values;
- Peak cell rate and cell delay variation tolerance for $CLP = 0$ and $CLP = 0 + 1$ traffic;
- Sustainable cell rate and burst tolerance for $CLP = 0$ and $CLP = 0 + 1$ traffic;
- QOS class.

The area of configuration management will need further study.

10.2.4 Accounting Management

Accounting management is responsible for collecting usage information in support of customer billing, customer network management, and network planning [14,15]. Billing is not addressed in ATM standards yet partly because it is expected that customer billing will be determined in large measure by individual network providers. Billing may be usage-insensitive (i.e., flat rate) or usage-sensitive. The latter depends on measurements of resource usage, and a preliminary strategy can be found in [10,15–18]. This strategy covers usage measurements, data formats, and data transmission. It is presented here as an expository example rather than a requirement.

For both directions of a virtual connection, usage measurements consist of these cell counts:

- Total number of user and OAM cells;
- Number of high loss priority (CLP = 0) user and OAM cells;
- Number of (F4 and F5) OAM cells;
- Number of high loss priority (CLP = 0) OAM cells.

Thus, billing can differentiate between user and OAM cells, and between high- and low-loss priority cells. While preliminary specifications postulate that the cell counts should be made at the egress UNI of the destination user (to measure the actual number of cells delivered successfully by the network), there is some question whether cell counts should also be made at the ingress UNI of the source user. The former case implies that cell counting must be performed in the output modules of an ATM switch; the latter case implies cell counting will be done in the input modules as well. The input modules or output modules will report the cell counts to the SM for record keeping and correlation (if necessary).

Usage measurements are supplemented by information about the connection. For (semi) permanent virtual connections, additional information may be:

- A connection identifier;
- Peak cell rate;
- Sustainable cell rate and burst tolerance;
- QOS class.

For switched virtual connections, additional information may be:

- Called- and calling-party numbers;
- Connect date, connect time, and elapsed time;
- Broadband bearer capability (contained in the *setup* signaling message);
- Peak cell rates (CLP = 0 + 1) in both directions;
- Cause indication (contained in the *release* or *release complete* message).

The information about connections resides largely in the CAC functional block. The CAC will pass this information to the SM.

Usage measurements are made over recording intervals whose lengths may be selected within a range of 15 minutes to 24 hours (30 minutes by default). The SM will collect the usage information and put them into a format called Bellcore Automatic Message Accounting Format (BAF) [15,18,19]. BAF records will then be sent to a so-called Revenue Accounting Office.

10.2.5 Security Management

Security management is responsible for protection of the switch and its database from security threats. Potential threats include:

- Someone assuming a false identity to gain access privileges;
- Disclosure of data without authorization;
- Unauthorized alteration of data;
- Unauthorized destruction of data.

The SM must first implement security measures to control access to data and system resources. Measures might include user identification, authentication (e.g., with a password), and session control (e.g., login timeouts or detection of unusual access activities). Also, users may be assigned privilege codes that restrict their access to certain system resources.

Another responsibility of the SM is data integrity. This includes duplicate backup of the database and encryption of data transfers.

Security management has not been addressed in ATM standards yet and needs further study.

10.2.6 Traffic Management

Recall from Chapter 4 that traffic management is concerned with the regulation of traffic flows to prevent and react to congestion. The main preventive mechanisms are CAC and UPC/NPC. Properly designed, these should ensure that the QOS for accepted connections will be within guaranteed limits and the probability of congestion will be small. In the event of congestion, low loss priority (CLP = 1) cells will be selectively discarded, and explicit forward congestion indication (EFCI) may be activated.

The CAC functional block is responsible for connection-level controls. UPC/NPC is performed in the input modules according to parameters provided to it by the CAC. Traffic management in the SM takes care of cell level controls consisting of congestion monitoring and congestion control.

Congestion must be monitored in all *congestable* parts of the switching system. These depend on the implementation of the switch. Of most concern is the CSF, which contains the routing fabric and cell buffers. However, other functional blocks may also be congestable, e.g., buffers and processors in the input modules and output modules. For each congestable component, a set of congestion measures can be determined. For example, congestion in the CSF could be measured by queue lengths, average utilization, cell loss due to buffer overflow, or queuing delays. These measurements must be made at the congestable component. For example, the buffer manager in the CSF measures congestion in the fabric.

Based on the congestion measures, the level (severity) of congestion is classified for each component, and the levels are reported to the SM. The reports may be made at regular periodic intervals or instantaneously when a high level of congestion is reached. The SM decides on the appropriate congestion control actions. The range of possible control actions depends on implementation but might include:

- Notification to network management to initiate manual controls;
- Congestion notification to users and other switches by EFCI or other means;
- Selective cell discarding;
- Rerouting;
- Internal flow control (within the CSF);
- Reconfiguration of the CSF;
- Adjustment of UPC/NPC, e.g., disable tagging.

10.3 MANAGEMENT INFORMATION

It is clear from the previous section that the SM will collect and maintain a variety of management information, including:

- Physical-layer and ATM-layer fault-management information;
- Physical-layer and ATM-layer performance-management information;
- Configuration information;
- Usage measurements and other accounting management information;
- Security information;
- Congestion measurements and traffic-control parameters.

Figure 10.1 shows a single (conceptual) database, but in practice, the information may very well reside in multiple physical locations.

All or part of the information may be made accessible to users or network management. The accessible information is stored in a *management information base* (MIB). A MIB is a conceptual repository of management information consisting of a structured collection of managed objects and their attributes (properties and values). Managed objects may be physical or logical (e.g., connection); the correspondence between physical resources and managed objects depends entirely on implementation. By reading the values in the MIB, a user or network manager can monitor the switch's resources; the resources can be controlled by modifying values in the MIB.

The structure of a MIB is defined in conjunction with a protocol for accessing information in the MIB. This section discusses the MIB in the contexts of two standard management information protocols, the simple network management protocol (SNMP) and common management information protocol (CMIP). SNMP and CMIP represent the two different management paradigms in the TCP/IP and OSI network architectures, respectively. The SNMP and CMIP protocols are described later in Section 10.4. Differences between the SNMP and CMIP paradigms are summarized in [20,21].

10.3.1 SNMP MIB

SNMP was introduced earlier in the context of the interim local management interface (ILMI) in Chapter 3. SNMP is a widely used protocol adopted by the Internet Engineering Task Force in 1989 to centrally manage large TCP/IP-based networks [4,22]. It actually includes the definition of an MIB and a protocol for accessing MIBs. The SNMP paradigm is shown in Figure 10.2. A central network management station (NMS) exchanges messages with agents residing in the network elements being managed. The agent in each network element maintains an MIB, which contains descriptions of managed objects (e.g., hardware, software, and connections).

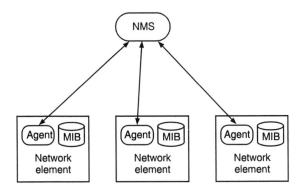

Figure 10.2 SNMP paradigm.

Each object has a name, a syntax, and an encoding. The name is an object identifier that uniquely specifies an object type. Object identifiers are assigned by an organization (e.g., ISO) that is authorized to administer a group of identifiers. An object identifier is a sequence of integers that identifies the location of an object type in a tree structure, as shown in Figure 10.3. The integers indicate the sequence of nodes along a path starting from the top of the tree. The tree is static, meaning that nodes (object types) are determined when the MIB is designed. In addition to providing unique identification of object types, the tree structure also shows groups of related objects under a single subtree. A text name (corresponding to object identifiers) is also assigned to object types for human readability.

The syntax defines the abstract data structure. A subset of Abstract Syntax Notation 1 (ASN.1) is used. ASN.1 is a language standardized by the ITU and ISO for defining data types and their properties. Encoding of objects follow the basic encoding rules associated with ASN.1. Descriptions of ASN.1 can be readily found in the literature.

Management data is indexed by the leaves located at the bottom of the tree. A leaf might refer to a single instance of an object type, where the management information takes a single data cell. Alternatively, a leaf might refer to multiple instances of an object type, in which case the management information takes the form of a table, with each row representing a separate instance.

For TCP/IP, the IETF has developed MIB-I [23] and a second version MIB-II [24]. For ATM, the IETF is working on an ATM MIB [25] and the ATM Forum has specified a UNI MIB for the ILMI [26]. The IETF has also defined a SONET MIB [27]. The IETF ATM MIB and ATM Forum UNI MIB are not the same, but there is a common subset, and attempts have been made to align the semantics and syntax.

The ATM Forum UNI MIB contains management information concerning:

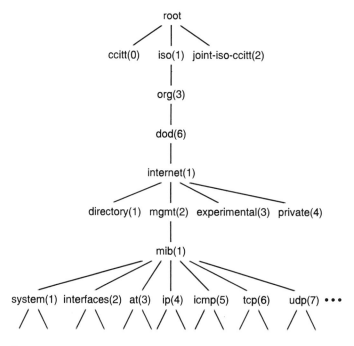

Figure 10.3 Tree structure of SNMP MIB.

- Physical layer;
- ATM layer;
- ATM layer statistics;
- VPCs/VCCs;
- Address registration.

For MIB object definitions, the reader is referred to [26]. The exchange of management information across the ILMI will be covered later in Section 10.4.

The proposed IETF ATM MIB is intended to be used to manage ATM interfaces, ATM virtual links, ATM crossconnects, and AAL5 entities. Managed objects are arranged in these groups:

- ATM interface configurations;
- ATM interface DS3 physical layer convergence procedure;
- ATM interface transmission convergence sublayer;
- ATM interface VP/VC link configurations;
- ATM VP/VC crossconnects;
- AAL5 connection performance statistics.

Details are contained in [25].

10.3.2 OSI MIB

The International Organization for Standardization (ISO) is, of course, well known for the seven-layer Open Systems Interconnection (OSI) reference archi-tecture model. ISO has developed an extensive set of standards for OSI systems management (network management), including specification of an OSI MIB that is accessed through CMIP [4]. It relies on object-oriented design concepts. Every (physical or logical) resource that is monitored and controlled is represented as a managed object. A managed object is defined by its attributes, operations that can be performed on it, notifications it can issue, and its relationships with other managed objects. Managed objects sharing the same attributes, notifica-tions, and management operations belong to the same object class.

There are three distinct and independent tree structures in OSI system management:

- ISO registration tree;
- Inheritance tree;
- Containment tree.

The ISO registration tree is a naming tree where object classes, attribute definitions, actions, notifications, and packages are registered. These can be re-used in different combinations to make new object class definitions. As in

SNMP, every object class in the registration tree has a unique object identifier that is a sequence of integers specifying a path down the tree.

The inheritance tree shows how the definitions of object classes are derived from other object classes. From any object class, multiple subclasses can be defined such that they *inherit* the characteristics of that class. The subclasses can be viewed as specializations of the parent class. Specialization can be done by adding new attributes, changing the range of an existing attribute, adding new operations and notifications, or changing the arguments to operations and notifications. All object classes can trace their inheritance ultimately to a single superclass at the top of the inheritance tree.

The containment tree specifies the MIB structure, which consists of identified objects and their hierarchy. Like the SNMP tree, this tree provides unambiguous referencing of object instances.

Further details of the OSI MIB can be found in [4,21]. Bellcore has offered detailed specifications for an ATM MIB [28]. The next section will discuss the CMIP protocol for accessing the OSI MIB.

10.4 COMMUNICATIONS

The SM maintains management information in the MIB for communication with users or a network manager. The MIB may be part of the entire SM database. Other information in the database may not be visible to users and network managers.

The communication of MIB information must obviously follow a protocol. Two leading candidates are SNMP and CMIP, which have been developed for the TCP/IP and OSI environments, respectively.

10.4.1 SNMP

SNMP is a simple polling protocol that allows a centralized NMS to query agents to retrieve and modify information in their MIBs [4,22]. It was originally adopted as a short-term approach for the Internet until the eventual implementation of CMIP over TCP/IP (so-called CMOT). However, the slow standardization and complexity of CMIP have inhibited its deployment. Meanwhile, the simplicity of SNMP has made it widely popular. It has become a de facto standard and appears likely to endure for many years. SNMP has been specified for the ATM ILMI.

For simplicity, SNMP consists of only three types of operations:

- *Get*: the NMS retrieves specific information from an agent;
- *Set*: the NMS alters specific information in an agent;
- *Trap*: an agent reports an event to the NMS.

Queries and control actions are initiated by polling by the NMS; the only exceptions are traps, which may be sent unsolicited to the NMS. There are no imperative commands; control actions occur as side effects of set operations. The three operations are performed with a set of only five types of messages, as listed in Table 10.1.

Table 10.1
Types of SNMP Messages

Message	Function
Get-request	Query to agent to fetch value of a variable
Get-next-request	Query to agent to fetch next variable after specific variable
Set-request	Query to agent to set value of a variable
Get-response	Response by agent to return value of a variable
Trap	Report of an event from agent

In 1993, a series of revisions to SNMP were put forward to address its limitations. A second version, SNMPv2, adds some enhancements to SNMPv1:

- New get-bulk-request allows the NMS to retrieve large blocks of data efficiently;
- New inform-request allows NMS-to-NMS communications;
- New SNMPv2 MIB and SNMPv2-M2M MIB (manager-to-manager);
- Security enhancements for authentication and privacy.

Interested readers are referred to [4,29].

10.4.2 CMIP

Like SNMP, CMIP is an application-layer protocol for exchanging management information between agents and network managers. However, there are many differences between the SNMP and CMIP paradigms [20,21]. In CMIP, agents and network managers communicate as peers. CMIP is connection-oriented, whereas SNMP uses the unguaranteed connectionless user datagram protocol over IP. Manager-agent communications are confirmed in CMIP but not in SNMP. CMIP allows dynamic changes to the MIB structure, operations on multiple objects at once, and imperative commands, whereas SNMP does not.

To enable more capabilities, agents and MIBs are much more complex in CMIP than SNMP.

Actually, CMIP is only part of the application-layer protocol, as shown in Figure 10.4. Agents and managers are peer applications that rely on the services provided by a *common management information service element* (CMISE). CMISE will:

- Report an event about a managed object to the other peer;
- Retrieve information from the other peer;
- Modify information at the other peer;
- Request action to be taken by the other peer;
- Create or delete a managed object at the other peer;
- Cancel a retrieval request.

CMISE consists of two parts, the *common management information service* (CMIS) and CMIP.

CMIS provides a set of service primitives to an agent or manager through an interface. CMIP provides for the exchange of messages called CMIP protocol data units. In turn, CMIP depends on the services of an *association-control-service element* (ACSE) and *remote-operations-service element* (ROSE). ACSE provides the capability to establish and terminate an *association* (similar to a connection) between two applications. For two applications sharing an association, ROSE allows one application to remotely invoke an action by the other

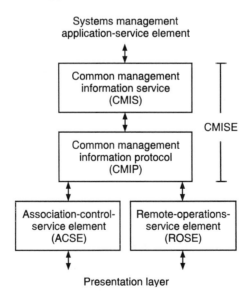

Figure 10.4 CMISE, ACSE, and ROSE.

application. ACSE and ROSE both depend on the services of the OSI presentation layer.

CMIP protocol data units are listed in Table 10.2. The role of these protocol data units in support of CMISE services is fairly apparent. For more details about CMIP and OSI system management, the reader is referred to [4,21].

Table 10.2
Types of CMIP Protocol Data Units

Data Unit	Function
m-Get	Request retrieval of management information or response
m-Linked-Reply	Intermediate response in series of multiple linked responses
m-Set	Request modification of management information or response
m-Set-Confirmed	Confirmation of m-Set
m-Action	Request for action by other peer
m-Action-Confirmed	Confirmation of m-Action
m-Create	Request creation of an instance of managed object by other peer
m-Delete	Request deletion of an instance of managed object by other peer
m-Cancel-Get-Confirmed	Request other peer to cancel a previous m-Get request
m-EventReport	Report an event about managed object to other peer
m-EventReport-Confirmed	Confirmation of m-EventReport

CMIP is favored by Bellcore for network management of broadband switching systems [10,28]. This is discussed further in Section 10.4.4.

10.4.3 Customer Network Management

It is expected that some users will perform network management on their side of the UNI (e.g., LAN management). Their network managers will be concerned with the communication services being provided by the network. They may well wish to monitor, and to some degree control, their services. The network may offer a customer network management service to aid the user. Essentially the aid may take two forms: the network exchanges management information with the user, or the network cooperates in supporting management functions such as ATM layer OAM.

In recognition of existing LAN network-management products, SNMP will be the management-information protocol between the user and network [14]. An expected scenario is shown in Figure 10.5. The NMS on the user side of the UNI can communicate via SNMP with an agent on the network side (this functional interface is designated as M(3) by the ATM Forum). The network agent resides on a LAN and interfaces to the ATM transport network through a router. The agent collects management information from multiple ATM switches concerning a user's service (see CMIP and next section). For a specification of information collected for (semi) permanent virtual connections, refer to [14]. The user NMS can exchange SNMP messages with the network agent through the router in two different ways: through the ATM network (UDP/IP over ATM), or by direct dialup to the router.

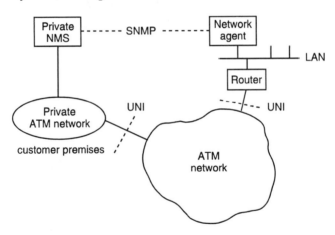

Figure 10.5 Communication between user NMS and network agent.

A similar but more limited service is provided by the interim local management interface (ILMI) that was introduced earlier in Section 3.4.2. Here, SNMP messages, encapsulated into ATM ILMI cells by AAL5, are passed across the UNI. This allows the user to access the MIB maintained by the ATM switch directly across the UNI. In this case, the accessible information is related only to that user's UNI and that access switch; the user cannot access complete information about his service. The UNI MIB is specified in [26].

Finally, customer network management may be considered to include layer-management functions. Physical-layer management consists of fault management and performance management using the SONET overhead exchanged across the UNI (see Chapter 6 and Section 10.2). ATM-layer management consists of F4 and F5 OAM cells exchanged across the UNI (see Sections 3.4.1 and 10.2).

10.4.4 Telecommunications Management Network

Network managers clearly need the capability to monitor and control a number of switches as a group. This means that each switch must communicate with one or more network managers. In data networks, a network manager is usually situated at a centralized computer-based network management station. In the telephone network, switches communicate with *operations systems* (OS) at operations centers. An OS is an application on a computer system that aids network managers by automating and carrying out specific management functions, e.g., collection of accounting data or logging alarms. Typically, switches communicate with OSs via an X.25 packet-switched network.

The separation of the switches (providing information transport) from the OSs (providing management functions) through a communications network exemplifies the *telecommunications management network* (TMN) concept. TMN principles have been studied by the ITU since 1985 and have been established in a series of standards [30]. The separation between transport and management functions is evident in the architecture shown in Figure 10.6. The telecommunications network consists of network elements that provide the switching and transmission of user information. The TMN is a functionally separate network consisting of a data communications network and OSs, interconnected to the telecommunications network at several points. In actuality, the TMN may share the transport facilities of the telecommunications network to carry management information.

Separation of management and transport is not the only principle, for it does not solve the problem of interoperability. Today, management systems are often proprietary and dependent on the switch implementation. Management systems from different manufacturers have difficulty working together. Hence, the TMN prescribes standardized Q-interfaces between all elements of Figure 10.6. The standardized interfaces allow full interoperability between OSs and multivendor network elements.

According to current standards, the Q-interfaces consist of a complete seven-layer OSI protocol suite [31]. One of the application layer protocols is CMISE over ACSE and ROSE. This is consistent with Bellcore specifications for the operations interface to broadband switching systems [10,28]. The lower layer protocol is currently X.25 but will likely include ATM and SONET in the future. SONET has data communications channels in the overhead for this purpose (see Chapter 6) [7].

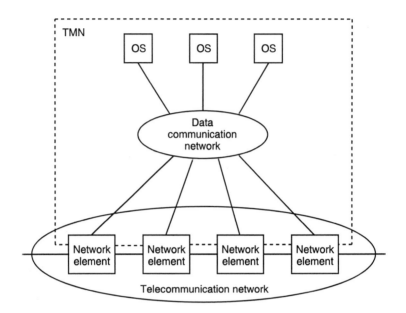

Figure 10.6 Telecommunications management network concept.

10.5 SUPERVISION AND COORDINATION

The discussions thus far have pointed out that the SM will be carrying out these activities:

- Specific management functions;
- Collection and administration of management information;
- Communications with users and network managers.

They are mostly independent but not entirely. Hence, there is a central functional block in the SM, designated as the supervision and coordination block in Figure 10.1, that handles the coordination of these activities. More specifically, it coordinates data and actions.

Perhaps the single most important responsibility of the supervision and coordination functional block is the management of data written into and read out of the database. It is evident that a copious amount of management information will be generated related to faults, performance, configuration, security, accounting, and congestion. The SM must coordinate the input of information into the database. In particular, the SM must:

- Resolve access conflicts;
- Filter unnecessary or redundant data;

- Check for data integrity and security (relying on security management);
- Change raw data to appropriate and consistent formats for storage;
- Correlate data and store in correct location(s).

The last item might be subdivided into at least two tasks. First, correlation analysis should detect cases where a single event is observed in a number of different measurements (e.g., a fault detected by fault monitoring and performance monitoring), so that it is not recorded as multiple events. Second, if the database actually consists of a number of separate specialized databases, it may be necessary to record data in more than one location. For example, a fault might be recorded in the fault-management database and the accounting-management database (if it interrupts a user's service).

Another responsibility of this functional block is coordination of control actions. For example, if fault management detects a failure, it may need to enlist actions by configuration management to isolate the failure. Coordination may involve:

- Resolving any conflicts between actions taken by different management functions;
- Establishing precedence and timing between different control actions;
- Establishing priorities among control actions;
- Activating or deactivating specific control mechanisms.

The supervision and coordination functional block will likely be implemented by a proprietary management application. Its complexity will depend on the implementation of the individual management activities. In any case, it would be desirable to clarify the working relationships between the various management activities; this area needs further study.

10.6 DISTRIBUTION OF SM

There are at least two compelling reasons to distribute SM functions to the other parts of the switch. First, the SM clearly involves a great amount of data collection and processing. If processing is centralized, it might become a limiting factor as the switch becomes larger or the SM becomes more complicated. Distributed processing may alleviate the potential performance bottleneck caused by centralized processing. This was the same motivation for the distribution of CAC functions (see Section 9.4).

Second, as mentioned earlier, some SM functions reside naturally in the other functional blocks in the switch. For example, the input modules handle physical layer OAM through overhead processing of incoming SONET signals. The input modules also perform ATM protocol monitoring by processing cell headers. With coordination by the SM, the output modules participate in physical layer OAM by generating the overhead in outgoing SONET signals. As another example, the CAC handles SAAL processing and the high-layer signaling protocols, which is part of performance monitoring.

Furthermore, some SM functions should be distributed to the input modules and output modules because of the nature of the functions. For instance, consider the ATM-layer performance-monitoring procedure: OAM performance management cells are embedded within the user cell stream. The OAM cells must maintain their relative positions within the cell streams as the cells pass through the switch. Hence, OAM cells cannot be extracted from the cell stream at the input modules and diverted to the SM for processing. It would be much more reasonable to process the OAM performance management cells *within the input modules* without extracting them from the user cell stream.

The portion of SM functions distributed to the input modules and output modules will be designated as IM-SMs and OM-SMs, respectively. The degree of distribution is an implementation issue that depends on a trade-off between performance and cost of duplication (IM-SMs and OM-SMs reside in every input module and output module). Natural candidates for distribution are the specific management functions described in Section 10.2, especially fault management, performance management, and accounting management. The SM database may also be distributed in practice, but we will consider it to be centralized conceptually. Then it would probably be reasonable to keep configuration management, security management, traffic management, supervision and coordination, and external communications (to network managers or TMN) in the centralized SM.

The IM-SMs have the opportunity to perform management functions on incoming cell streams and report information to the central SM. An IM-SM might contain these functions:

- Processing of physical layer OAM information in SONET overhead;
- Automatic physical-layer fault protection;
- Processing of OAM fault-management cells;
- Monitoring of user data cells for ATM-layer performance monitoring;
- Processing of OAM performance-management cells;
- Cell-header processing for ATM protocol monitoring;
- AAL processing and AAL protocol monitoring (e.g., for ILMI cells);
- Ingress cell counts.

Some of these functions will reside in the input modules naturally, and the others are a matter of choice for implementation. It should be noted that the IM-SMs could become rather complex and assume a great amount of processing burden. In this case, the input modules could become a very costly part of the overall switching system.

The OM-SMs will report management information to the central SM and generate management information in outgoing traffic. An OM-SM might contain these functions:

- Generate physical-layer OAM information in SONET overhead;
- Automatic physical-layer fault protection;
- Generate OAM fault-management cells;
- Monitor outgoing user cells for ATM-layer performance monitoring;
- Generate OAM performance-management cells;
- AAL processing and AAL protocol monitoring (e.g., for ILMI cells)
- Egress cell counts.

Some of these functions will reside in the output modules naturally, and the others are a matter of choice for the switch designer.

10.7 CONCLUSIONS

The SM is a complex but important functional block that represents the wide-ranging functions of the management plane of the B-ISDN protocol reference model. It carries out specific management responsibilities, namely:

- Fault management;
- Performance management;
- Configuration management;
- Accounting management;
- Security management;
- Traffic management.

These management activities involve a variety of management information that the SM maintains in a database. All or part of the database is made accessible to users and network managers for purposes of control, planning, and provisioning. The accessible information is stored in a MIB. By reading from and writing into the MIB, objects (logical resources) within the switch can be monitored and controlled.

The SM supports access to the MIB through the management-information protocols SNMP or CMIP (in which cases the MIB is an SNMP MIB or OSI MIB). SNMP is currently specified for customer network management, including the ILMI. On the other hand, CMIP is favored for network management via the TMN (without the involvement of users).

It was observed that some SM functions naturally reside in the other functional blocks in the switch. Indeed a precise partitioning of SM functions from the other functional blocks is difficult. In addition, some SM functions—

such as ATM-layer OAM performance management—should be distributed to the input modules and output modules because of the nature of these functions. The precise distribution of SM functions to the input modules and output modules depends on the trade-off between cost and performance. It is worthwhile to note that the input modules especially could become rather complex and assume a great amount of processing burden. In this case, the input modules could become a very costly part of the overall switching system.

References

[1] Rey, R., ed., *Engineering and Operations in the Bell System*, 2nd ed., AT&T Bell Laboratories, Murray Hill, NJ, 1983.

[2] Haenschke, D., and D. Kettler, "Network Management and Congestion in the U.S. Telecommunications Network," *IEEE Trans. on Communications*, Vol. COM-29, April 1981, pp. 376–385.

[3] Tow, D., "Network Management—Recent Advances and Future Trends," *IEEE J. on Selected Areas in Communications*, Vol. 6, May 1988, pp. 732–741.

[4] Stallings, W., *SNMP, SNMPv2, and CMIP: The Practical Guide to Network Management Standards*, Reading, MA: Addison-Wesley, 1993.

[5] Terplan, K., *Communication Networks Management*, Englewood Cliffs, NJ: Prentice-Hall, 1987.

[6] ITU-T Rec. I.610, *B-ISDN Operation and Maintenance Principles and Functions*, Helsinki March 1–12, 1993.

[7] Bellcore, *Synchronous Optical Network (SONET) Transport Systems: Common Generic Criteria*, TA-NWT-000253, Issue 8, Oct. 1993.

[8] Bellcore, *Broadband User to Network Interface and Network Node Interface Physical layer Generic Criteria*, TR-NWT-001112, Issue 1, June 1993.

[9] ITU-T Rec. I.432, *B-ISDN User-Network Interface—Physical Layer Specification*, Helsinki March 1–12, 1993.

[10] Bellcore, *Generic Requirements for Operations of Broadband Switching Systems*, TA-NWT 001248, Issue 2, Oct. 1993.

[11] Bellcore, *Broadband ISDN Switching System Generic Requirements*, TA-NWT-001110, Issue 2, Aug. 1993.

[12] Bellcore, *Asynchronous Transfer Mode (ATM) and ATM Adaptation Layer (AAL) Protocol Generic Requirements*, TA-NWT-001113, Issue 2, July 1993.

[13] ITU-T Rec. I.363, *B-ISDN ATM Adaptation Layer (AAL) Specification*, Helsinki, March 1–12, 1993.

[14] Bellcore, *Generic Requirements for Exchange PVC CRS Customer Network Management Service*, TA-TSV-001117, Issue 1, Sept. 1993.

[15] Bellcore, *Guide to Generic Requirements for Usage Information to Support Billing for ATM Broadband Networking*, SR-NWT-002941, Issue 1, Dec. 1993.

[16] Bellcore, *Generic Requirements for Exchange PVC Cell Relay Service*, TA-TSV-001408, Issue 1, Aug. 1993.

[17] Bellcore, *Generic Requirements for Exchange Access PVC Cell Relay Service*, TA-TSV-001409, Issue 1, Nov. 1993.

[18] Bellcore, *Generic Requirements for Exchange SVC Cell Relay Service*, TA-NWT-001501, Issue 1, Dec. 1993.

[19] Bellcore, *Bellcore Automatic Message Accounting Format (BAF) Requirements*, TR-NWT 001100, Issue 2, Feb. 1993.

[20] Aidarous, S., and T. Plevyak, eds., *Telecommunications Network Management into the 21st Century*, New York, NY: IEEE Press, 1993.

[21] Yemini, Y., "The OSI Network Management Model," *IEEE Communications Mag.*, May 1993, pp. 20–29.

[22] Case, J., et al., "Simple Network Management Protocol," *Internet Working Group Request for Comments 1157*, May 1990.

[23] McCloghrie, K., and M. Rose, "Management Information Base for Network Management of TCP/IP-Based Internets," *Internet Working Group Request for Comments 1156*, May 1990.

[24] McCloghrie, K., and M. Rose, eds., "Management Information Base for Network Management of TCP/IP-Based Internets: MIB-II," *Internet Working Group Request for Comments 1156*, March 1991.

[25] Ahmed, M., and K. Tesink, eds., "Definitions of Managed Objects for ATM Management Version 8.0," *Internet draft draft-ieft-atommib-atm-07.txt*, June 15, 1994.

[26] ATM Forum, *ATM User-Network Interface Specification Version 3.0*, Sept. 10, 1993.

[27] Brown, T., and K. Tesink, eds., "Definitions of Managed Objects for the SONET/SDH Interface Type," *Internet Working Group Request for Comments 1595*, March 1994.

[28] Bellcore, *Generic Requirements for Operations Interfaces Using OSI Tools: ATM/Broadband Network Management*, TA-NWT-001114, Issue 2, Oct. 1993.

[29] Case, J., et al., "Introduction to Version 2 of the Internet-Standard Network Management Framework," *Internet Working Group Request for Comments 1441*, April 1993.

[30] ITU-T Rec. M.3010, *Principles for a Telecommunications Management Network*, Geneva, Oct. 5, 1992.

[31] Widl, W., "CCITT Standardization of Telecommunications Management Networks," *Ericsson Review*, 1991, pp. 34–51.

Appendix A
ATM Adaptation Layer Type 1

ITU-T Recommendation I.363 specifies ATM adaptation layer type 1 (AAL1) to support constant bit-rate services above the ATM layer. Essentially, AAL1 at the transmitter will divide a continuous fixed-rate bitstream into small segments and add the AAL1 information to each segment. Each segment is carried by the ATM layer within ATM cells. At the receiver, AAL1 extracts the segments from the ATM cells and reassembles the continuous bitstream using the AAL information. The receiver may have to handle cell-delay variation, lost or misinserted cells, error detection, and source clock frequency recovery.

As usual, AAL1 consists of two sublayers: the segmentation and reassembly (SAR) sublayer and the convergence sublayer (CS). The SAR and CS functions are first described for *unstructured data transfer*. In this mode, the user data is viewed by AAL1 as a continuous bitstream without any internal structure, such as byte-aligned blocks or internal framing bit patterns. No information about the internal structure is conveyed. An overview of the SAR and CS functions is shown in Figure A.1.

At the transmitter, the user data bitstream is divided into segments of 47 bytes. Each segment forms a CS protocol data unit (PDU) without any additional CS information. The CS PDUs are then passed to the SAR sublayer. Each segment is prefixed with 1 byte of SAR information consisting of a 4-bit sequence number (SN) and 4-bit sequence number protection (SNP). The resulting 48 bytes, now an SAR PDU, are submitted to the ATM layer to be encapsulated into an ATM cell.

The purpose of the SN field is to identify the sequential order of SAR PDUs for reassembly. The SN field consists of a convergence sublayer indicator (CSI) bit and a 3-bit sequence count (SC). The CSI bit is actually reserved for use by the CS. It is used to indicate the existence or absence of a CS function. The sequence count is assigned to the CS PDUs to detect lost or misordered PDUs.

The SNP field provides the SN field with single-bit error correction or multiple-bit error detection. The SNP field consists of a 3-bit CRC and an even parity bit. The CRC is the result of a CRC calculation across the 4 bits of the SN

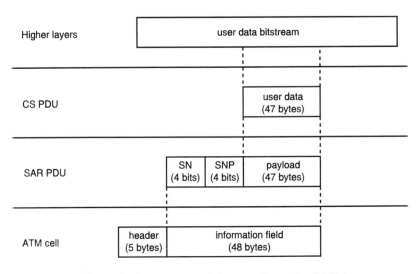

Figure A.1 Protocol data units in *unstructured data transfer* mode of AAL1.

field; i.e., it is the remainder of the product of the SN multiplied by x^3 and divided by the generator polynomial $x^3 + x + 1$. The even parity bit is inserted after the CRC calculation.

The receiver has the more complicated responsibility of reassembly of the continuous bitstream from the received SAR PDUs. Specifically, the AAL1 at the receiver must:

- Examine the CRC and parity bit for error detection;
- Correct single-bit errors in the SN field;
- Declare the SN invalid in the event of multiple-bit errors;
- Reassemble the CS PDUs in correct sequence using the sequence numbers;
- Discard misinserted CS PDUs and generate dummy information for missing CS PDUs;
- Buffer the received CS PDUs to compensate for cell delay variation through the ATM layer.

The amount of buffering necessary is under study. It is to be expected that buffer overflow or underflow may be possible. In the event of buffer overflow, an appropriate amount of data may have to be discarded to maintain the integrity of the reassembled user data bitstream. Likewise, in the event of buffer underflow, an appropriate amount of dummy bits may have to be inserted.

Bits must be output from the buffer at the same bit-rate as the original user data bitstream. The receiver uses a service clock, which may or may not be synchronized with a network clock. If the service clock is not synchronized with a network clock, AAL1 must convey timing information from the transmitter to the receiver using the *synchronous residual time stamp* (SRTS) method.

At the transmitter, it is assumed that a network reference clock is available, but the source clock is not synchronized with it. The SRTS method conveys a measure of the frequency difference between the reference clock and source clock. The frequency of the network clock is divided by some integer (to be determined) to generate a derived network reference clock. Within a time interval of N source clock cycles, suppose there are M cycles of the derived network reference clock. There is a nominal value M_{nom} (fixed and known for the service) but the actual value of M may vary anywhere within a certain range around this nominal value. The actual value of M will be the sum of M_{nom} and a residual part. By transmitting the residual part, the receiver has enough information to reconstruct the source clock.

It turns out that for the clock accuracies associated with DS1 and DS3 services, only the least significant bits of the residual part are needed. The SRTS method uses four bits for the residual part (the residual time stamp). These four bits can be conveyed in the CSI bits in SAR PDUs, which have odd SN values; if these bits are not used, they are set to zeros. The CSI bits in SAR PDUs with even SN values are used for structured data transfer (described below). For more details about the SRTS method, the reader should consult ITU-T Recommendation I.363.

An adaptive-clock method can be used when a common network reference clock is not available. At the receiver, data is received in a buffer that is read with a local clock. The content level of the buffer is used to control the frequency of the local clock. The content level around the medium level is continuously measured to drive a phase-locked loop providing the local clock. The content level of the buffer may be maintained within an upper limit and lower limit to prevent buffer overflow and underflow.

AAL1 also provides *structured data transfer* for conveying information about the internal byte-aligned structure of the user data bitstream. Essentially, the AAL1 CS uses a pointer to delineate the structure boundaries. This is supported by two types of CS PDUs, called non-P and P format, as shown in Figure A.2. The non-P format CS PDU is filled entirely with user data (as in unstructured data transfer). In the P format CS PDU, the first byte is a pointer field and the remaining 46 bytes are filled with user data. The P format CS PDUs are indicated by CSI = 1, and hence this format can be used only in SAR PDUs with even SN values (because the SRTS method uses the CSI bits in SAR PDUs with odd SN values).

The first bit in the pointer field is reserved for future uses (to be determined). The other 7 bits are the offset measured in bytes between the end of the pointer field and the start of the structured block in the 93 bytes consisting of the remaining 46 bytes in this CS PDU and the 47 bytes of the next CS PDU.

This offset may range from 0 to 93. An offset value of 93 is used to indicate that the end of the 93 bytes coincides with the end of a structured block that does not start within the 93 bytes.

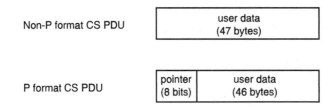

Figure A.2 Formats of CS protocol data units for *structured data transfer* mode of AAL1.

Appendix B
ATM Adaptation Layer Type 3/4

ITU-T Recommendation I.363 specifies ATM adaptation layer type 3/4 (AAL3/4) to support Class C or D variable bit-rate services above the ATM layer with error detection. It is much more complicated than AAL5 and, unlike AAL5, allows multiplexing of data from multiple AAL3/4 users (higher layer applications).

As usual, AAL3/4 consists of two sublayers: the segmentation and reassembly (SAR) sublayer and the convergence sublayer (CS). The CS is further subdivided into a common part convergence sublayer (CPCS) and service-specific convergence sublayer (SSCS). Different SSCS protocols may be defined for specific higher layer applications, and sometimes the SSCS may be null (e.g., for Class D connectionless services). The CPCS provides unguaranteed transport of variable-length frames of up to 65,535 bytes. Errored frames may be discarded or optionally delivered with an error indication. This appendix discusses only the common part of AAL3/4, consisting of the CPCS and SAR sublayers.

There are two ways in which the CPCS receives the variable-length frame from the higher layers. In *message mode service*, the higher layers submit a frame in its entirety to CPCS. In *streaming mode service*, the higher layers submit a frame in one or more parts that can be separated in time. The CPCS may transmit the parts separately as they are submitted; all segments of the same data frame are collected by the CPCS at the receiver. A partially transmitted frame can be aborted upon request by the higher layers.

The basic operation of the AAL3/4 common part is shown in Figure B.1. At the transmitter, the CPCS adds header and trailer information to the variable-length data frame to construct a CPCS protocol data unit (CPCS PDU). This is divided by the SAR sublayer into 44-byte segments, and a header and trailer are added to each segment to make 48-byte SAR PDUs. The SAR PDUs are carried in the information fields of ATM cells.

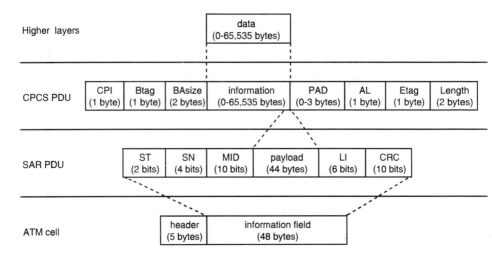

Figure B.1 Protocol data units in AAL3/4 common part.

The CPCS PDU contains these fields in the header and trailer:

- *CPI (common part indicator)*: indicates the measurement units for the BASize and Length fields (only CPI = 0 has been defined so far, meaning the units are bytes);
- *Btag (beginning tag)*: indicates misassembly if different from the Etag field (this field will have different values in consecutive CPCS PDUs);
- *BASize (buffer allocation size)*: indicates the maximum buffering requirements to receive this CPCS PDU (greater than or equal to the length of the user data in the information field; in message mode, BASize is the length of the user data frame);
- *PAD*: 0–3 bytes of padding to make the entire CPCS PDU an exact multiple of four bytes;
- *AL (alignment)*: a byte of zeros to make the trailer (AL, Etag, and Length) aligned with four bytes;
- *Etag (end tag)*: indicates misassembly if different from the Btag field;
- *Length*: number of bytes in the information field.

It can be seen that the main purpose of the header and trailer in the CPCS PDU is detection of misassembly.

The CPCS PDU is divided into one or more 44-byte segments. A header and trailer are added to each segment to construct 48-byte SAR PDUs. The first and last segments are identified explicitly by the segment type (ST) field in the SAR PDU header. They are designated as beginning of message (BOM) and end of message (EOM), respectively. Intermediate segments are designated as continuation of message (COM). If the CPCS PDU results in only one segment, it is designated as single segment message (SSM). The ST field uses these codes:

- ST = 10: BOM;
- ST = 00: COM;
- ST = 01: EOM;
- ST = 11: SSM.

The other fields in the SAR PDU are:

- *SN (sequence number)*: sequential position of each SAR PDU belonging to the same CPCS PDU, modulo 16;
- *MID (multiplexing identification)*: identifies the CPCS PDU when SAR PDUs from different CPCS PDUs are multiplexed together (the MID number should be the same for all SAR PDUs belonging to the same CPCS PDU, and MID = 0 if no multiplexing is used);
- *LI (length indication)*: length of user data in payload (in bytes);
- *CRC*: CRC-10 calculation over the entire SAR PDU for error detection (using the generator polynomial $x^{10} + x^9 + x^5 + x^4 + x + 1$).

Note that the payload may not be entirely filled with information; the remainder is filled with zeros.

The receiver collects all SAR PDUs belonging to the same CPCS PDU identified by the MID field (if no multiplexing is used, it collects all SAR PDUs from BOM to EOM). It then checks the correct sequential order of SAR PDUs using the ST and SN fields. Errors may be detected from the CRC field. If there are no errors, the payloads of the SAR PDUs are extracted to reassemble the CPCS PDU.

Misassembly error may be detected by a mismatch between the Btag and Etag fields. If bit errors have been detected, the CPCS PDU may be discarded, or, as an option, it may be passed to the higher layers with an error indication.

Appendix C
ATM Adaptation Layer Type 5

ATM adaptation layer type 5 (AAL5) is a simple AAL that supports variable bit-rate data services with error detection above the ATM layer. Essentially, AAL5 at the transmitter will append AAL5 information to a variable-length user data frame (up to 65,535 bytes) and segment the result into a sequence of ATM cells. The receiver extracts the segments from the cells and reassembles the variable-length frame. The AAL information is used for error detection but not correction. Unlike AAL3/4, AAL5 does not support multiplexing of data from multiple higher layer applications.

AAL5 consists of a common part (AAL5 CP) and a service-specific part (AAL5 SSP). The common part of AAL5 provides unguaranteed connection-oriented transport of variable-length frames with error detection. The service-specific part provides additional functions as required by the higher layers, and may sometimes be null. An example of the service-specific part is the SAAL service-specific convergence sublayer (see Chapter 9). Only the AAL5 CP is described here.

The basic operation of the AAL5 CP is shown in Figure C.1. Like AAL3/4, AAL5 supports a *message mode service* and *streaming mode service*. However, since no applications for streaming mode service have been identified yet, only the message mode service is illustrated. The user data frame may be up to 65,535 bytes in length. At the transmitter, AAL5 appends these fields to construct a CP protocol data unit (CP PDU):

- *PAD*: 0–47 bytes of padding to make the entire CP PDU an exact multiple of 48 bytes;
- *UU*: AAL5 user-to-user information;
- *CPI (common part indicator)*: reserved for future functions;
- *Length*: number of bytes used in the data field;
- *CRC-32*: calculated over the entire CP PDU to detect errors.

The UU field allows the AAL5 users to exchange a byte of information in addition to the user data frame; this byte is carried transparently by AAL5.

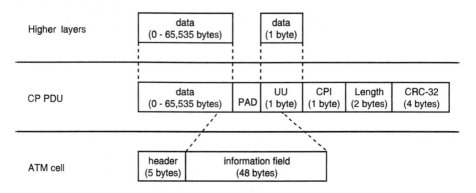

Figure C.1 Protocol data units in AAL5 common part.

The CP PDU is then segmented into 48-byte units, which are carried in the information fields of an ATM cell stream. All cells within the stream have the code PT = 000 in the headers, except for the last cell, which has the code PT = 001 (this might change if the cells experience congestion within the network, in which case the network will change PT = 000 to PT = 010 and PT = 001 to PT = 011). The CLP bit of the cells are determined by the loss priority requested by the AAL5 user.

At the receiver, the reverse AAL5 functions are performed to reconstruct the CP PDU. The last cell in the sequence is identified by the code PT = 001 or PT = 011, and the next cell is inferred to be the first cell of the next CP PDU (AAL5 does not allow multiplexing from several connections). The CRC-32 and Length fields are used to detect errors or information loss. Detected errors and information loss are reported to the higher layers, which have the responsibility for recovery.

List of Acronyms

A

AAL	ATM adaptation layer
ABR	available bit rate
ACSE	association-control-service element
AIN	advanced intelligent network
AIS	alarm indication signal
APS	automatic protection switching
ARPA	Advanced Research Projects Agency
ASN.1	abstract syntax notation 1
ATD	asynchronous time division
ATM	asynchronous transfer mode

B

BAF	Bellcore automatic message accounting format
BIP	bit-interleaved parity
B-ISDN	broadband integrated services digital network
BISUP	broadband ISDN user part

C

CAC	connection admission control
CBR	constant bit-rate
CCITT	Comite Consultatif Internationale Telegraphique et Telephonique
CLP	cell-loss priority
CMIP	common management information protocol
CMISE	common management information service element
CPCS	common part convergence sublayer
CRC	cyclic redundancy check

CS   convergence sublayer
CSF   cell switch fabric

D
DCC   data communication channel
DQDB   distributed queue dual bus

E
EFCI   explicit forward congestion indication
EOC   embedded operation channel
ESS   electronic switching system
ETSI   European Telecommunication Standards Institute

F
FDDI   fiber distributed data interface
FDM   frequency-division multiplexing
FERF   far end receive failure

G
Gbps   gigabits per second
GCRA   generic cell rate algorithm
GFC   generic flow control
GOS   grade of service

H
HEC   header-error control

I
IDN   integrated digital network
IETF   Internet Engineering Task Force
ILMI   interim local management interface
IM   input module
IN   intelligent network
IP   Internet protocol
ISDN   integrated services digital network
ISO   International Organization for Standardization
ISUP   ISDN user part
ITU   International Telecommunication Union
ITU-T   ITU Telecommunication Standardization Sector

K

Kbps   kilobits per second

L

LAN   local area network
LOF   loss of frame
LOP   loss of pointer
LOS   loss of signal
LTE   line-terminating equipment

M

MAN   metropolitan area network
Mbps   megabits per second
MIB   management information base
MIN   multistage interconnection network
MTP   message transfer part

N

NDF   new data flag
NMS   network management station
NNI   network node interface
NPC   network parameter control

O

OAM   operations and maintenance
OAM&P   operations, administration, maintenance, and provisioning
OC-N   optical carrier N
OM   output module
OS   operations system
OSI   open systems interconnection

P

PDU   protocol data unit
PL-SAP   physical layer service access point
PM   physical medium
PT   payload type
PTE   path-terminating equipment

Q

QOS   quality of service

R

RDI	remote defect indication
RFI	remote failure indication
ROSE	remote-operations-service element

S

SAAL	signaling ATM adaptation layer
SAR	segmentation and reassembly
SCP	service control point
SDH	synchronous digital hierarchy
SM	system management
SMDS	switched multimegabit data service
SNMP	simple network management protocol
SONET	synchronous optical network
SPE	synchronous payload envelope
SRTS	synchronous residual time stamp
SS7	signaling system number 7
SSCF	service-specific coordination functions
SSCS	service-specific convergence sublayer
SSCOP	service-specific connection-oriented protocol
SSP	service switching point
STE	section-terminating equipment
STM	synchronous transfer mode
STP	signaling transfer point
STS-N	synchronous transport signal-level N

T

Tbps	terabits per second
TC	transmission convergence
TCP	transmission control protocol
TDM	time-division multiplexing
TMN	telecommunications management network

U

UME	UNI management entity
UNI	user-network interface
UPC	usage parameter control

V

| VBR | variable bit rate |

VC	virtual channel
VCC	virtual-channel connection
VCI	virtual-channel identifier
VP	virtual path
VPC	virtual-path connection
VPI	virtual-path identifier
VT	virtual tributary

W

WAN	wide area network

About the Authors

Thomas M. Chen received the Ph.D. degree in electrical engineering from the University of California at Berkeley and the M.S. and B.S. degrees from the Massachusetts Institute of Technology. In 1989, he joined GTE Laboratories in Waltham, Massachusetts, where he is currently a senior member of technical staff working on research in ATM switching and network control. Dr. Chen is an active member of the IEEE Communications Society and serves as an associate technical editor for IEEE Communications Magazine. He taught at the University of Massachusetts at Lowell as an adjunct professor in 1993.

Stephen S. Liu received the B.S. and Ph.D. degrees in electrical engineering from Cheng-Kung University in Taiwan and Georgia Institute of Technology, respectively. He joined GTE Laboratories in 1981 and has since been working on packet-switching technology. He is a principal member of technical staff in the Network Transport System Department. Dr. Liu's current interest is in wide-area ATM transport for broadband multimedia services. He is a senior member of the IEEE.

Index

2 × 2 switching element, 149–50
  examples of, 150
4 × 4 banyan network, 150–51
8 × 8 Batcher-banyan network, 152

Abstract Syntax Notation 1 (ASN.1), 220
Access signaling, 178–87
  message formats, 184–87
  messages, 43–44
  meta-signaling, 182–83
  point-to-multipoint connections, 182
  point-to-point connections, 179–82
  See also Signaling
Accounting management, 215–17
Advanced intelligent network (AIN), 13
Advanced Research Projects Agency (ARPA), 4
Alarm indication signal (AIS), 48, 118
  downstream, 118–19
  line AIS (AIS-L), 118
  STS path AIS (AIS-P), 118–19
  VT path AIS (AIS-V), 119
Alarm surveillance, 116–18
American National Standards Institute
  (ANSI), 24
APS channel trouble, 117
ARPANET, 4
Association-control-service element (ACSE),
  224–25
Asynchronous, 21
Asynchronous transfer mode (ATM), 17–35
  advantages, 11, 22
  cell format, 25, 35
  concept of, 21–23
  disadvantages of, 23
  history of, 1–5
  information flows, 37–54
  motivation of, 20
  as multiplexing technique, 22

principles, 21–22
  protocol monitoring, 213–14
  standards, 23–30
  subnetwork, 21
  as switching technique, 22–23
  See also ATM adaptation layer (AAL);
     ATM networking; ATM switching
ATM adaptation layer (AAL), 19
  appendixes, 20
  protocol monitoring, 213–14
  signaling (SAAL), 40, 42, 176, 192–95
  sublayers, 19–20
  type 1 (AAL1), 235–38
  type 3/4 (AAL3/4), 239–41
  type 5 (AAL5), 243–44
ATM networking, 30–34, 35
  aspects of, 30
  ATM-layer cell transport, 31
  ATM-layer management, 34
  connection-admission control, 32–33
  traffic control, 33, 57
  VPs and VCs and, 31–32
ATM switching, 34, 35
  CAC and, 77
  control-plane considerations, 83–85
  defined, 143
  functional requirements, 82–87
  identification of, 85
  management-plane considerations, 85–87
  traffic-control considerations, 87
  user-plane considerations, 82–83
  See also ATM switching architectures
ATM switching architectures, 77, 81–95
  CAC, 87, 90
  cell switch fabric, 87, 89–90
  defined, 143
  distribution of functions, 90–95

in resource management, 69–70
Virtual path connection (VPC), 32
    connecting points, 39
    connectivity testing, 49
    multiple, 196
    QOS of, 50
    semipermanent, 32–33, 40
    statistically multiplexing, 198
    status information on, 177
    switched, 40, 177
Virtual peak rate, 202
Virtual scheduling algorithm, 65
    illustrated, 66
Virtual tributaries, 113, 114

The Artech House Telecommunications Library

Vinton G. Cerf, Series Editor

Terrestrial Digital Microwave Communciations, Ferdo Ivanek, editor

Transmission Networking: SONET and the SDH, Mike Sexton and Andy Reid

Transmission Performance of Evolving Telecommunications Networks, John Gruber and Godfrey Williams

Troposcatter Radio Links, G. Roda

UNIX Internetworking, Uday O. Pabrai

Virtual Networks: A Buyer's Guide, Daniel D. Briere

Voice Processing, Second Edition, Walt Tetschner

Voice Teletraffic System Engineering, James R. Boucher

Wireless Access and the Local Telephone Network, George Calhoun

Wireless Data Networking, Nathan J. Muller

Wireless LAN Systems, A. Santamaría and F. J. Lopez-Hernandez

Writing Disaster Recovery Plans for Telecommunications Networks and LANs, Leo A. Wrobel

X Window System User's Guide, Uday O. Pabrai

For further information on these and other Artech House titles, contact:

Artech House
685 Canton Street
Norwood, MA 02062
617-769-9750
Fax: 617-769-6334
Telex: 951-659
email: artech@world.std.com

Artech House
Portland House, Stag Place
London SW1E 5XA England
+44 (0) 171-973-8077
Fax: +44 (0) 171-630-0166
Telex: 951-659
email: bookco@artech.demon.co.uk

F